RUDOLF STEINER'S

Bernard Nesfield-C[...]
is Principal of Hawkwoo[...]
independent centre for adult education in
Gloucestershire, and a member of the
Anthroposophical Society. He was educated at
a Rudolf Steiner school in London
and at the universities of Jena, London,
and Bristol.

Also available:

RUDOLF STEINER
Essential Readings
Selected and edited by Richard Seddon

RUDOLF STEINER
The Man and His Vision
Colin Wilson

By the same author:
WILLIAM BLAKE
Prophet of Universal Brotherhood

RUDOLF STEINER'S
VISION
OF LOVE

Spiritual Science
and the Logic of the Heart

BERNARD NESFIELD~COOKSON

First published by The Aquarian Press 1983
This edition 1989

© BERNARD NESFIELD-COOKSON 1983

British Library Cataloguing in Publication Data

Nesfield-Cookson, Bernard
Rudolf Steiner's vision of love
1. Anthroposophy. Theories of Steiner,
Rudolf, 1861–1925
I. Title
299'.935'0924

ISBN 1–85274–063–9

*Crucible is an imprint of The Aquarian Press, part of
the Thorsons Publishing Group, Wellingborough,
Northamptonshire, NN8 2RQ, England*

Printed in Great Britain by Woolnough
Bookbinding Limited, Irthlingborough,
Northamptonshire

3   5   7   9   10   8   6   4   2

ACKNOWLEDGEMENTS

I owe a special debt to Benedict Wood, who found the time and energy to read the manuscript in its various stages of development. His many useful suggestions have been incorporated into the text to its great improvement. I have also to thank my wife Ruth for her encouragement and criticism — and for her painstaking typing and retyping of the manuscript.

Hawkwood College, June 1981

CONTENTS

Dedicated — in love — to the memory of
Eileen and Father Andrew; and to Margit,
Anna Kristina, Christian, and my wife, Ruth.

INTRODUCTION

In Love lives the seed of Truth,
In Truth seek the root of Love:
Thus speaks thy higher Self. [1]

Love is the only passion which must not be discarded in the search for truth. [2]

An all-embracing comprehension of truth satisfies and unites all humanity and makes love and peace possible among men. [3]

In the human Heart
there lives a part of Man
which contains matter
more spiritual than in any other organ;
also a part of Man
of which the spiritual life
is made more manifest in matter
than that of any other organ.

Hence in the Microcosm that is Man
Sun is the Heart,
and in his Heart is Man united
most of all with the deepest fount —
the fount of his true Being. [4]

In the life of the heart we have a far more intimate indication of the invisible than in the life of concepts. [5]

INTRODUCTION

An objection often raised against spiritual science (Anthroposophy) [5a] is that Steiner's pathway to supersensible knowledge is far too difficult for most people and, moreover, that it is only suitable for the intellectual. Rudolf Steiner himself is the first to admit that it is a testing path. But it is not the lack of intellectual erudition that is the origin of these difficulties: 'Erudition and scientific training are not preconditions for the unfolding of higher senses. They can develop in the simple-minded person just as in the scientist of high standard'. [6] It can readily be conceded that qualities of clear thinking need to be nurtured — mark well, 'clear', not 'clever' — but it is above all moral qualities that we need to develop to a higher degree than we usually possess if we are to attain direct perception of the spirit-world and of our own spirit-being. Indeed, we could say that it is those simple qualities of soul Christ exhorts us to develop in the Sermon on the Mount that we find most difficult of attainment.

The golden rule of genuine spiritual science Steiner formulates in the following way: 'For every *one* step forward that you take in seeking knowledge of occult truths, take *three* steps forward in the development of your own character.' [7]

In his basic book *Knowledge of the Higher Worlds. How is it attained?* Steiner emphasizes that the spiritual investigator should not lose himself in intellectual speculations. Such intellectualizing diverts him from the right path. 'He should look out on the world with fresh, healthy senses and a keen power of observation, and then give himself up to his feelings.' [8] In a footnote to this passage Steiner adds: 'It should be remarked that *artistic* feeling, coupled with a quiet, introspective nature, is the best preliminary condition for the development of spiritual faculties. Artistic feeling pierces through the surface of things, and by so doing reaches their secrets.'

Elsewhere, discussing feeling as a guide to knowledge, Steiner states that, above all, our innate and 'infallible feeling for truth must be the active principle in the verification of knowledge'. He then goes on to characterize the nature feeling must have if it is to

act as a stimulus not merely to thought about the sense-perceptible world but to thought concerning worlds that we cannot
apprehend with our usual senses: 'When feeling strives towards
some other thing, when the human soul seeks feelingly to
embrace some other thing, such feeling is called love. This love is
not only possible, it is indispensable before the unknown can be
penetrated by the light of thought.' Devotion, too, can be directed
towards the unknown before thought can attain knowledge of it:
'The union of devotion and love gives rise to religiousness in the
true sense of the word. Religious devotion may be regarded as the
"leader" to knowledge of the spiritual world, for love and
devotion are no less important where the supersensible world is
concerned than in ordinary, everyday life.' [9]

On another occasion, speaking in this instance of devotion in
relation to the human ego, [10] Steiner makes a statement that
clearly illustrates the point already made in regard to the
necessity of the clarity of thought. 'Devotion can prove salutary
for the human soul only when it is aglow with the ego — a
devotion in which we immerse ourselves in some being or thing
without parting with our ego.' And, in answer to the question,
what is it that can preserve the ego from self-loss, he continues:
'Thought and nothing but thought can preserve the ego from
self-loss when we seek contact with the world through the
channel of devotion'. [11] In particular, when the will directs the
soul beyond the confines of the sense-perceptible the illumination of thought is essential, otherwise we become little more
than marionettes. If the will to think is lacking, then the will to
devotion is threatened by the danger of self-loss. [12] We can then
so easily fall a prey to illusion and hallucination; to inimical
forces, too, over which we have no control.

In the same lecture to which reference has just been made,
Steiner also considers the possibility of love being exposed to a
similar danger. 'What,' he asks, 'what becomes of love when the
ego fails to bring to bear the light of thought and of reasonable
judgement upon the unknown' — be this unknown of the
sensible or the supersensible world? His answer is well worth
heeding: 'Such love becomes mere gush. Such love for the
unknown, lacking the will to powerful thought, finally involves
the soul in mere gush and sentimentality'. [13] Moreover, 'all errors
and superstitions, all false and untruthful methods of entering the
supersensible worlds can be traced to a refusal to let consciousness be illuminated by the light of *creative thought*'. [14]

To enter more deeply into what Steiner means by active, creative thinking — which is not to be confused with arid intellectualism — is not our present task; but it seems prudent to bring to the notice of the reader unfamiliar with Steiner's work the importance he attaches to the activity of thinking as, with the exception of a short chapter and a few passing references here and there in the following pages, relatively little mention is made of this all-important quality of the human soul. [15]

In the final lecture of a cycle entitled *Macrocosm and Microcosm*, Steiner makes the point that the goal of spiritual science (Anthroposophy) is to guide the whole of man to a knowledge of the spiritual essence of the world and himself, not merely the thinking man but also the man of feeling and of will. 'Anyone who professes to have knowledge of the spirit and remains indifferent in his feeling and will has not been rightly affected by this knowledge.' [16] Knowledge gained through spiritual scientific investigation must be received into the heart. 'When the heart is involved, man feels himself drawn to other hearts.' [17]

True love is rooted in the spirit. Only when we find our fellow-men in the spirit do we find them with indissoluble, unswerving love. This is the life-giving element in all human existence. Spiritual science brings a formative, life-giving force into the soul. And when through what would otherwise remain dispassionate, intellectual knowledge we feel warmed in soul to such a degree that this warmth brings individuals closer to one another, then we have received such knowledge in the right way. Even a presentiment of transition from the logic of thinking to the logic of the heart will tend to bring individuals together. The logic of thinking may lead to intense egoism, but the logic of the heart overcomes egoism and makes all men participants in the life of mankind as one whole. [18]

In short, Steiner emphasizes the necessity of transforming 'head-thinking' into 'heart-thinking' if we are to gain true knowledge not only of the physical world around us, including our fellow-men, but also of the spiritual world. Our quest for knowledge, grounded in active, creative thinking, must be guided by love and devotion. Indeed, we could say that without love and devotion, without the warmth of feeling and the power of the will, creative, active thought is not possible.

*   *   *   *

Commenting on the misrepresentation of other people's work and thoughts and on judgements based on inadequate knowledge of the subject matter, Steiner once stated that spiritual progress will only be possible when such things do not happen, when they are impossible. A sense of honour and love for others demands that it should be impossible. No progress is made in the search for truth if judgements are formed on an inadequate basis, and it is the 'duty' of spiritual scientists to note such things. It is loveless to speak of universal love of humanity and, at the same time, to act towards a fellow-seeker in what amounts to a loveless way. [19]

These are stern statements and remind us of the enormous responsibility anyone has who undertakes, in any measure, to speak or write about such matters as knowledge of the spiritual worlds, spiritual self- and world-evolution, and so on. The present author is only too well aware of his own inadequacies, but in the following pages he has never knowingly misrepresented, though he readily admits he may have misunderstood.

Those already familiar with Rudolf Steiner's work will easily recognize the attempts made to follow up indications given by him in his written works and many lectures. The following of a thread between one indication and another is a heart-warming and illuminative task — and the author sincerely hopes that he has not woven threads where, in the hearts and minds of those wiser than he, no threads exist. Here and there, let it be confessed, greater stress has been laid on the soul-spiritual quality of love than may seem apparent in the book or lecture to which reference is being made. In defence, it would be said that such stress has seemed warranted, either because of a particular passage's relation to the wider context of a book, lecture, or cycle of lectures, or because of something stated by Steiner in quite a different context, time and place.

*   *   *   *

Man and Cosmos form one totality and it is therefore impossible to departmentalize this or that aspect of such a theme as the power of love. This power flows into every aspect of life — human and cosmic — and there are points of 'fusion', as it were, where the various strands of this power cross over one another.

Rudolf Steiner made many statements regarding the all-embracing and all-penetrating power of love in a great many different contexts. Some of these statements are to a greater or lesser degree identical. It need not surprise the reader, therefore, to find a statement in one chapter that has already been encountered in an earlier chapter. Such similar statements have been deliberately quoted for two reasons: first, they serve to underline the importance Steiner attaches to the power of love; second the present author is not concerned to present his own version but to give as authentic a panaroma as possible of Steiner's own words and views. In connection with the second point it should be mentioned that only in those cases where it has seemed desirable has any attempt been made to interpret Steiner's statements. As much as possible the goal has been pursued to allow Steiner to speak directly to the reader. Hence, of course, the numerous quotations. Moreover, no attempt has been made to use what some readers might consider to be a more 'modern' terminology, nor to relate what Steiner has to say to the insights and world-conceptions of other great men and women.

There are many instances in the following chapters where a more comprehensive exposition is called for in order that misunderstandings should not arise. Wherever possible, therefore, references are made in the notes to specific passages in Steiner's books and lectures to enable the reader to follow up and verify in greater depth what otherwise might remain a question-able statement. In view of this possible need, references and quotations have been limited to works that are readily accessible to the English reading public.

Clearly such a study as the following is one-sided. The emphasis is on one aspect of the complex nature of the human soul. But the author has long felt that there is a widespread and distressing misunderstanding of Rudolf Steiner's conception of man and the universe — that, as already indicated, it is considered to have appeal and make sense only to the 'head', and that the 'heart' cannot draw spiritual nourishment from it.

It is hoped that these pages will help to dispel this erroneous view of Steiner's spiritual science and that they may contribute to the realization that he worked and spoke out of his whole being and that it is with *our* whole being, centred in the heart, that we need to respond to him.

In bringing these introductory paragraphs to a close the author would stress that he lays no claim to originality. All that he has endeavoured to do is to highlight the profound significance Rudolf Steiner attaches to the power of love in man's striving towards spiritual reality.

1.

THE MISSION AND ESSENCE
OF SPIRITUAL SCIENCE

*Love must not forget
That she is wisdom's sister.* [1]

1.

People lightly reproach anthroposophical spiritual science for being merely theoretical and concerning itself with cosmic evolution, for instance, rather than with love. 'They do not see,' says Steiner, 'that cosmic evolution is the expression of love, but prefer to talk of "love", of universal love, of how and what man should love, and they have been talking thus for years. Many do not understand that, at the present time, the fruition of love is to be comprehended through the study of cosmic evolution.' [2] If we allow spiritual science to take hold of the human soul we can soon perceive how love arises in the human heart. Love cannot be preached, nor grafted upon the heart; it grows if properly cultivated. Love is a child of the spirit.

Steiner again and again makes it abundantly clear that it is not enough merely to know about supersensible things. We must 'understand with feeling', and 'feel with understanding'. Love-filled wisdom, wisdom-filled love. Leonardo da Vinci's statement is true: 'Great love is the daughter of great understanding'. He who is not prepared to understand will not learn how to love. [3]

True spiritual science is not merely something theoretical. It is a living thing. The contents of spiritual teachings do not remain conceptions and ideas. The spiritual ideas we make our own become part of us and are active as invigorating, life-giving forces — even though we may not be conscious of them. [4]

Even if what spiritual science has to say is not now recognized as being true, the time will most certainly come when its truth *will* be recognized. Truth may be suppressed, but not destroyed. It will always be re-born, for truth is intimately and vitally bound up with the human soul. The human soul and truth are twin sisters and even if there are occasions when dissension reigns between them, mutual love and recognition must always reassert themselves between the soul and truth, for they have a common origin. Their origin is in the spirituality that rules throughout the universe — the reunion with and rediscovery of which is the very task spiritual science sets itself.

Steiner makes an interesting statement regarding the future of spiritual science and its acceptance in a lecture in which he refers to and quotes from an address given by a Catholic priest who was professor to the theological faculty at Vienna University during the later part of the nineteenth century. In this address we find the following:

> Thus a new conception of the world appeared [reference is being made to the Galileo-Copernican world-view'], which in many points was apparently at variance with opinions regarding which it was asserted, with very questionable right, that they proceeded from the doctrine of Christianity. It was much more a question of the contrast of the widened world-consciousness of the *modern* age to the more limited one of the *antique,* a contrast to the Greek, but not to the rightly understood Christian conception of the world, which perceived fresh marvels of divine power and wisdom in the newly discovered worlds, whereby the miracle of divine love accomplished on earth could but acquire greater importance.

In a similar way, Steiner says, in respect of the relation of spiritual science to orthodoxy, it may be said that this spiritual science is often apparently at variance with opinions often held to be inherent in Christianity, but which with 'very questionable right' assert their origin in the doctrines of Christianity. It is more a question of the contrast of the world-consciousness of our modern age — which has extended into spiritual reality — to the narrowly limited natural-scientific consciousness of the last few centuries, than to the rightly understood Christian conception of the world, which should perceive in the spirit-worlds of spiritual science new marvels of divine power and wisdom, whereby the miracle of divine love accomplished in the sense-perceptual world can but acquire enhanced significance.

As soon as in certain directions there is a fundamental insight into spiritual science — such as was possessed by the above mentioned Roman Catholic priest and theologian into modern natural science — the attacks and criticism that are often directed in such an unfounded manner against spiritual science from the bastions of orthodox religion will cease. [5]

In a lecture given in Vienna in 1923, Steiner makes the following statement which everyone, both those who are entering upon the path of spiritual striving and those who are sceptical of the use and necessity of such endeavour, could do well to take to heart: 'Since supersensible knowledge leads us, not to abstractions, but to forces of life, it can "flow over" into our whole conduct of life, permeating it with that which lifts man above his everyday mode of existence, lifts him out of the sense-perceptible into the supersensible . . . Such knowledge can bring him to the stage where he becomes, in consecrated love, one with the Spirit of the World, with the Christ, thus attaining truly religious piety.'[6]

To reiterate: spiritual science is not mere theoretical learning. The ideas it presents are not meant as, and are not, abstract theory. 'Spiritual scientific ideas are vessels fashioned by love',[7] states Steiner quite simply. Spiritual science must bring the light of true humanness to shine forth in living, creative ideas that bear love's imprint. Indeed, spiritual science itself can only be 'grasped' by the power of love.

So long as we approach and treat spiritual science as though it were mere theoretical knowledge, it will have little value for life. It must be *applied in practical life*. Then our views and ideas go through a complete transformation. Knowledge then no longer remains abstract theory, for, when it is spiritualized, it permeates and transforms the whole of our life and our work. We begin, for instance, to understand our fellow-men as individualities, and our knowledge also enters into communion with the sphere of feeling, with the forces of the heart, expressing itself then as love, respect and esteem. It is all too readily thought that life can be treated as if all human beings were made in accordance with one stereotyped pattern. Such a thought can only arise when true spiritual knowledge is lacking. Spiritual science and spiritual knowledge must so permeate our everyday life, in particular our life of feeling, that we are able to understand the depth of the riddle confronting us in each individual human being.

Basic to an understanding of this riddle is that loving harmony should reign between men. The riddle of the human being in the general sense may be tackled by abstract ideas, says Steiner, but not the riddle of the *individual*. To each human being we must bring *direct* understanding rooted in love. Such is the foundation upon which we can create a social life worthy of the spiritual essence of man. Love-filled wisdom is the true basis of social life. Spiritual science must work in this way — not through preaching or moralizing. It gives us the 'tools' with which a social life can be created in which we can know and understand the inner core of our fellow-men.

In every respect we can learn to know the individual human

being through spiritual science. We can, for instance, discover and treasure the peculiar, enigmatical qualities of the individuality of a child entrusted to our care in our capacity as teachers, gradually realizing how he or she should be approached. Nor, Steiner says, can we help loving a man 'if, ceasing all attempts to fathom him intellectually, we let his whole being work upon ours, and if our spiritual knowledge lends wings to our feelings and our love'. [8] This is a true and fruitful basis of human love. It is the basis upon which we can seek and find the innermost kernel of being in each individual fellow- man. Such a discovery of the essence of a fellow human being can only be made when our approach, our understanding of life, is born of the spirit. No materialistic conception of man can reach his spiritual being. 'The science of the Spirit must develop for the reason that man enter into relationship with man. But man is spirit. Man can enter into relationship with man only when the approach is from the spirit.' [9]

Spiritual scientific knowledge only becomes an 'art of life' when it permeates the very fibres of our being and our every thought and deed. The 'most beautiful relationships can grow between human beings when a man beholds another and is not only able to fathom the riddle he presents but understand how to let love flow between them'. [10]

> Love is the blossom and fruit of a life quickened by spiritual science. That is why spiritual science may justly claim that it creates the soil for *human love*, the fairest goal of the human race. Our sympathy, our love, the way we meet and behave towards each individual man, all this will teach us a true art of life. [11]

Love must permeate and be active in the process of knowledge if we desire to penetrate beyond the world of sense perceptions, the only world the intellect is capable of grasping. What is beyond the sphere of the senses can only be experienced when we have devotion for the world, when we surrender every aspect of ourselves to which any form of egoism adheres. In short, to penetrate beyond the world of sense perceptions, the self, the ego, as we experience it in *ordinary life*, must be given up. [12] We then find that, in a very special way, the spirit manifests itself in the physical world — it manifests itself in love, the capacity for love, the capacity for sympathy, for sharing both joy and sorrow with others. [13]

In our present civilization we need, above all things, a new *knowledge of Christ* — Steiner stresses this time and again. This new knowledge is to be gained increasingly through the effects spiritual science has upon us. We have to recognize that a 'school' of unselfishness is needed for our present culture. A renewing of a sense of responsibility for all creation, a deepening of our moral life, can come into being only through a training in unselfishness. Before our inner vision stands, as the archetypal phenomenon of selflessness in the entire evolution of the world, the appearance of Christ on earth.

Under the influence of materialism the 'natural' unselfishness of mankind has disappeared to a large extent. But by contemplation of the Mystery of Golgotha, by consciously permeating our knowledge of it with all our heart-feeling, we may acquire again with our whole soul-being an education in unselfishness.

In relation to our moral life and to all the activities of our conscious life, we must become selfless first of all. This is a 'duty' of our present culture to the future. Mankind must become more and more selfless, for therein lies the future of right living and of all the deeds of love possible to earthly humanity. [14]

Our conscious life must evolve towards unselfishness. It is now man's task to learn unselfishness in his moral and intellectual life through his understanding of St Paul's words: 'Not I, but Christ in me'.

2.

LOVE AND ITS MEANING IN THE WORLD

The fruits of Love can only come to man
when they are brought to him from realms divine. [1]

2.

A lecture with the title of this chapter, 'Love and its Meaning in the World', given in 1912, [2] exemplary for its clarity, profundity and wisdom, illustrates many aspects of Steiner's insight and experience of the meaning of love for the world. Its full impact can clearly only be felt by reading it in its totality and taking its contents into one's heart. All the following resumé can purport to do is to indicate some of the significant points (most of which will be taken up again in the following pages).

The older we grow, the more we nourish love for the wisdom life reveals. Love of such wisdom is not of an egoistic nature, or, rather, grows less and less egoistic the older we grow; for this love increases in intensity the closer we draw near to the end of our earthly life, that is to say, it increases, but the expectation of gaining something from our wisdom decreases. In youth this is seldom the case, for then we gather knowledge, pass through experiences, and cherish hopes for the future — in short, in our youthful years, consciously or unconsciously, we harbour expectations of some gain or other.

Our love, then, for this content of our soul, for wisdom, steadily increases as we go through life and yet, in this respect, Steiner warns, spiritual science may actually become a source of temptation, in so far as we may be led to acquire wisdom in this life on earth with a view to self-advancement in the next one. The effect of spiritual science may be 'an extension of egoism beyond the bounds of this present life, and therein lies danger'; [3] hence the need for the constant experience of 'Not I, but Christ in me'.

Love of wisdom acquired from life-experience may be compared with the formation of a seed when the plant has reached the relevant stage of maturity. When a plant has completed its vegetative growth through the year the seed for the next year is formed and remains. So it is, too, in regard to the wisdom acquired from life. Man passes through the Portal of Death and the spiritual core of his being, in its process of ripening, is the seed of the next life. In the wisdom revealed by life, man forms the seed of his next life.

If we grasp the meaning of the law of reincarnation we recognize the signficance of love in the world. When we speak of karma, we mean that which as cause in the one life has its effect in the next. However, we cannot speak of love, of spiritualized love, in terms of cause and effect. We cannot speak of a deed of love in terms of its eventual compensation, reward. True, the deed, as cause, will have its compensation, its effect; but this has nothing to do with love. A deed of love does not seek a return, either in this life or in the next. A 'deed of love' that looks for reward is not a deed of love, but a deed of egoism. This is the point. The only actions from which we gain nothing directly in the future are those we perform out of true spiritualized love. We gain from the loving deeds of others; others gain from our deeds of love. We could say — in fact, Steiner does so — that, seen in the context of a greater whole than the immediate present, or even than a present life, we are paying off debts by everything we do out of love.

To work without compensation, without reward, is not something modern man at all willingly undertakes — and 'that is why deeds of pure love are done so unwillingly, why there is so little true love in the world'. [4] We need to attain quite an advanced stage of inner development before we can experience joy in performing deeds of love from which there is nothing tangible to be gained. It is clear that our egoism gains nothing from deeds of pure love, but the world gains all the more: 'Love is for the world what the sun is for external life'. [5] No human soul could thrive if love departed from the world. 'Love is the "moral" sun of the world'. [6] Would it not be absurd, Steiner asks, if we were to delight in the flowers growing in a meadow and yet to wish that the sun would vanish from the world? Answering the question in terms of the moral life we could say: our deep concern must always be to disseminate love over the earth in the greatest measure possible, to promote love on the earth — that, and that alone, is true wisdom. As a corollary to this we can say: lack of interest in the world is egoism in a gross form. Interest in the earth's evolution, in the evolution of man, past, present and future, in the nature of the spiritual forces working and weaving in these evolutionary processes, and interest in the invisible world, in the world of the spirit, should form the spiritual seed of love for the world. '*A spiritual science without love would be a danger to mankind*', is Steiner's categorical statement. 'Deeds of love and spiritual science should be inseparably united.'

Love mediated by way of the senses is the wellspring of creative power, of that which is coming into being. Without senseborn love, nothing created by man in the material world would exist. Likewise, without spiritual love, nothing spiritual can arise in evolution. When we offer love, cultivate love, then creative forces pour into the world. [7]

To our intellect this conception is quite unintelligible — such a spiritual fact is beyond the compass of our intellect. And this is so because, as Steiner points out, the creative forces of love, of divine love, poured into the universe before we ourselves and our intellect came into being. Only the purified power of love within ourselves can 'understand', can 'perceive' the creative power of Cosmic Love. As egoists — we could also say, as intellectuals — we can certainly deprive the future of creative forces, but we cannot eradicate the deeds of love and the creative forces of the past. We owe our very existence to deeds of love wrought in the past. The qualities and various aspects of our being, moral integrity, courage and vision, with which we have been endowed by these deeds of creative love, are a manifestation of our debt to the past. Whatever love may flow forth from us is, in this sense, a payment of debts we owe for our existence. In the light of this we can understand the loving deeds of a man who has reached a high stage of spiritual development, for he has greater 'debts' than the ordinary man to pay to the past. He pays his debts through deeds of love — and herein lies his wisdom. The higher the stage of spiritual knowledge, the greater is the creative power of love. The one great exception to this is the Christ Being. His is the greatest love, yet he owed no debts to the past.

The meaning and effect of love in the world may be understood in the following way: as already indicated, no profit accrues to ourselves from our deeds of love in the world. Indeed, we have to leave our deeds of love, the effects of our deeds of love, behind us when we pass through the Portal of Death; but in the world of humanity they continue to be creative, they continue to act as spiritual factors in the flow of world happenings. The world grows richer through our creative deeds of love. When we seek to discover whatever is creative we find that the source is love; love is the creative foundation of everything that lives. *'Love is the creative force in the world'*. [8]

Reference is made elsewhere to Steiner's statement that pure love is not capable of diminution or of augmentation; that, by its

very nature, it is quite different from the other two great powers
in the world — wisdom and might. In the case of pure love we
cannot speak of enhancement in the same way as we can speak of
the augmentation of knowledge into omniscience, or of might
into omnipotence. Progress in the development of wisdom and
might is attained by degrees, but pure love did not enter the
stream of evolution by degrees. Pure love flowed into mankind,
into evolution, through Christ, in complete, perfect wholeness. It
is true that we receive into ourselves the Christ Impulse by
degrees, gradually; but the Divine Impulse of pure Love itself
came once and forever in its fullness as a gift to humanity, a gift
born of the very essence of love. [9]

A man, says Steiner, who inwardly knows that any manifestation of pure love implies the paying of debts and brings no profit
in the future for himself, a man who understands the radical
difference between the nature of wisdom and might and that of
love, such a man, even though he has no insight into the meaning
of the Mystery of Golgotha, has no knowledge of the Gospels,
such a man is a true Christian. 'To understand the nature of love
— that is to be a Christian'. [10]

Spiritual science alone, with its teachings of karma and
reincarnation, can, Steiner reiterates again and again, make us
into egoists unless we are imbued with the impulse of love, with
the Christ Impulse. Spiritual science, cultivated without the
Christ Impulse, without the impulse of love, will increase the
power of egoism, will actually breed an egoism that lasts even
beyond death. The striving towards the realization within oneself
of selfless love and an understanding of the essential nature of
love must form integral elements of any spiritual scientific
training; they are the very foundation stones upon which such a
training needs to be based.

Love is essential for any understanding of the Mystery of
Golgotha. Only when love streams into wisdom — and wisdom
flows into love — is it possible to grasp inwardly the nature and
meaning of this Mystery.

Philosopy, philo-sophia, is, in its original Greek meaning, love
of wisdom and, in the light of what has just been indicated, we can
say that the pre-Christian wisdom, the ancient wisdom of the
East, was not philosophy for it did not come to birth through love
but through revelation. We could, indeed, say that there is no
such thing as a philosophy of the East; wisdom of the East, yes;
but not philo-sophia. Philosophy, in the true sense of the word,

manifested itself in the evolution of mankind through the incarnation of the Christ. There we have the entry of wisdom emanating from the impulse of love, which came into the world as the Christ Impulse. It is incumbent upon us, today and in the future, to recognize that the impulse of love must be carried into effect in wisdom itself.

Christ, Who came forth from the realms of the spirit, united wisdom with love — and this love will overcome egoism. Such is its aim. But — and we shall have cause to mention this in greater detail later on — this love must be offered freely from one being to another. The cosmos itself has its source and origin in the love of the Father. Now, strange as it may sound on first hearing, because man was given freedom of choice (described in *Genesis* as the Temptation in the Garden of Eden), egoism was the offshoot of this love. Expressing this more succinctly: separation from the divine source — and separation, too, among men — had its origin in the love of the Father. The Son, the Christ Impulse, the impulse of love, manifest on earth, will, with time — and through our conscious striving — overcome this element of separation, of egoism, and each one of us will gradually become a participant in this creative force of love, the very essence of which is the creation of communion.

In our daily lives we can feel love pouring into our hearts when we bring alive within us the words of Christ:

Where two or three are gathered together in My Name, there am I in the midst of them.

In like manner, Steiner reminds us, does the Rosicrucian saying resound into the love that is wedded with wisdom: *In Christo Morimur* — In Christ we die.

*   *   *   *

Originally, men were in a state of complete union with the divine. Then, as a consequence of what Steiner calls the Luciferic temptation (see Appendix), which promotes selfishness — and through which we live as personalities, — separateness came into being. Together with selfishness, evil came into the world. This had to be so, states Steiner, because without the element of evil as a real force in the world men would not be able to grasp the good consciously. Separateness is a prerequisite of clarity of ordinary consciousness. When we gain victory over the evil within ourselves, the unfolding of love can begin to manifest itself. To man in the clutches of increasing egoism, Christ brought the impulse for this victory over himself. The deeds of Christ were gifts to men, spiritual forces with which separateness, a consequence of egoism and selfishness, could be overcome and a new oneness among men — and with the All — consciously regained. As time progresses, the evolution of mankind will be imbued more and more with new spiritual life, a spiritual life born of Christ's divine deed of love on Golgotha — a deed enacted wholly out of the spirit of purified love. *Per Spiritum Sanctum Reviviscimus* — Through the Holy Spirit we live again.

*　　*　　*　　*

Spiritual perfecting of oneself is certainly a goal for earthly man, but, as we have already seen, nobody who understands what the nature of true deeds of love is will claim that his own striving for perfection is wholly selfless. There is a certain element of egoism involved in such striving. It imparts inner strength to our being; but our real value for the world, for humanity, must be seen to lie in deeds of love, not in deeds carried out for the sake of self-perfection. Steiner emphasizes that we should be under no illusion about this. Further, we should be quite clear in our minds that, when we endeavour to be of service to mankind, only so much of the wisdom we apply in our deeds takes real effect as is imbued with love.

Wisdom steeped in love, which at once furthers true spiritual development and leads the world to Christ, also precludes the lie, precludes all falsification, chicanery and pretence. The lie is always in opposition to the actual facts, to the reality, and those who speak and act in loving accord with the facts are incapable of any form of deceit. Deceit, the lie, has its roots in egoism — always and without exception.

We find the path to wisdom through love. We acquire ever greater wisdom through the increasing power of self-conquest, through selfless love. Along the path of love to wisdom we also grow into true free individuality. Only those who are free in this sense are true Christians. [11]

3.

KNOWLEDGE OF THE HIGHER WORLDS

What'er this world engenders in man's heart
Born tho' it be of love or bitter hate
And howsoever direful its results:
The spirit-seeker must attain the power
In all these things to stand unmoved, serene,
Casting his gaze all unperturbed and calm
Upon the scene where such contentions rage. [1]

Thus speaks the power of love, which bindeth worlds
And filleth beings with the breath of life:
Let warmth flow in his heart that he may grasp
How by the sacrificing of that vain
Illusion of his personality
He doth draw near the spirit of the world.
His sight from sleep of sense thou hast set free;
Love's warmth will wake the spirit in his soul;
His Self from carnal covering thou hast drawn;
And love itself will crystallize his soul
That it may be a mirror to reflect
All that doth happen in the spirit-world.
Love too will give him strength to feel himself
A spirit, and will fashion thus his ear
That it can hear and know the spirit-speech. [2]

3.

In a work which is probably more widely known than any other of his, and which is basic to his conception of man's ability to attain *direct knowledge* of the spiritual world, his *Knowledge of the Higher Worlds*, Steiner stresses the importance and necessity of developing the power of love. Already in the first chapter, entitled 'How is knowledge of the Higher Worlds achieved?', with the subtitle 'Conditions', he states clearly that just as there are laws of Nature so are there also laws in the spiritual life. Acquaintance with the most rudimentary requirements for spiritual development brings the realization that every feeling of true devotion, every manifestation of true love, harboured in the soul develops a power that leads, sooner or later, to a higher stage of knowledge.

Whoever 'by nature' harbours feelings of true devotion — or has been fortunate enough to have had them inculcated by a living education (see Chapter 17) — brings a good foundation with him upon which to base his search for access to higher knowledge. Failing such a preparation in early life the aspirant to higher knowledge must, right from the start, undertake a rigorous self-education to engender within himself the attitude of loving devotion. This is by no means as simple as it sounds, for it is a very widespread and engrained tendency in our modern civilization to give free course to criticism and condemnation rather than nurturing and encouraging the growth within one's soul of devotion and selfless veneration.

To obviate any misunderstanding here, it should be stressed that Steiner is not harbouring negative criticism here towards modern civilization, or, rather, against modern man's well-developed critical faculty. For it is just to this critical faculty, born of the intellect, to this conscious sense of human judgement, that we owe the greatness of our civilization. We would never have been able to develop the technology, science, industry, commerce, system of civil rights, etc., if man had not exercised his critical faculty and sense of judgement. But what we have gained in the various forms of external civilization we have had to pay for, as it were, with a corresponding loss of higher, spiritual

knowledge. It is to the conscious regaining of the latter that
Steiner addresses himself.

Without the fundamental attitude of the soul, which the
spiritual investigator calls the *path of veneration*, of devotion to
truth, no one can embark rightly on the path towards higher
knowledge. Whoever seeks higher knowledge must bring the
feelings of veneration, reverence and wonder — all founded on
and rooted in love — to life in himself.

This cannot, of course, be done by means of study; it can only
be achieved through living. As pupils seeking higher knowledge
we must constantly seek whatever can command our admiration
and respect — in our environment, in our fellow-men, in our
experience of life. If, for instance, I meet someone and blame him
for his failings, I deprive myself of the power of higher
knowledge; but if I earnestly endeavour to understand his
qualities, I nurture this power. In this connection, however, it is
essential to realize that the withholding of negative criticism must
not be a mere 'external' rule of life — that is, merely an unspoken
thought — but must become an integral element of our inmost
soul. Man has the power of perfecting himself and, as time goes
on, of completely transforming himself; but this transformation
must take place in his inmost soul, in his life of thought.

At the outset of his spiritual training the pupil must bring
devotion, love, into his life of thought. He must be wary of
thoughts of disrespect and adverse criticism and constantly
endeavour to cultivate thoughts that imbue him with wonder,
respect and veneration — with love — for the world and for life. [3]

Man has in him the possibility of metamorphosis, of transformation, just as the plant seed contains the possibility of growing
into a complete plant. But whereas the plant goes through the
various stages of transformation because of the objective law
inherent in it, the human being remains in an incomplete,
imperfect state, unless he undertakes inner transformation
through his own initiative. Such a transformation cannot be
forced upon us: we have to undertake it out of our own free will.
Nature makes man no more than a natural being; society makes
of him a law-abiding being; only he himself can raise himself
above the realm of the natural into that of the spiritual — and the
central force in and fundamental to this process is love. [4]

One of the basic conditions of esoteric training is the
development of a feeling of gratitude for everything that one
meets in life — a feeling of gratitude for one's destiny, no matter

how hard the blows may be. It is essential to realize that our existence on earth — with all that earthly existence entails — is a 'gift' from the universe, a cosmic gift. The right development of such a feeling of gratitude can start in quite a simple way. Gratitude to the farmer who grows the grain, to the man who collects the refuse, to the sun and the rain, and so on. 'He who is incapable of developing such an attitude of thought and feeling is also incapable of developing the *all-embracing love that is necessary for the attainment of higher knowledge.*' Only that which I love will reveal itself to me; and every revelation must fill me with gratitude, for each one makes me inwardly the richer. [5]

'The most beautiful way for one's soul to be led to the supersensible is when the path leads through the feeling of thankfulness to life — gratitude not only for the joys but also for the sorrows which life has brought and continues to bring to us.' [6]

When we look at our life 'through the heart', not with the intellect, our expression of thankfulness could assume a form something like this: I am grateful for all that has come towards me in my life because only as a result of the various 'ups' and 'downs' have I grown into the being I am. I cannot know whether, if things had been otherwise, if I had had more gladdening and less saddening experiences, I might have become of more or less account than I am now.

If the soul in its purity — that is, unsullied by emotions tinged with egoism — judges life, then gratitude always arises. Though much of what life may bring to us may be deplored, we can see through the eyes of gratitude that regret is nearly always the expression of misunderstanding of what we are. For, again, if what we regret had not taken place we should not be what we actually are. I and my destiny are one. Whatever life has denied me, it has at all events brought me something, and for that 'something' I must develop the feeling of gratitude.

'Thankfulness gives birth to love and when love is born of thankfulness to life it opens the heart to the spiritual powers permeating all existence. Thankfulness is a way into the supersensible, and finally it becomes veneration and love for the life-bestowing spirit of man.' [7]

At the beginning of the lecture from which the lines just quoted have been drawn, [8] Steiner draws a comparison between the full intensity of the moment an event is experienced — say, the death of someone dear to us — and the usually somewhat 'shadowy' memories of the event that rise up in us several years later. However intense our feelings may have been at the time of an event, the memory picture that remains with us grows dimmer, increasingly void of feeling, as time goes by. Our relation, in the sphere of feeling, to memory is but a pale shadow in comparison with that we have to the experience at the time of the event.

Now when, through actual experience, we develop gratitude and love to the life-bestowing spiritual Powers, our feeling is quite different from anything associated with memory. We experience vividly and with intensity; in memory our experiences become dull in comparison, for it is a characteristic feature of memory that, as time passes, 'feeling and also impulses of will are more and more sifted out of it'. [9]

Memory owes its existence to past experiences. Though they may be shadowy, they are essential to our awareness of the continuity, intrinsic value and reality of our Ego in earthly life. For our everyday-consciousness, our Ego is grounded in the memory. At higher levels of consciousness, when through the power of love we ascend into the spiritual world, we become aware of our true Being, the spiritual essence which our Ego in reality is, and we 'see' that 'we do not experience our "I", our Ego, with very great intensity in everyday-level consciousness on Earth', [10] that the Ego accessible to such consciousness is but a shadow of the Spiritual Essence, of the Higher Self, discernible to spiritual vision, to exact clairvoyance.

This clarification of the nature of the Ego may help us to understand the following indication given by Steiner. When we, in love and gratitude, consider the experiences that have come to us in life we are not concerned merely with our shadowy memories; we are concerned with something far more powerful — not with the shadow of the Ego flowing through time, but with creative powers underlying the eternal in our Ego. Meeting us, from 'outside', are events to which we owe our existence, and when we consider these events in loving gratitude we can but acknowledge them to be powerful creative forces imbuing and forming our Ego. 'We stand in the midst of these events with our Ego; "behind" us, if we look into our soul, we see shadowy after-images, memories of our experiences; "before" us there is weaving destiny, the successive experiences of destiny which form and mould our Ego.' [11]

Steiner indicates further that the transition from head-thinking to heart-feeling belongs, in fact, to this vivid experience of the shaping of destiny, for thankfulness and love can be experienced only in the realm of feeling: 'It is to this thankfulness and love that there comes a presentiment of a ruling destiny. When we have divined the existence of this ruling destiny, having experienced thankfulness and love, we begin to feel the power of the events that have made us what we are.' [12]

The fulfilment of this condition, i.e. the right development of a feeling of gratitude — together with that of others which Steiner elucidates in *Knowledge of the Higher Worlds* — is absolutely essential if the pupil is to be able to meet the further demands that his training will inevitably make upon him — demands which, because of their severity and difficulty, would otherwise render him hesitant and apprehensive. If he fails to meet the basic conditions the pupil will lack the faith in and love for humanity that he needs. All striving for truth along the path of esoteric training must be grounded in love for and faith in one's fellow-men. This love of man must, of course, gradually widen into love that embraces all beings, indeed all existence. Genuine selfless love for everything is both upbuilding and creative and imbues us with a strong inclination to refrain from all forms of negative destructiveness. Such love prevents us, indeed, from destroying merely for the sake of destruction — not only in our actions, but also in our spoken utterances, our feelings and our thoughts. Such love allows us to lend our aid to destruction only when we see that, through a process of destruction, we shall be able to create, or help to create, something afresh, when we can actively support and encourage new life, new growth. Even in what is evil, love leads us to seek out those aspects through which we may transform evil into good. 'Anyone', states Steiner, 'who develops within himself the propensity for creative activity (a propensity founded in love) will be able to deal with evil in the right way.'

He who embarks upon esoteric training has to realize right from the start that its purpose is to create, not to destroy. He must, therefore, cultivate the will for sincere and devoted work, not for criticism and destructiveness. Work upon oneself and devotion to others, are fundamental demands made upon the pupil striving for spiritual knowledge. It is often the experience of those embarking upon esoteric training, Steiner reminds us, that no real progress is being made, in spite of constant activity. A common reason for this lack of progress is that the true nature and purpose of work and devotion have not been rightly grasped. Seen in the light of esoteric training and the attainment of higher spiritual knowledge and faculties, work undertaken for the sake of success will be the least successful, and learning pursued without love, without devotion, will manifest the least progress. Love of the work itself, not of success, leads to success; love of learning itself, not of progress, leads to the greatest progress. [13]

*   *   *   *

Steiner speaks of four attributes that must be acquired on the probationary path for the attainment of higher knowledge. Only short mention of them can be made here and the reader is referred to the book *Knowledge of the Higher Worlds* for closer study. The first is the faculty to *discriminate in thought* between semblance and truth, between mere opinion and truth. Here a short reference to Chapter VII in *The Philosophy of Freedom* is pertinent. This chapter shows that when thinking is understood in the sense Steiner presents it, we cannot speak of limits to knowledge, only of limits to sense perception. We could say that the problem is not that there are limits beyond which our thinking cannot go, but rather that the problem is how to grow inwardly strong enough to accompany our thinking, with our full Ego-consciousness, on its journey through the veil, i.e. beyond the limits set to sense perception. Here we need to recognize that we are confronted with a realm fraught with dangers unless rightly and consciously entered. Those, for instance, who indulge in mediumship and spiritualism leave their Ego-consciousness behind them, with the result that they can so easily be beset by illusion, by a whole world of illusions, for without clear Ego-consciousness they are lacking in the faculty of discrimination.

The second attribute is the faculty to *value* rightly the true and the real — as against the apparent.

The third consists in the practice of the following six qualities: control of thought, control of actions, perseverence, tolerance, faith and equanimity. [14]

Clearly much could be said in regard to these six qualities and the significance of their realization in our endeavours to attain knowledge of the higher worlds, but to dwell at length on them here would lead us beyond the limits of our present thesis. However, Steiner makes some remarks in respect of tolerance that we may well consider here. They have particular relevance to our day-to-day living with our fellow-men. The essence of Steiner's statement is this: He who would be a memeber of a truly

Christian community must strive to attain tolerance towards, and understanding of, his fellow-men. Such understanding and tolerance does not mean, however, that we should adopt an uncritical attitude towards weaknesses and faults we may perceive in others. Such an attitude would lead us to a denial of the truth. If we practise true tolerance and understanding then they give birth within our souls to love for our fellow man. Out of this love we may then speak to him of his faults and errors. If this love is selfless, then in many cases we can readily experience that he who is criticized becomes aware of this love flowing towards him and that his response — expressed or otherwise — is that of gratitude. If, however, we rebuke such a person with cold, loveless indifference, then — and this we can easily recognize — he 'recoils' from our lack of warmth and understanding. In such situations we can often become the cause of the birth of a feeling of antipathy, of hatred even, towards us. Selfless love is always constructive. Loveless indifference and intolerance can but give rise to a negative, destructive reaction. [15]

The fourth attribute, particularly relevant to our theme, is the *selfless love of inner freedom*: 'A mere intellectual grasp of what lies in these attributes is of no use. They must be so deeply integrated into the soul that they become the basis of inner habits.' [16]

With reference to the fourth attribute — selfless love of inner freedom — Steiner emphasizes that once it has become habit, we increasingly free ourselves from everything that is concerned *only* with the faculties of our personal nature. We cease to view things from an egocentric viewpoint, and the limits of our narrow self-centredness, which fetter us to this or that opinion, disappear. The 'secrets' — the 'open' secrets Goethe would have called them — of the spiritual world begin to reveal themselves to the inner self, the inner self imbued with spiritualized love, and the process of liberation begins; the fetters that *compel* us to view things according to our personal idiosyncrasies fall away. It is from this narrow, personal viewpoint, as distinct from a universal, cosmic, all-embracing way of viewing things, that the pupil undergoing esoteric training seeks freedom. [17]

Among the general demands that, Steiner says, every aspirant for spiritual development must make of himself, among the conditions that must form the basis of all esoteric training, is the habitual cultivation of a 'positive attitude' to life in all its manifestations. This exercise implies that we always look for the good, praiseworthy, beautiful, and so on, in all experiences.

Steiner characterizes this attitude of soul by recounting a Persian legend concerning Christ. One day as Christ was walking with his disciples, they saw a dead dog lying by the roadside in a state of advanced decomposition. All the disciples turned away from the disgusting sight; Christ alone did not, but looked thoughtfully at the putrefying corpse and said: 'What beautiful teeth the animal has!'

In a certain respect we can see that this exercise is closely connected with that of 'abstention from criticism' (see p.36). This is not, Steiner points out, to be understood that we should be prepared to call black white or white black. No, the point to bear in mind is that there is a significant difference between a judgement which, proceeding merely from one's limited personality, is coloured by an element of personal sympathy or antipathy, and an attitude which lovingly approaches the phenomenon. Such an attitude would ask, for instance: How has it come to be like this or act like this? Such an attitude, imbued with love, will, by its very nature, be more inclined to offer help to that which is imperfect than simply to find fault and negatively criticize. [18]

Among the many meditative verses Steiner gave to those who asked for them is the following. Held in our consciousness for some five minutes, immediately upon waking in the morning, it can help us cultivate the 'positive attitude' just described:

> In purest outpoured Light
> Shimmers the Godhead of the World.
> In purest Love towards all that lives
> Outpours the god-hood of my soul.
> I rest within the Godhead of the World;
> There shall I find myself,
> Within the Godhead of the World.

For those who have German the original is included here — for no matter how well done the translation into English, something of the mood and intention in Steiner's words is lost:

> *In den reinen Strahlen des Lichts*
> *Erglänzt die Gottheit der Welt.*
> *In der reinen Liebe zu allen Wesen*
> *Erstrahlt die Gottlichkeit meiner Seele.*
> *Ich ruhe in der Gottheit der Welt;*

Ich werde mich selbst finden
In der Gottheit der Welt. [19]

As part of the meditative 'rounding off' of the day, Steiner gave a complementary verse:

Within the Godhead of the World,
There shall I find Myself
Wherein I rest.
The god-head of my soul outpours
In purest Love toward all that lives,
Shimmers the Godhead of the World
In purest Light outpoured.

In der Gottheit der Welt
Werde ich mich selber finden,
In IHR ruhe ich.
Es erstrahlt die Göttlichkeit meiner Seele
In der reinen Liebe zu allen Wesen,
Es erglänzt die Gottheit der Welt
In den reinen Strahlen des Lichts. [20]

On occasion Steiner gave a commentary on such meditative verses and, because of its relevance to our present theme, a few extracts, given more or less verbatim, are included here. Prefacing his commentary on the verse beginning with the words 'In purest outpoured Light' he said that his comments are to be regarded as being an imaginative presentation of the single strophes:

In purest outpoured Light
Shimmers the Godhead of the World . . .

The Godhead pours himself out, as it were, in silver-shining moonlight over the outer world: we feel as if this light is streaming through us, flowing around us.

In purest Love towards all that lives
Outpours the god-hood of my soul . . .

After expanding into the outer world, where we sought to know the Godhead, we sink deeply within our being, and through the love that unites us with all beings we find the link with the Godhead and feel the divine element in our own soul.

I rest within the Godhead of the World . . .

Ich ruhe in der Gottheit der Welt . . .

The word '*ruhe*', as Steiner points out, has magic power — a power which is not present to anything like the same extent in the English word 'rest'. The pupil who succeeds in concentrating himself in this word, '*ruhe*', in 'entering' right into it, into the sound of it and into its inner content, will have the experience of being pervaded by and bathed in peace and rest. In that we feel within ourselves the connection with the Godhead; we find this rest and this peace within us. Rest and peace encircle us and penetrate us.

> There shall I find myself
> Within the Godhead of the World.

And now, continues Steiner, there arises in us an image of a point of light, a gleaming spark shimmering towards us from afar, to which we strive and wherein we shall find ourselves in the bosom of the Godhead. [21]

One of the most beautiful — and certainly untranslatable — little poems Goethe wrote can give us in a most wonderful way this experience of being imbued with peace and rest and held 'in the bosom of the Godhead'. It has meant a great deal to the present writer since his boyhood days and he may, therefore, be forgiven for self-indulgence in quoting it here:

> *Über allen Gipfeln*
> *Ist Ruh,*
> *In allen Wipfeln*
> *Spürest du*
> *Kaum einen Hauch;*
> *Die Vögelein schweigen im Walde.*
> *Warte nur, balde*
> *Ruhest du auch.*

*   *   *   *

Referring once again to the 'positive attitude' to life, which the pupil embarking upon an esoteric, a spiritual scientific training, must cultivate, the following comment by Steiner may serve to meet an obvious objection: 'Man learns little by little to love all things. This does not mean that he should give his heart *without discrimination* to everything he encounters.'[22] As we all know, experience can at first be deceptive; but if we take pains to fathom a fellow human being down to his divine foundation, then we also begin to love him. This does not mean, however, that if a depraved person confronts us, we should love his depravity. We should be in error to do so and, moreover, we should not in any way be helping him. On the other hand, if we ponder over how this person may have arrived at his depraved state, and if we make every effort to help him to grow out of and overcome it, then not only do we help him but we ourselves also struggle through to the truth. 'We must search everywhere for the *right way* to love[23] . . . I am not straightaway to love the external aspect of a being or a thing, for this is deceptive and I could then easily love his error. But behind all illusion lies truth, and truth we can always love. And if the heart seeks the love of truth in all beings, then there lives the "Spirit in the heart". Such love is the garment that the soul should ever wear. Then the soul weaves the divine into things.'[24]

Taking up the statement 'the soul weaves the divine into things', which leads on to some aspects of our theme that are the concern of the next chapter, we may here consider the following: If someone, out of love, does me a kindness, it is true that the deed, as such, 'passes away'. But what the deed plants in my heart and soul remains. Nor does the bond of love that has united him with me pass away. Indeed, whatever we experience is always the source in us of something that lasts, so that even when we pass through the Portal of Death and are thus transplanted to an entirely different scene of action we take with us the fruits of what we have garnered here on earth, and our 'deeds' in the spiritual world will be 'woven out of the memories' of this world — for, as Steiner succinctly puts it, 'there is no seed that does not bear fruit'.[25] If, for instance, we are united with someone on earth by love, then this love is a seed and we experience its fruit throughout the future, for we belong together with and are an integral part of such a person throughout the future. 'Thus there lives in each one of us something which is interwoven with the divine power that binds all beings together into the eternal fabric of the universe. This "something" is our higher Self.'[26] The eternal core of this higher Self is spiritualized love.

*   *   *   *

Steiner advances a most important argument in respect of the limits of man's cognitive faculty, of man's purely natural knowledge — as distinct from his spiritual organism in the form of cognitive activity and inner experience to which the term 'limit' cannot be applied in the same sense. In so far as we are only considering the former, i.e. man's theoretical cognitive faculty, Steiner would agree with Kant that limits should be recognized — but for quite other reasons than those advanced by Kant. [27]

Assuming, argues Steiner, that man's theoretical cognitive faculty, by which he connects his concepts with observations and the results of experiments in order to arrive at the laws of the universe, could also penetrate without difficulty into the organic realm; if it could advance as far as life (which Steiner shows in, for instance, *A Theory of Knowledge Implicit in Goethe's World Conception*, [28] that it cannot in fact do), there would be little reason why it should stop short of the higher modes of existence — the realms of soul and spirit. Assuming, therefore, that the ordinary consciousness we employ in the sciences and work with in ordinary life were able not only to comprehend the inorganic world and the 'externals' of life, but also to penetrate below the surface of things into their inner being; assuming this were possible and that there were thus no limits to knowledge based on ordinary lucid thinking, what, asks Steiner, would the soul-spiritual constitution of man look like? His answer to this question is startling: 'Though this may appear paradoxical to some people, a dispassionate observer of life and of the relationship of man to the world will realize that a being whose ordinary everyday consciousness was unlimited would inevitably lack the capacity to love.' [29]

If we reflect, continues Steiner, on the significance of this capacity for our whole life — and on what we are in life just because we can love — then we have to conclude that we should not be true men if we did not have this capacity to love. But — and this is the essential point to which attention is drawn on several occasions in these pages — love demands that we should meet other individuals as self-contained entities. We should not, 'must not invade other individuals with our clear, lucid, logical thinking'. On the contrary, at the very moment when we develop love, our inner essence must become active — that 'part of us which is beyond logic', beyond concepts formulated by our everyday consciousness, our everyday cognitive faculty of intellectual thought. 'The moment we invade another individual with clear and lucid concepts, love dies.' [30]

Since, as elsewhere discussed, man must develop more and more into a being of love by virtue of his task on earth (see Chapter 14), we can see that he definitely 'needs' limits to his knowledge of the outside world if he is to fulfil his task here on earth. 'The property that enables man to be a creature of love has its obverse side in his ordinary knowledge. This knowledge has to stop at the limit that is set for us in order that we may be creatures capable of love.' [31]

Inasmuch as we love, our relationship to the world around us is not one of cognition based on ordinary consciousness, operating through the senses, the intellect and the faculty of logic, but one of reality, a real relationship of being. It is, states Steiner, only by developing 'vital thinking' (see Introduction) that we are able to carry over our experiences into the reality of things. By developing plastic, vital thinking and then creating what Steiner calls an 'empty consciousness', [32] we advance further and further into the spiritual world. Compared with ordinary consciousness, we feel in a supersensible act of cognition of this kind as if we have been awakened from sleep. 'We eavesdrop on our being as it becomes a living thing.' 'At a certain stage of higher cognition, we must pour out our own self — as being — into the outside world. This goes hand in hand with the experience that the act of cognition now transforms mere knowledge into real life, or, differently expressed, into a real symbiosis with the outside world.' [33]

At first, Steiner warns, the development of the faculty of higher, spiritual cognition is linked with 'an appreciable intensification of the sense of self'. He explains this in the following manner:

In ordinary cognition of the outside world, our ego goes as far as the frontiers of nature. Here the ego is 'repulsed'. We feel surrounded on all sides by psychic walls, so to speak. This, in turn, has repercussions on the sense of self. The sense of self has its own strength, and it finds its right nuance of expression precisely through the fact that, along with this feeling of something like 'confinement', there is interwoven that quality of self-surrender to the world and its creatures that comes of love. In supersensible cognition the self is made even stronger and there is, we may say, a real danger that it will transform the love that rightfully exists on earth into a selfish submersion in things, that it will effusively thrust and insinuate itself into things'.

That, in other words, it will oust the power of love as a force of knowledge, oust the self-less outgoing into the things and processes of the world. 'By so doing, the self will expand.' [34]

This is why, in his fundamental book, *Knowledge of the Higher Worlds*, Steiner attaches so much weight to the preparatory exercises on the path towards higher knowledge. These exercises are aimed at self-discipline in relation to the sense of self, and, at the same time, at helping us to develop the necessary capacity for love in ordinary life and consciousness, before attempting to move into the supersensible world by means of higher knowledge.

In a lecture with the title 'Recent Results of Occult Investigation into Life between Death and Rebirth', [35] Steiner gives a graphic picture of two characteristic differences that prevail between our experience of the spiritual world, on the one hand, and of the sense world, on the other.

If we reflect upon our experience in the sense world of objects around us, we recognize that what we perceive by means of our senses, say our eyes and ears, comes 'towards us' — a sound impinges upon our ear, our ear does not seek out the sound, and so on. It is only in the 'higher realms' of life, so to speak, in the spheres of metaphysical knowledge and imaginative art, that *we* have to exert ourselves to participate in drawing things towards us. Everything that impinges on our senses and our intellect comes towards us. Our everyday thought is dependent on a perception of the sense-world. Every moment of everyday life is filled with *impressions* and, apart from the exceptions mentioned, we do not have to make the effort to bring them about.

This stands in acute contrast to our *actions* in the physical world. For then we have to be active, we have to move from place to place, be on the go. *We* have to go 'towards' things.

What is presented to our perception comes to us without our activity — apart from 'receptivity', of course; what we ourselves wish to achieve, however, in the sense-perceptible world can only be brought about if we are active, if we are outgoing.

Now, says Steiner, strange as it may appear, the opposite is true in the spiritual world, in our clairvoyant existence in this world. There we cannot be active in the same way as we are on earth. We cannot say that this or that happens in the spiritual world as a result of our being on the go, of our going towards things. On the contrary, for something to happen in the spiritual world it is essential that there be absolute calmness in our soul. The 'quieter' we are, the more things can happen through us in the spiritual world. We need to develop loving participation in a mood of soul-calmness for what is to happen, and then wait patiently to see how things come to pass. This attitude of soul is essential in any genuine spiritual striving towards higher knowledge. It is a quality of calmness and patience that in the spiritual world is creative and hardly has its equal in ordinary everyday physical life. We could say that it is somewhat similar to the quality of soul an artist or a creative thinker needs. For instance, the creative artist who cannot wait, patiently and with inner calm and receptivity, for the right moment of inspiration, until the intuition comes to him, will not be able to create the highest of which he is capable. He who seeks to create according to some previously thought out plan will produce works of inferior quality — that is, inferior to the best of which he is capable. Also, he who seeks to create, be it the smallest work, prompted by an outer stimulus will not succeed as well as he would do if he were to wait quietly and with loving devotion for the moment of inspiration —'We might say for the moment of grace.' [36] The same is true of the spiritual world. In it there is no rush and excitement, no sense of urgency, only calmness of soul.

What has to *happen*, then, *through* us, in the spiritual world, in our experience of this world has to be awaited in silence. What, on the other hand, we have to do in the spiritual world in order to know, we do here in the physical world in order to act. For instance, in the physical world the rose we find along the wayside gladdens our hearts. This does not happen on the spiritual plane. There something similar to a rose would not appear unless we had *exerted ourselves* to enter a particular realm of the spirit in order to draw it towards us. 'Only the higher activities of man, for example, creative artistic effort, where the spiritual world weaves into the physical, afford a reflection of the events in the spiritual world.' That is why, Steiner tells us, it is essential, if we wish inwardly to understand what is imparted by spiritual science, to develop two qualities of soul. 'First, love for the spiritual world, which leads to an active grasping of the spirit — and is the surest way of enabling us to bring the things of the spirit towards us. And, secondly, inner rest, a calmness of soul, a silence free from vanity or ambition anxious to attain results, but capable of receiving grace, able to await inspiration.' [37] Anyone who attempts to force the citadels of the spiritual worlds through lack of inner preparation imbued with love and humility falls a victim to the enticements of either Lucifer or Ahriman (see Appendix), or an alliance of both.

In practice this patient mood and inner attitude of open expectation is not easy, but Steiner, out of his experience of the spiritual worlds and of the 'laws' underlying all genuine spiritual striving, gives us many indications, often in the forms of exercises, that can help us to overcome obstacles. In this particular instance he gives a thought that is difficult for us at first to accept because it strikes deeply against our vanity — a strong Luciferic element within us. The thought, which should grow into a living force within us, is this: in the overall, universal pattern and destiny of mankind it is of no importance whatsoever whether something is achieved by me or by someone else. This does not mean, of course, that we should grow inwardly lethargic, nor should it prevent us from doing our duty, but it should 'prevent us from hurrying to and fro. How glad every individual feels that *he* is capable, that *he* can do it! A certain resignation is necessary for us to feel equally glad when someone else can and does do something.' In other words, we should not love something because we have done it ourselves, but love it because it is in the world irrespective of whether we or someone else has done it. If we ponder this thought, and endeavour to live up to it, it will 'lead most certainly to selflessness'. [38]

Such moods of soul are essential elements in our striving to become cognisant of spiritual events and realities.

4.

LOVE — THE BRIDGE BETWEEN TWO WORLDS

Upward to thee strive the love of my soul,
Upward to thee flow the stream of my love!
   May they sustain thee,
   May they enfold thee
   In heights of Hope,
   In spheres of Love. [1]

Into the fields of Spirit will I send
The faithful love we found on Earth,
Uniting soul with soul.
And thou wilt find my loving thought
When from the Spirit-lands of light
Thou hither turn thy seeking soul
To find what thou does seek in me. [2]

4.

As an introductory statement, which will subsequently be enlarged upon, the reader is referred to a lecture given by Steiner in London in the early 1920s. [3] Summarizing the relevant passages, what he says is this: All relationships woven on earth between human beings, between soul and soul, are laid aside in their earthly form when the soul enters the purely spiritual world after physical death. But the fruits of these ties of love and affection that have been unfolded here on earth do not disappear. They are transmuted after death into those spiritual experiences which then help to form a later physical life. In this activity the departed human being is not working for himself alone but for — and in communion with — those souls who were esteemed and loved by him on earth.

Indeed, the communion between two souls, one of which is in the spiritual world, can be closer and more intimate than between two human beings here on earth, for it may be said that in the physical world there is an unbridgeable abyss between two souls, since their meeting takes place in the physical body and even the most spiritual relationships between them are determined and limited by the conditions of an existence in bodily form. But when a human being himself is in the spiritual world, the physical body belonging to the one whom he loved and has left behind on earth does not constitute any obstacle to a living communion with the soul. The human being who has passed through the Portal of Death can penetrate through the physical body of the one he has loved and left behind and thus enter into direct communion with his soul.

Mention was just made of 'an unbridgeable abyss between two souls' in earth existence, in spite of the most spiritual relationship which may exist between them. In an early written work, which in English bears the title *The Threshold of the Spiritual World*, [4] and in a series of lectures, *Occult Reading and Occult Hearing*, [5] given shortly after the publication of the book, Steiner approaches this problem from a different angle and what he says on these occasions may appear to contradict what was stated above. But the essential point to bear in mind is that in both instances Steiner is concerned to show what we have to do to evolve the faculty of 'growing into the spiritual world'. This is a faculty of the future in the sense in which Steiner is speaking.

Part of the process involved is that we 'emerge' from ourselves and identify ourselves with another being. But, says Steiner, this is only the beginning, this is not sufficient in itself. It is necessary not only to be able to identify ourselves with other beings — which is difficult enough — but also to go a stage beyond this and be able to *transform* ourselves inwardly into other beings so that we do not remain what we are but are able to metamorphose ourselves into other beings — 'actually to become that, *inwardly*, into which we penetrate'. [6]

A good preparation for this future faculty is to practise again and again a loving interest in everything that is around us in the world. We have already had occasion to see that this cannot be emphasized too strongly. It is only too easy for the necessary power of interest to be centred in oneself. Honesty compels us to admit that real, selfless interest is far from being as constant as it should be. However, to give up all interest in ourselves as individual entities would be, Steiner states, counter to the cosmic law that decrees that, whilst on earth, man must have interest in himself too. [7] But if we are to grow into the spiritual world, it is essential that this self-interest is transmuted in increasing measure into selfless interest. We are beings of the earth, as well as of the spirit, and not to take any interest in ourselves is clearly not natural to the earth-plane. Steiner illustrates the kind of transmutation he means by the following simple example. A man falls seriously ill. He is not specially interested in the fact that it is *he* who has this illness. What does interest him is the 'how' and the 'why' of the origin of the illness in the Cosmos. How and why at some point in cosmic evolution something arose that now finds expression in him, is within his own body. In such a case as this the man is interested in a severe illness in the same way as if it were nothing to do with him physically, as if it were something *outside* himself. His interest, in short, may be called selfless. [8]

This cultivation of selfless interest is a vital and necessary step along the path towards a conscious entry into the spiritual world. Steiner admits that for most of us this fundamental step is very difficult. It is difficult to contemplate the most ordinary things we experience *within* us, in our senses and our thoughts, as though they were objects outside ourselves. The task set before us is this:

we have to transform our inner attitude of soul in such a way that we are no longer merely an interesting *subject* for ourselves, but, in increasing measure, an interesting *object*.

Now to the same extent to which we ourselves begin to become an object to ourselves, we begin also to be selflessly interested in the world around us and its phenomena. When loving devotion to the world and its phenomena deepens more and more, the mood of soul is also able to intensify to the point where we not only 'pass out' of or 'emerge' from ourselves, but are also able to metamorphose ourselves into other beings, other objects. Gradually, we shall become capable of doing this. [9]

5.

LINKS BETWEEN THE LIVING AND THE DEAD

*For intercourse with the dead, some
things in life are more favourable, others
less so. And we may ask: What can really
help our intercourse with the dead? The
manner of our intercourse with the dead
cannot be the same as the manner of our speech
with the living; the dead neither hear nor
take in this kind of speech . . . What makes
it possible to ask questions of the dead or
to communicate something to the dead, is that
we unite the life of feeling with our
thoughts and ideas . . . Any question to the
dead must be put in a particular way; it
must not merely be a thought or an idea,
it must be imbued with feeling — and with
will. Your relationship with the dead must
be one of the* heart, *of* inner interest.
*You must remind yourself of your love for the
dead when he was alive, and address yourself
to him not abstractly, but with real warmth
of heart.* [1]

5.

During the course of a series of lectures, *The Forming of Destiny and Life After Death*, [2] Steiner elucidates certain aspects of earth life in order to bring us understanding of some of the experiences of the soul in the spiritual world. He begins by asking us to consider how, in life on earth, we are confronted with events of nature that run their course and then expire, this being characteristic of any happening 'tied' to the laws of necessity, laws of nature, indeed of all human activities out of which human history is woven in the world of 'necessity'. But beyond this there is something in us which seeks that which has nothing to do with the immediate necessities of life. We are aware that, if nature and history merely ran their course solely in relation to the fulfilment and satisfaction of human needs and the necessities of nature, life would indeed manifest itself as bleak and barren. Man creates on earth something that is not subject to the laws of nature and necessity. For instance, we can think of the whole realm of art as something that we, as creative beings, call into existence and that is of a different reality than that pertaining to nature and history. The artist within us creates something which need not of necessity exist; or, differently expressed, artistic creation is something quite other than that which underlies the unfolding of the laws of nature. If art were non-existent, the necessities of nature would not suffer — 'natural' life would still pursue its course. In art we have something that 'extends' beyond the life of nature and necessity. We could say that we have two progressive processes: the *necessities* of nature and history obeying definite laws *and* the *freely-flowing* stream of artistic creation.

Now, says Steiner, 'As far as the "dead" are concerned, the spiritual world would run its course without any memories living in the souls here, memories born of love and of all our human relationships. But then the world of the dead would be to them as a world would be to us in which we could find nothing transcending ordinary reality'. [3] This, continues Steiner, is an extraordinarily significant connection between the living and the dead; for, through thoughts of love, through loving memories, and what is thus active in our souls in connection with those no longer in the physical world, there is created for the dead 'something analogous to artistic creation here on earth'. However, there is a very distinct difference. Whereas here in the physical world *we must give birth to* artistic creation out of our own souls, in the spiritual world quite the opposite pertains: that which for them has similar significance as art has for us, namely love, *must be brought to* them. Without this love streaming up to them from our hearts, the world of the 'dead' would be as this world of nature and necessity would be to us, if it were to run its course without art, without all that we create 'above and beyond' the immediate physical reality. Such would our world be for the dead if we on earth held no loving memories of them. [4]

Steiner gave the following meditation to be used in our endeavour to bring to the 'dead' the warmth and spiritual nourishment they need:

> Upward to thee strive the love of my soul,
> Upward to thee flow the stream of my love!
> > May they sustain thee,
> > May they enfold thee
> > In heights of Hope,
> > In spheres of Love.

> *Es strebe zu dir meiner Seele Liebe,*
> *Es ströme zu dir meiner Liebe Sinn.*
> *Sie mögen dich tragen,*
> *Sie mögen dich halten*
> *In Hoffnungshöhen,*
> *In Liebessphären.* [5]

'Each time that a dead person contacts a remembrance of himself in the soul of a man who was in some way connected with him on earth, it is always as if something streamed over to him which beautifies his life, and enhances its value.' [6] Just as on earth beauty and soul-enrichment come to us through the inspired creations of artistic genius, so to the dead beauty and enrichment stream from the hearts of those who hold them afresh in loving memory.

A short digression may be permitted here. We can see from what has just been discussed that life on earth has significance not only for those who are active on earth but also for those who have left it and are in the spiritual world. Spiritual science, in short, does not — and should not — lead us to deplore earth existence. On the contrary, it gives us the insight to consider earth life, with all that this entails, as a part, a vital part, of the whole life of the cosmos. We could, indeed, say with Angelus Silesius:

> I know that without me God can no moment live;
> If I come to naught, He must needs give up the Ghost. [7]

'The Kingdom of the Heavens is nourished by the effluence of human love. The interest of the Gods is the element of human love by means of which their life is sustained.' [8]

The spiritual world would not appear in its perfection without human life on earth. When, therefore, we realize that 'beauty' must issue forth from the physical world, that is to say, that love must stream from our hearts to those who have died, we also realize that 'the spiritual world would lack this beauty, if there were no physical world, if there were no human souls who, while still in the physical body, were able to evolve thoughts full of love for those no longer on earth'. [9]

A person who has died before us and whom we completely forget finds it almost impossible to reach us. The love, the constant sympathy and warmth we feel for the dead, creates a path by which a connection can be made with those who remain on earth. It is only over the 'bridge of love' which we build that those who have departed earth existence can find a connection with us. [10]

Concerning communion between the living and the dead, Steiner gives us some interesting facts regarding the effects of the dislike or hatred we have harboured for someone who has died. When the clairvoyant investigator follows the soul of the departed through the Portal of Death into the spiritual worlds and then 'looks back' at someone who, on earth, hated or was antipathetic to the one who has died, he finds that, in general, the departed soul has a very clear perception of the soul-quality of hatred in the living. The clairvoyant can also perceive what such hatred means to the dead. It creates an obstacle to his good intentions in his spiritual environment, comparable to the obstacles we may encounter on earth that stand in the way of the attainment of our aims. The dead sees my hatred, my antipathy, as an actual hindrance to his good endeavours.

Now, it is an interesting phenomenon, observes Steiner, that if we have hated or disliked someone who has died, we often find that we cannot continue to hate or dislike him to the same extent. Indeed, if our hatred or dislike extends beyond the moment of death we often have a feeling of shame in regard thereto. We can understand, therefore, why, if we search into ourselves but a little, hatred, even if seemingly quite justified, will 'die out' because of the shame it entails after the death of the hated person. It is true that we may not always be aware of the connection, for it is only the clairvoyant who will 'see' the reason for the shame; but he who has hated nevertheless more often than not has an instinctive feeling that he is being observed — that the dead person perceives the feelings of hatred. He may even feel that this hatred forms an obstacle in the way of the good intentions of the soul in the spiritual world.

'Many feelings rooted deeply in the human soul are explained when we [in exact clairvoyance] rise into the worlds of spirit and recognize the spiritual facts underlying these feelings.' [11] Just as on earth we may do certain things which we would not wish others to observe — and in fact refrain from doing them if we know ourselves to be observed — so we do not go on hating or disliking a person after his death if we have the feeling that we are being observed by him.

On the other hand, the sensitive soul can also feel that love, or even a gentle sympathy for the dead, removes obstacles from the path of those who have passed through the Gates of Death. Their spiritual journey is made easier. They feel a certain relief because of the love that flows up to them from the earth. [12]

Another example, often discussed by Steiner, of an obstacle being placed before the soul of the dead in his attempts to come into communion with those he has left behind on earth is probably more readily accepted by ordinary thought than the example just discussed. It is this: clairvoyant vision sometimes reveals to us human souls suffering, in the life between death and a new birth, because those they have known — including those dearest to them — harbour only materialistic thoughts.

Suppose, for instance, we find in the spiritual world a man who has recently passed through the Gates of Death, whom we knew personally during his earth life, and who left behind members of his family also known to us. Clairvoyant vision now reveals that the man, whose wife was very close to him on earth and who had genuine human love for him, is nevertheless inaccessible to him. He cannot 'see' into her soul because she has no spiritual thoughts — either in her head or in her heart. He cannot find her. This is an example of a soul, in the life between death and rebirth, looking towards someone still on earth, someone who had loved him but whose love was not united with belief in the soul's continued existence after death. This also illustrates the widespread view that as far as consciousness is concerned the dead pass over into a kind of void. A person who holds such a view can only think of the dead in materialistic terms — not with any fruitful thoughts. In such cases, at the very moment after death — and during the early stages of the spiritual journey — when the 'wish' arises in the soul of him who has died to 'see' those whom he loved on earth, all vision is extinguished. 'The living human being on earth cannot be found, nor can any link be established with him, although it is known that he could indeed be contacted, if spiritual thoughts were harboured in his soul.' [13]

The eyes of the spirit of the dead person, who, incidentally, may also have been a materialist, [14] cannot 'see' what they experience when they turn to those still on earth if there is no spiritual life in their souls: 'spiritual life alone throws light up into the spiritual worlds'. Without spiritual life on earth, darkness reigns between souls living in the two worlds.

In the lecture entitled 'Links Between the Living and the Dead' — essential reading for those concerned to establish the reality of such links — Steiner makes the point that in our present materialistic age the dead are cut off from the living more drastically than they were a comparatively short time ago (he would be speaking in terms of several centuries) [15] and this makes it more difficult for them 'to perceive what is astir in the souls of those left behind'. This belongs, says Steiner, to the evolution of humanity. But we must now consciously rediscover real intercourse between the living and the dead. 'It will be one of the practical tasks of spiritual scientific life to ensure that the bridge is built again between the living and the dead.' [16]

On one occasion Steiner introduced the question of communion with those who have passed through the Portal of Death in the following way. Many think nothing of enriching themselves at the expense of others: 'Not only do they live in such a manner without any moral self-criticism, but they simply do not think about it at all.' In due course, Steiner remarks, there will develop the consciousness that such a way of living is immoral and that the happiness and prosperity of the individual will be quite impossible unless the community, mankind as a whole, also enjoys happiness and prosperity. 'This must gradually become a fundamental principal of true human ethics.' [17] The feeling of community will gradually increase, said Steiner just over sixty years ago, and with it the feeling that the life of the whole community is similar to that of any living organism in which each element works in harmony with all the others. In a living organism, unless such harmony rules between the various parts, disease [18] — a conflict of interests, etc. — is inevitable.

Such a feeling as just indicated can be greatly intensified; it can develop into an intimate perception, a heart-sensitive perception, of the unity of all things.

One way in which we can cultivate the feeling of unity with all things is to bring to our consciousness the idea that when we have performed some deed — however insignificant it may appear on the surface — something of it remains in us, something, for instance, of what we have understood in the doing of it. A certain active force remains in us from the doing of something — either alone or with someone else; from the forces with which we do a thing, something remains connected with our indestructible Ego. If we can experience this, then we bring to our consciousness what otherwise remains in our subconscious — namely, the fact that we leave our distinctive mark on all things and that we are intimately bound up with the people with whom we have come in touch in our deeds.

This feeling of unity must become an integral element in our soul-life if we are to make it possible for someone we have loved and who has died to bring himself to our consciousness. Only when we are able to re-experience what we have had in common with someone with whom we were and continue to be karmically united, even after his death, only when we are able to think (and feel) about the person who has crossed the Threshold (in the same way as we think when we have) this feeling of unity, of at-oneness, are we ready, inwardly, for the discarnate person to reach us — and we to reach him.

We can picture this to ourselves in this way. We think of something that took place between ourselves and the one who is dead — right down to the slightest detail. How, for instance, we sat at a particular table and broke homebaked bread with him, discussed a book we had both recently read, and so on. The whole occasion gave rise to a rich and warm feeling of at-oneness with him. We visualize, in thought, this situation as strongly as we are able, and then we turn our whole soul-life in the direction of this thought. If we can but develop, in thought, a communion of soul with the dead that is in accordance with the 'feeling of unity' we had on the occasion outlined, then his gaze from the spiritual world can find the reality from these thoughts, just as our thoughts can find the reality to which they are directed. If we allow such thoughts of the dead to develop in our soul, to the degree that they are filled with love, the soul-spiritual gaze of the living 'encounters' that of the dead. [19] Through such encounters the dead can 'speak' to us, be with us.

We learn, as it were, to feel our karma when we begin to sense how we leave behind us everywhere the stamp of our thought in everything in which we have been involved; we learn to identify ourselves with these things — in love — and thus we develop the feeling that brings us into increasing conscious union with the dead. A love-filled consciousness of being at-one with the dead clears the way for them to 'speak' to us.

Steiner gives us many details of the obstacles that prevent communion with the dead. One in particular — in connection with materialistic thought — was mentioned earlier. To go into detail regarding others is not our task, [20] but mention will be made of the following. If the dead wish to 'speak' to us, it is necessary that — in addition to the feeling of unity previously mentioned — we take into our consciousness something of the feeling of loving gratitude for all that reveals itself to us. If there is none of this feeling within us, if we cannot realize that life on earth is a 'gift', the dead cannot find a common soul-spiritual 'air' with us, cannot 'speak' with us. We cannot arouse this feeling of gratitude if, having lost a loved one, we wish him back in earth life; we should feel gratitude that he was with us on earth, even if only for a short time. The very feelings we so frequently have towards those we love who have passed into the spiritual world are a hindrance to their finding and 'speaking' to us. Most often we have far too little of the feeling of loving gratitude that they have meant a great deal to us in life. We should not hold fast to the idea that we have them no longer with us in a physical sense, for that is a feeling of ingratitude, considered in the wider sense of Life. Our feeling of 'having lost' them is a burden to those who have died. To lighten their burden as much as possible, we must think selflessly of what they were to us and not lose ourselves in feelings of loss. The better we can selflessly feel what a loved one meant to us during his life, the sooner will it be possible for him to 'speak' to us by means of the common soul-spiritual 'air' of loving gratitude. [21]

At the end of a lecture dealing with occult development Steiner gives a succinct answer to the question: Is there any value in reading Masses for the dead? His answer is: 'Good thoughts are balm for the dead. It is not selfish love that we should send them, not mourning because we no longer have them here; this harms a dead person and weighs on him like lead. But love that endures, that does not lay claim to the dead person by wanting him back again — this nourishes him and augments his happiness.' [22]

In a lecture entitled 'The Dead are with us' [23] Steiner mentions the significant difference between the relationship we can have with those who have died old and those who have died young.

The secret of communion with children who have died can be expressed by saying that in the spiritual sense we do not lose them; they remain with us. When children die, particularly in very young years, they continue ever present with us — spiritually — to a very marked degree. Of older people who have loved us and whom we have loved, the reverse may be said. Those who have died in advanced years do not lose *us*. *We* do not lose little children. Older people when they die are strongly drawn to the spiritual world, but this also gives them the power so to work into the physical world that it is easier for them to approach us.

The meaning of this difference can also be considered in another connection.

When friends die, we mourn and feel pain; [24] but in regard to this pain and sorrow, people make no distinction as to whether it is caused by the death of a child or of an older person. Spiritually speaking, Steiner tells us, there is a great difference.

When little children die the pain of those who mourn is really a kind of compassion. The souls of children who die remain together with us and, because we have been physically united with them, they convey their pain to our souls. 'We feel *their* pain, for they would fain still be with us on the physical plane.' Their pain is eased, however, when we share it with them. The child feels in us. 'It is good when a child can share his feelings with us; his pain is thereby relieved.' [25]

Of quite a different nature, however, is the pain we feel at the death of an older person. This can be called 'egoistical pain'. An older person does not lose us and the feeling he has is therefore quite different from that present in a child. He is drawn strongly to the spiritual world and would not 'fain still be with us on the physical plane'. It is we who feel we have lost him — the pain is, therefore, only *ours*, not his. It is egoistical pain. We do not share his feelings as we do in the case of children; we do not ease *his* burden; on the contrary, we feel the pain *for ourselves*, not for him — as we do for children. [26]

On several occasions Steiner speaks of the experience of self-reproach those may have who 'meet' each other again in the spiritual worlds. After death, we do, in fact, encounter all those with whom we were connected on earth. In varying degrees of intensity we are, after death, still involved in earthly affairs — an involvement that grows less in vividness the further 'out' we expand into the spiritual cosmos. [27] We still know what we have done on earth and what we have thought; but, says Steiner, recollection may be painful. [28] It is all the more painful in the spiritual worlds because although, in earth-existence, we may have done a person some injustice or not have loved him as much as we should have done, we do have the possibility of correcting this; but, after death, in the spiritual worlds, this possibility does not exist. [29] In other words, in spiritual recollection we behold these earth-relationships. They remain as they were, we cannot alter them. What was established on earth remains. This experience gives rise to the self-reproach. However, this reproach in the spiritual world bears within it the seed for 'improvement' in the next earth-life. [30]

Elsewhere, regarding relationships between those who loved one another, or who harboured friendship for one another, Steiner says that on a foundation of knowledge, of spiritual science, 'the clairvoyant can see how, as men pass through the Gates of Death, they find themselves once more together. He sees how, just as the physical body — which impedes our sight of the spirit — disappears in the spiritual world, so too in that world every impediment to continued friendship and love disappears. He sees how the friendships and relationships of love that came into being on the physical plane continue into the spiritual world, where they can be spiritually experienced; where men are, indeed, closer together in friendship and love than they ever were in the flesh.' [31]

Picking up the theme of 'clairvoyance' and life after death, Steiner refers on one occasion to a discussion that ensued after he had been talking about certain matters concerning the higher worlds. Someone in the audience stood up afterwards and said: 'Matters such as these must always be tested by Kant's philosophy and we then find that all these things cannot be known here; for we can only know them when we have died.' [32]

After answering the point as to whether it is possible or not to 'know these things here' clearly in the affirmative, Steiner then goes on to elaborate on whether we can 'know them when we have died'. His answer is most illuminating and certainly germane to our main theme. The content of his answer is this: It is not so, that we merely have to die in order to experience certain things in the spiritual world. Indeed, a person who goes through the Portal of Death does not experience anything for which he has made no preparation. 'The life between death and rebirth is absolutely a continuation of the life here on earth . . . Therefore, as human beings, after death, we can only "obtain" from the beings of the higher hierarchies that for which *we have prepared ourselves* here on earth.' [33] How, we could ask, could we possibly receive impulses from the cosmic forces of love if, on earth, we had filled our souls with hatred?

This process of self-education, self-preparation, is the general rule. There are, however, Steiner says, exceptions. One of these may be described as a form of mediation between the soul who has passed over the Threshold and the beings of the higher hierarchies. This act of mediation can be performed by those still on the earth plane who loved him who has left this existence. For instance, a man has died who, during his earthly life, rejected, even abused, any form of knowledge concerned with the spiritual worlds. In short, he did not prepare himself to receive impulses emanating from the higher hierarchies. Now, if out of selfless love — which, as we have previously seen, forms a strong bond between the living and the dead — the soul of the discarnate being is made acquainted with spiritual matters through, say, his wife, then a remedy, which extends beyond 'death', is provided for something that has been neglected on earth.

Upon this love-filled act by the living is founded what Steiner calls 'Reading to the Dead'. We can do them a great service by this, even though the departed soul formerly wished to know nothing about the spiritual world. [34] We can do this either in the form of thought concerned with some spiritual matter, or we may take a spiritual scientific book, picture the person who has died, and read to him. If this is carried out with genuine selfless love, the dead can then 'perceive', 'hear' what is being thought or read, and as a consequence will also 'sense' a certain relief and an openness to his spiritual environment not previously manifest.

In connection with the undertaking of reading to the dead,

Steiner makes the following observation: 'It is a fact that a simple person, who may have had little contact with spiritual science, may well be better able to read to a deceased person whom he genuinely loved than the seer who, though able to find the soul of the dead, had no affectionate connection with him in his earthly life.' [35]

Often the question arises in one's mind and heart: 'What can I do to help him who has just died?' There are, of course, many ways we can be of help. Some we have briefly outlined. Another concrete form of help we on earth can render to the dead person is to endeavour to carry to a conclusion a task he had set himself to do but was prevented by death from completing. In this way we release the dead person from an earthly bond, for if he had set his heart on the task in question he will 'cling' to it after his death. Also, if we realize that the departed soul feels anxiety for a living person, it will help this soul in his further development to relieve him of this anxiety. We ease the life of someone who has died by relieving him, for instance, of anxiety about a child whom he has left behind unprovided for. By doing something for the child, we relieve the dead of anxiety. Deeds of love of this nature are a blessing to those who have died. [36]

What has just been said leads on quite naturally to the question: Does a relationship between two souls, one who has gone through the Gates of Death and the other who remains on earth, endure? Steiner gives an affirmative answer to this question and, in a lecture dealing with the Theosophy of the Rosicrucians, gives two concrete examples. He opens by saying: 'There is community of life, not only among men on the physical earth but also in the higher worlds. Just as the activities of human beings in the spirit-realm reach down into the physical world, so all the relationships and connections that are established between men on earth stretch up into the spiritual world.' [37]

One of the concrete examples Steiner mentions is that existing between a mother and child. He states quite categorically that an enduring relationship exists beyond the physical death of one or the other; indeed it is, 'a much more intimate, much firmer relationship than can ever be established here on earth'.

Mother-love, to begin with, is a kind of natural instinct; it has, we could even say, something of an animal-like character. As the child grows up, however, this relationship grows into an increasingly moral, ethical and spiritual one. When mother and child learn to think together, when they share experiences, inner experiences, then 'instinctive love', the natural instinct, increasingly diminishes in strength. Such love has merely provided the opportunity for the forging of that beautiful bond of 'at-oneness' that can exist in the reciprocal feeling of love and high esteem between mother and child as they progress through life together. Now the mutual understanding and love which thus unfolds continues on into the regions of the spiritual world, even though, as the result of one of them dying earlier than the other, they seem for a time to be separated from each other. [38] After this period of apparent separation, when they are both in the spiritual world, the link that was once on earth is forged again, and is equally, if not more, vital and intimate. In the spiritual world, indeed, all the purely animal, natural instincts no longer exist. The feelings and thoughts which 'weave between one soul and another on earth are not hindered — in the spiritual world — by the restrictions imposed on the soul by the physical, natural life and body'.

In the spiritual world we meet those who have been dear to us on earth, but now we are released from all the obstacles and hindrances of temporal and spatial existence which, in earth-existence, lie like veils over soul-relationships. In the spiritual world, soul confronts soul directly. Recognition is never in doubt, even when one soul precedes the other in passing into the spiritual world: 'Recognition of those one has loved on earth meets with no difficulty in the world of the spirit, for each soul bears his inner, spiritual reality inscribed upon his spiritual countenance.' [39]

Although, as we have previously seen, communion is possible under certain conditions between a soul in the spiritual world and a soul still inhabiting a physical body, [40] it is nevertheless only possible to have unhindered communion between two souls when they are both in the spiritual world. For instance, the soul that has departed first from the physical world cannot 'directly' perceive the actions of the ensouled body of the one still living in the physical world. Such a discarnate soul cannot, for example, see physical colours and forms natural to the earth because in the realm of spirit he has no physical organ of perception; but everything in the physical world has its spiritual counterpart and that is what is perceived by the disembodied soul. Every movement of the hand in the physical world, every will-filled thought, every creative thought, every change in the physical human being, because it is preceded by an impulse of will, by a spiritual activity — either conscious or unconscious — can be 'perceived' in the spiritual world by the soul whose 'death' preceded that of the beloved one still living in the sense-perceptible world. To reiterate: existence in the spiritual world is far from being a kind of dreaming or sleeping; there the soul leads an active and highly conscious life. It is in the spiritual world, Steiner states, that a human being develops the predisposition and impulses that enable the bonds with those whom he loved on earth to remain more intimate in order that, in a later incarnation, he will find them again. 'In many respects the purpose of incarnation on earth is to forge bonds of ever greater warmth and love.' [41]

   Steiner approaches this conception of 'forging bonds of ever greater warmth and love' from a most instructive viewpoint in a lecture entitled, 'Human Soul and Body from the Viewpoint of the Science of Spirit'. In this lecture he points out that all the actions we perform and all the close relationships we have by virtue of living and working together with another person in the 'outer' world have an 'inner' counterpart that forms a new relationship, or, rather, sows the seed of a new relationship that has to be realized in the future. In other words, between birth and death we form hidden, inner conditions of life that demand new situations. During the time we live between death and a new birth we live through 'outwardly', in the spiritual world, what we, in the previous life on earth, have experienced inwardly in connection with another human being. In the spiritual world 'my previous inner life and the other person's previous inner life become "outwardly" perceptible'. Through this reciprocal perception the 'path' is created that leads towards a situation where the possibility prevails to build on the foundation already established in a previous earth-life — a foundation that is not purely spiritual and that can only be 'built on' by our Ego when it is active through a physical body.

   The reciprocal spiritual perception in the spiritual world gives rise to an experience in that world through which we develop a power that draws us to future situations in a renewed relationship in the physical world. This experience is shared by those who are involved in a particular relationship and they use the spiritual power just mentioned so that situations are brought into being in which it is possible to realize the impulses, the seeds, that have been sown in a previous life. 'Hence,' says Steiner, 'people who have been together in one earth-life will be united again in another so that they may bring the impulses of an earlier life to fruition.' [42]

A further example Steiner mentions in connection with the inter-relationship between earth and spirit-world existence is this: Friendships are born here on earth on the foundations of a kinship of souls — a foundation that was 'woven' in a previous 'life' in the spiritual world. This affinity, this friendship, continues in the spiritual world after death, and from it the social connections arise for the next life on earth. [43] We can say, Steiner states: 'By establishing close connections with souls here on earth, we are also working at the form which life in the spiritual world will take.' [44] We could say we are working here at the form which the spiritual world receives. We have all worked in this way if bonds of friendship, of love, were forged between ourselves and other men here on earth — and we are thereby creators of something which not only has significance for life on earth, but which also 'shapes conditions in the spiritual world'.* 'What happens here as the fruit of love, of friendship, of mutual inner understanding — all these things are building stones of temples in the spiritual regions above — and men who have this certainty cannot but be inspired by the knowledge that when, here on earth, bonds are forged from soul to soul, this is the foundation of an eternal "becoming." [45] If we, therefore, try to visualize the whole human race and the bonds of friendship and love that have been woven, then we have also to picture these relationships as a great network or web, which is just as actual and present in the spiritual world.

In conclusion, Steiner draws our attention to the spiritual fact that only a planet such as the earth, where bonds of love are forged between human beings, can have a spiritual world rich in content and variety. An essential element in this richness and variety is the greater or lesser degree of consciousness of communion a being has, in the spiritual world, with those who have remained behind on the earth.

It is a mistake, says Steiner repeatedly, to assume that the consciousness of the human being in the spiritual world is dim or shadowy. Through his spiritual organs he has a clear consciousness of what is happening in the sphere of the earth. 'Occultism reveals that the human being in the spiritual world lives together with what is taking place on the earth.' [46]

Of vital importance is the imperative to harbour not only loving thoughts but also 'correct' thoughts about the souls of those we

* See p.61.

have loved on earth and who are in the spiritual world. When we cease to regard this world from our earthly egoistical standpoint we can 'see' it as a condition of existence of infinite blessedness — even apart from the fact that all freedom from the physical body, freedom from the 'lower nature', brings with it, for the soul of him who has left the physical plane, a feeling of intense relief. Existence in the spiritual world is a time of 'expansion and expression in all directions; there is a richness and an absence of restriction that are never experienced on the earth'. [47]

There will come a time, says Steiner, when we shall not merely have memory pictures in our minds of our dead friends, but shall feel them as real assistants in our activities on earth. The souls of those we have loved and who have passed into the spiritual worlds will then live on in our consciousness. That this is not yet experienced by many, says Steiner, is because spiritual scientific development is as yet only really beginning. It has not yet 'implanted' in souls the capacities and power that can act freely out of selfless love and love-filled wisdom.

The path to such an experience of the presence and help of the 'dead' will gradually open for many souls in the future. We may think of the 'dead' while about our daily work; we may awaken in our hearts all the selfless love we harboured for them, and the moment will surely come when we have the clear, conscious experience that the one who has 'died' is helping us, as if he kindled our ardour for the work we are doing, as if he or she were working through our very hands and fingers. This clear feeling, this conscious inner experience, that spiritual influences work down from the spiritual worlds into our physical earth-lives, is a fruit, a living fruit, that comes to those souls who, in selfless surrender, in spiritualized love, tread the path of spiritual development. [48]

*   *   *   *

During the war years 1914-18, Steiner would frequently begin a meeting or a lecture with the following meditative verses — the one for those who were suffering or were engaged in some capacity or other in a dangerous or difficult task, no matter what their nationality, and the other for those who had passed through the Gate of Death:

Spirits of your Souls, ever-active Guardians,
May your wings carry
Our souls' appealing love
To those on Earth committed to your care;
That, united with your power,
Our prayer may radiate with help
To the souls it seeks with love.

and

Spirits of your Souls, ever-active Guardians,
May your wings carry
Our souls' appealing love
To those in the Spiritual World committed to your care;
That, united with your power,
Our prayer may radiate with help
To the souls it seeks with love. [49]

Both these verses are used today by many people throughout
the world in their meditative life when directing their thoughts
and feelings towards friends and loved ones.

Among other such meditative verses given by Steiner is the
following:

May love of hearts reach out to love of souls,
May warmth of love ray out to Spirit-light.
Even so would we draw near to you,
Thinking with you Thoughts of Spirit,
Feeling in you the Love of Worlds,
Consciously at one with you
Willing in silent Being. [50]

6.

MAN AND HIS ANGEL

In my body lives the seed of the Spirit.
And I shall endow my Spirit
With supersensible eyes,
That with them I may behold
The light of the Spirit-Beings.
And I shall weld in my Spirit
Wisdom and Strength and Love,
That through me the Beings may work
And I may become
The conscious instrument of Their Deeds.
In my body lives the seed of the Spirit. [1]

6.

In the second lecture of a short course of three given in Oslo in 1919, Steiner gives a most illuminating account of man's relationship to his Angel — and of some of the consequences of the nature of this relationship. [2]

From the time of falling asleep until we wake, each one of us can have a particularly close connection with a spiritual being who is allotted to us as our own Angel. Even when we have no awareness of this relationship, it is nevertheless there.

Now just as in the physical world, if we are attentive and deliberately train our powers of observation and of thinking, we see more than when we are unobservant and hasty, i.e. our connection with the three kingdoms of Nature can be either intimate or superficial; so also will our connection with the world of spiritual beings vary according to our inner attitude of soul.

For instance, if our thoughts are entirely dedicated to matters of the physical world, if we never desire to acquaint ourselves with moral ideas extending beyond the utilitarian, if we have no desire to experience true human love, if we, in our daily lives, have no devotion to the divine-spiritual world, then, during the state of physical sleep, we have no inner forces to enable us to come into contact with our Angel. Whenever we fall asleep, our Angel is 'waiting' for the content of the idealistic, love- and devotion-filled feelings and thoughts we have nurtured and cultivated during the day. The greater this content is, the more intimate is our relationship with our Angel while we are asleep.

Now when we pass through the Gate of Death into a new form of 'life' in the spiritual worlds, all sense perceptions cease. In a similar manner, we learn from Steiner, the thinking that is connected with sense perception is extinguished, for its realm is the etheric body. This etheric body remains with the astral body and the Ego * for only a few days after physical death. Its 'tissue' dissolves away into the universe, just as the ordinary, everyday thoughts acquired from the world of the senses pass away from

* See chapter 13, note 14.

us. All purely utilitarian thoughts, all thoughts connected with the material aspects of the world, drift away from us when we pass through the Gate of Death. But the idealistic thoughts and feelings, the pure human love, the religious feelings of devotion that have arisen in us and been cultivated by us during our waking life — and have united us, in sleep, closely with our Angel — these thoughts and feelings 'accompany' us when we pass into the spiritual worlds.

This has a very important consequence for us during the period between death and a new birth. The more we have 'delivered over' to our Angel in our communion with him, the more *conscious* life is this Angel able to infuse into us when we are beings of soul-and-spirit; the more 'gifts' can be bestowed on us by the third Hierarchy (Angels, Archangels and Archai) and the higher Hierarchies through our Angel. What our Angel thus bestows upon us is for our consciousness in the spiritual world what our eyes and ears, our senses, are in the physical world; and the more idealistic and loving the thoughts and feelings we have brought to our Angel, the clearer does our consciousness become in the spiritual world.

Steiner, the exact clairvoyant, has described the period through which we live between death and a new birth from many different viewpoints, notably in a cycle of lectures he gave in Vienna entitled *The Inner Nature of Man and the Life between Death and a New Birth* [3] and in another cycle, given in Berlin, with the title *Between Death and Rebirth*, [4] but nowhere else does he speak in such detail about certain aspects of the relationship between man and his Guardian Angel as he does in the Oslo lecture from which the material for this chapter has been culled. Some aspects of this relationship, more specific than that just mentioned, are of particular relevance to the theme of the power of love.

There is an important moment, Steiner tells us, when, after a somewhat lengthy period has elapsed after physical death, our Angel has to 'hand over' to the Archangels what he has received from us through our 'idealistic' experiences. This activity, which unfolds between our Angel and the Archangels, must under all circumstances take place; but there is a great difference as to how the human soul grows into the spiritual world, how that which the Angel 'hands over' to the Archangel is treated. At this important moment our soul will have a definite experience, either of the warmth of acceptance or the chill of rejection. If during our earth-life we have brought idealistic and loving thoughts and feelings, human love and piety to our Angel we shall be able to follow consciously what takes place between the Angel and the Archangels. We are, as it were, in harmony with the spiritual beings and experience an embracing warmth. If, on the other hand, our consciousness in earth existence has been devoted more or less exclusively to a materialistic conception of things and, as a result, we have been able to have little or no contact with our Angel, we shall not be endowed by the Angel with sufficient conscious life to participate, as a soul-and-spirit being, in what takes place between the Angel and the Archangels. We cannot, in other words, experience harmony at this important moment with the spiritual beings and, as a consequence, we feel continually rejected and chilled by a world which would, if we had cultivated love, piety and reverence in earth-life, receive us with warmth. For man should be received with loving sympathy into the world of the Archangels at this important moment of the Angel's offering to the Higher Spirits, for then he will be led in the right way towards what Steiner calls 'The Midnight Hour of Existence'. [5]

To follow the soul's 'journey' through the various spheres in the spiritual world is not our present task and the reader is referred to Steiner's own works. [6] Here we must content ourselves with his statement that, up to the Midnight Hour of Existence, man has become more amd more estranged from earthly existence and that he has grown more and more into the spiritual world — either being received lovingly, or going through the experience of being rejected, chilled by it. But when the Midnight Hour of Existence has passed, then our soul begins gradually to long for earthly life and starts on the journey of 'descent'. Once again we encounter the spiritual realm of the Archangels and, here again, is another important nodal point in the life between death and a new birth. In a man who has brought through the Portal of Death little or no idealistic thoughts or feelings, little or no human love or true piety, something of the soul-and-spirit has perished as a result of the antipathy and chilling reception meted out by the world of the Archangels. Such a man will be imbued with a longing for earthly life that to a greater or lesser degree remains unconscious, with the result that in his new earth existence he will be far less effective than he who, because of idealistic and loving strivings in a previous earth-life, is able to approach the realms of the Archangels on his descent in the right way. The latter receives into his soul-spiritual being the power to work effectively, constructively and positively, in his subsequent life on earth.

A very great deal depends upon the two meetings with the archangelic world. For instance, Steiner tells us, upon it depends to what people, to what mother-tongue, a man descends in his forthcoming earth-life. The urge towards a particular people and mother-tongue may have been implanted in him deeply and inwardly or more superficially; more deeply and consciously in the man who in a previous life has cultivated idealistic thoughts, warmth of love and true piety, more superficially in him who has been to a greater or lesser degree devoid of such tendencies and qualities. In other words, on our descent into a new earth-existence, we are either permeated with a deep and inward love for what will become our mother-tongue, or we enter more 'automatically', more unconsciously, into what we shall have to express through our organs of speech.

He who before his new earthly life, during his 'descent' through Archangelic-Angelic realms, can be permeated with a really inward love for his mother-tongue, assimilates it into his very being. He thus grows into his language and into his race as into a natural home, and his love for both is born of his soul. If, however, a man has the urge to incarnate implanted in him more superficially, he arrives on the earth loving his language and his race, nation, merely out of instinct and 'lower' impulses. For instance, lacking the true, inward love for his language and his people, he will be prone to an aggressive patriotism.

A true and inward love for language and nation expresses itself naturally, and is thoroughly consistent with real and universal love. Chauvinism, a superficial and aggressive form of patriotism, finds no soil for growth in such an attitude of soul. A genuine feeling for internationalism or cosmopolitanism is never stultified by a natural, inner love for a language and people. When, however — and this can hardly be emphasized enough — a man grows into his mother-tongue and people more 'automatically', when through his instincts and ego-centred impulses he develops an animal-like, overfervid love for his language and nation, we can readily recognize false nationalism and chauvinism arising, with an exaggerated emphasis upon race and nationality.

'All over the earth a false attitude is being adopted to nationality, race and language' [7] — this is as true today as it was when Steiner expressed this thought nearly sixty years ago. Examples are all too blatant to need specific mention. Much of what has arisen in the catastrophes of devastating wars, for instance, is readily explicable when studied against a knowledge of the 'happenings' in the spiritual world.

A study of life today in the light of spiritual science leads us to the realization that, in their former earth-life, men — particularly in the western hemisphere — became increasingly enmeshed in materialism and manifested little real human love and idealism and that, as a result, in their second encounter with the realms of the first Hierarchy between death and a new birth the seeds were sown for much that arises today in various malevolent forms.

7.

ST LUKE'S GOSPEL OF LOVE —
BUDDHA AND CHRIST

At the turning point of Time,
The Spirit-Light of the World
Entered the stream of Earthly Evolution.
Darkness of Night
Had held its sway;
Day-radiant Light
Poured into the souls of men:
Light that gave warmth
To simple shepherds' hearts,
Light that enlightened
The wise heads of Kings.

O Light Divine!
O Sun of Christ!
Warm thou our hearts,
Enlighten thou our heads,
That good may become
What from our hearts we would found
And from our heads direct
With single purpose. [1]

7.

Rudolf Steiner states quite categorically that the spiritual science he presented to mankind is not to be regarded as being merely a body of new teaching, but far more as an 'instrument' — involving the whole man, not merely his intellect — for comprehending life and its mysteries. Thus, for instance, it is an instrument for understanding the Christian revelation. [2]

Steiner was one of those who, through his own love-filled heart, could receive and assimilate the words of the Gospel of St Luke, which resounded when the spiritual world opened to the simple shepherds: 'And peace be in the souls of men in whom there is good will.'

Through his ceaseless and loving endeavour Steiner gives to mankind, in his spiritual science, a gift for full self-discovery and self-realization, rooted in wisdom and love.

Through his spiritual perception of the inner reality of the Mystery of Golgotha [3] and his love-filled living into the message contained in the Gospel of St Luke, Steiner shows us the path along which we can experience that this Gospel is able, more than any other religious text, to pour into the human soul that warmth-giving love through which peace can reign on earth — and that, he says, is the most beautiful mirror-image of divine mysteries revealed on earth. What can be revealed must be mirrored on earth and, as mirror-image, rise up again to the spiritual heights. Love and peace — here is the most beautiful mirror-image on earth of what streams down from the heights.

* * * *

The Gospel of St Luke is an expression of the principle of love and compassion. [4] It is the Gospel to which especially those who long to be imbued with Christian love and compassion turn their minds and hearts, because here the power of love is revealed more potently and clearly than in any other Christian document. Whereas much inner preparation is called for before the full power of St John's Gospel can be experienced, it may be said of St Luke's Gospel that no one of us is too immature to be aware of the loving warmth streaming from it. Anyone who allows this Gospel to work upon and live in his soul will discover that, from beginning to end, it gives living expression to the principle of love and compassion.

The Gospel of St Luke contains Buddhism in a new form, 'as though springing from a fountain of youth'; [5] hence it expresses the religion of compassion and love in a form immediately accessible to the simplest souls.

Steiner frequently emphasized the importance of an understanding of Western man for the teaching of Buddha — and of the recognition of the relationship of Buddhism to Christianity.

In Buddhism we can see the purest teaching of compassion and love. From Buddha flowed a 'gospel' of love and compassion into the spiritual evolution of the earth and mankind. This gospel lives in the true Buddhist when his heart *feels* the suffering confronting him in the world in all living creatures. This is Buddhistic love and compassion in the fullest sense of the word. But from the Gospel of St Luke flows an element that enriches, and is more than, this all-embracing feeling of love and compassion. We could describe this element as being the translation of love and compassion into *deed*. Compassion, in the highest sense of the word, is the ideal of the Buddhist; the ideal, the aim of one who lives according to the spirit of the message of the Gospel of St Luke is to unfold love that *acts*. The true Buddhist shares in the sufferings of the sick, but he is not called upon to heal. From the Gospel of St Luke rings the call to take active steps to do whatever is possible to alleviate suffering and to bring about healing.

Although in this Gospel there resounds the purest Buddhism, we may perceive the Christian element of *love translated into deed* as being a sublimation of Buddhism. [6]

Buddha brought the *teaching* of love to the earth; Christ, Steiner emphasizes, brought love itself as a *living power* to the earth. That is the great difference.

The teaching of compassion and love brought by Buddha is given expression in the Eightfold Path. If every precept of this Path is obeyed, then man's Ego [7] will reach the greatest degree of purification, perfection and ennoblement conceivable. The point of importance here is that it is work carried out by the Ego for its own perfecting — not merely for its own sake, for the sake of the Ego-bearing individual, but, above all, for the sake of the perfection and ennoblement of humanity. If, therefore, we were to develop in ourselves that which Buddha set in motion as the 'Wheel of the Law', our Egos would gradually become possessed of wisdom at a high level — wisdom in the form of thought, contemplative thought.

Buddha, a soul imbued with the highest degree of enlightenment, gave birth to the lofty doctrine of compassion and love. But there is a significant difference between wisdom in the form of *thought* and wisdom as *living power*. There is a difference between perceiving, knowing what the Ego must do, on the one hand, and on the other, allowing the living power to flow into our innermost being so that it may stream forth again from the Ego into all the world, as it streamed from Christ.

The impulse given by the great Buddha endowed humanity with the knowledge of the teaching of compassion and love. What Christ brought, however, is above all a *living power*, not a teaching. He sacrificed His very Self. He descended into earth existence in order to flow not merely into the souls of men, but also into the spirit, the Ego, so that the Ego itself should have the power to ray out love as 'substantiality'. Christ brought to humanity the 'substantiality', the living essence of love, thus enhancing the wisdom-filled content of love taught by Buddha. [8]

The faculty to unfold love as a living power we owe to the Deed of Christ on Golgotha. He poured love itself into men and it will grow from strength to strength. When men have reached the end of their evolution in the distant future, wisdom will have revealed to them the full content of the doctrine of compassion and love — and this they will owe to Buddha. But, at the same time, they will possess to perfection the faculty of letting love stream out from the Ego over the whole of the earth and mankind — and this they will owe to Christ. Thus Buddha and Christ work in close co-operation during the course of evolution. Indeed, the fulfilment of Buddha's teaching may be said to be dependent on the incarnation of Christ on earth. On one occasion, Steiner asks us to imagine that Christ Jesus had, in fact, not come into earth existence. What would have happened to man during the course of his evolution? Man, Steiner says, would certainly have developed a fully self-conscious Ego, but this Ego would have led him irrevocably into egoism and to the disappearance, the extinction of love on the earth. Men would have become 'Egos', but utterly egotistical beings.

When Christ Jesus came to the earth man was ready for the

development of the self, the Ego. Without the Mystery of Golgotha it would have developed into an 'empty' Ego, concerned with itself alone and having no impulse to act out of love for others. To give this Ego a real content, to stimulate its development so that the power of love could gradually stream more and more from it, was the divine mission of Christ Jesus on earth. Without Him the Ego would have become an empty vessel; through His coming it can evolve into a chalice filling itself more and more with the life-creating warmth of the power of selfless love. [9]

*   *   *   *

In the light of the foregoing we could now ask: What is it that is proclaimed to the shepherds from on high? It is the manifestation of the wisdom-filled God from the Heights that is proclaimed. But this is not all. If it were, then the 'step' from Buddha to Christ would not have been taken. To this proclamation the all important words are added in the Gospel of Love of St Luke: 'And peace be to men on Earth who are filled with good will' — that is, to men in whom the living power of love is germinating. It is this that must gradually become reality on earth through the new impulse given by Christ. To the 'revelation from the Heights' He joined the living, creative, healing power of love. The Christ-bestowed power that can fill the human heart to overflowing is called in the Gospel of St Luke — and in the other Gospels too — the power of faith. This is what the Gospels mean by faith, says Steiner. A man who receives Christ into himself so that the Christ *lives* in him; a man whose Ego is not an empty vessel, but is filled to overflowing with love - such a man has Faith. [10]

*   *   *   *

Why could Christ be the supreme illustration of the power of 'healing through the word?' Because, states Steiner, He was the first to set in motion the 'Wheel of Love' (as distinct from Buddha's 'Wheel of the Law') as a freely creative power of the human soul; because love in the very purest form was within Him — love brimming over in such abundance that it could pour into those around Him who needed to be healed; [11] because the words He spoke — no matter whether He said 'Stand up and walk', or 'Thy sins are forgiven thee' — issued from a 'vessel' of perfect love. His words were uttered from overflowing love, from a love

transcending the limits of the Ego; and those who were able to
some extent to experience this were called by Christ the faithful.
Faith is the capacity to transcend the self, to transcend what the
Ego can achieve.

Christ's mission was not solely concerned with the task of the
achievement, by the Ego, of the greatest possible purification, of
perfection. This, as we have seen, is the task, the goal, the
Buddhist sets himself. The task Christ set humanity over and
above this was the transcendence by the Ego of its limits. How, we
may now ask, can the Ego overflow? Christ Himself gives an
answer to this in simple words: it is not enough to give something
only to those of whom you know that they will give it back to you.
Such an action has not been prompted by overflowing love. But if
you give something knowing that it will not come back to you in
any form, then you have acted out of love, out of pure love. Or,
expressed differently, pure love is that which the Ego does not,
indeed cannot, keep enclosed within itself, but releases as a
formative force that flows forth from within in infinite abundance.

The words of the greatest warmth in the Gospel of St Luke,
Steiner stresses, are those that tell of this overflowing love. The
Gospel itself, written by Luke the Healer, will be found to contain
this overflowing love, if we let its words work upon us in such a
way that the love pervades all our own words, enabling them to
exert their healing power upon our fellow-men. [12]

In the Gospel of St Matthew we find the expression that
epitomizes the many powerful and beautiful passages about love
contained in the Gospel of St Luke: 'Out of the abundance of the
heart the mouth speaketh'. This expresses one of the very highest
Christian ideals. The mouth speaks from the overflowing heart,
itself a central element within the circulating blood, which is the
expression of the Ego. [13] The meaning for us today of St
Matthew's words can be reformulated: Speak from an Ego that
overflows and rays forth the power of love-filled faith, then do
your words contain the healing Christ-power. This, a cardinal
principle of Christianity, should also permeate all spiritual
science. [14]

As has already been indicated, if man were to remain at the
stage of spiritual evolution where he, in a meditative, contemplative way, ponders upon the teachings of the Buddhist Eightfold
Path, he would never gain within his soul the living, overflowing,
active power of love. To impart this power of love Christ

descended to the earth. He descended for three years only, never having been embodied on the earth before and never to incarnate again into a physical sheath. * The very presence of the Christ on earth for three years — from the Baptism by John until the Mystery of Golgotha — means that love will flow in ever increasing measure into the human heart, into the human Ego, so that at the end of earth evolution the Ego will be filled with the power of Christ.

Just as the teaching of compassion and love had first to be kindled to life through the Buddha, so the 'substance' of love had to be brought down from heavenly heights to the earth by the Being who — through the Mystery of Golgotha — made it possible for this 'substance' of love to become the possession of the human Ego itself in the future.

We may not, of course, say that love was not previously in existence prior to the birth of Christ — the experience of the Buddha, for instance, shows that this was not the case. What was not present in the stream of evolution before the coming of Christ, however, was the love that could be the 'direct possession of the human Ego'. [15]

The writer of the Gospel of St Luke, the Gospel of spiritualized love, perceives this 'possession' of the purified Ego as the out-streaming love that forgives the most terrible of all wrongs the physical world can inflict. [16] Words expressing this ideal of love resound from the Cross on Golgotha: 'Father, forgive them, for they know not what they do!'

*   *   *   *

Steiner underlines the essential difference between Buddha's teaching and the Deed of Christ by drawing our attention to the essence and meaning of suffering as it presents itself to the soul of the Buddhist and that of the Christian.

Through observing old age, illness and death, the truth concerning suffering dawned on the Buddha. He then taught the cessation of suffering and release from suffering through the elimination of the desire for birth, for physical incarnation.

To the soul after the Mystery of Golgotha the truth that life is suffering presents itself quite differently.

Is it true that to be born is to suffer, as the Buddha, the teacher of love and compassion, declared? For the Christian, who

* See chapter 14, note 39.

inwardly gazes at Christ upon the Cross, at the Representative of Man who dies and through His death brought life, the answer is 'No'. For, out of selfless love, Christ entered into our earth existence; birth, therefore, leads us to an earth able, from its own elements, to provide a raiment for the Christ and we gladly tread the earth upon which Christ has walked. Union with Christ brings the recognition that birth is not suffering but the portal through which we can find and experience the Redeemer, who clothed Himself with the very same earthly substances that compose the bodily sheath of every human being.

Rather than look upon illness as suffering — as the Buddha teaches — the Christian sees in illness an opportunity to overcome an obstacle by unfolding the Christ Power. Through the Life and Deed of Christ the Healer, the power of healing exists in every one of us — that is, the power of selfless love that has been kindled by the Christ Impulse. His Power embraces everything that out of the spiritual can unfold the healing force to overcome illness. In uniting himself with the Christ Impulse, man spiritualizes his life and thereby makes himself whole, heals himself.

We need to arrive at a similar understanding about the infirmities and frailties of old age. Only in respect of the physical body need we speak of suffering. In our real Self we grow, through the power of selfless love, stronger, more powerful and beautiful. The more the feebleness of our limbs increases, the more we can grow in the spirit. Seen in this light, age is not suffering, for with every day that passes we grow into the spiritual world, we gain increasing mastery over the physical through the Christ Power dwelling in us. The appearance of Christ on the earth is the great turning point when man can ascend again from the physical into the spiritual world.

So, too, death is not suffering for it has been conquered in the Resurrection, through the Event of Golgotha. Death has been overcome by love-filled life, has been vanquished by life, by the spirit.

To be separated from the being one loves is not suffering in the Buddhistic sense. Souls permeated with the Christ Power know that love can forge links from soul to soul that transcend all material obstacles and limits, links in the spiritual world that cannot be severed. There is nothing, states Steiner, in the life between birth and death or between death and re-birth to which we cannot spiritually find the way, if we are truly imbued with the

Christ Impulse. If we permeate ourselves with the Christ, then permanent separation from the being we love is inconceivable. He leads us to union, re-union with those we love. He who has taken the Christ Impulse into his soul is never separated from the one he loves — for Christ has brought a light into earth existence and into the life of man, that bridges the physical and the spiritual world.

The Buddha taught that to be united with that which one does not love is suffering. For the Christian this cannot be so. He recognizes, experiences, that Christ kindles in his heart a universal love that embraces every being, every object according to its intrinsic value. In Christ there is nothing we do not encompass with love.

For the condition of suffering, which Buddha proclaimed and recognized, the remedy has been given through the universal, selfless Love of Christ. The Event of Golgotha signifies the gradual elimination of the facets associated by the great Buddha with suffering. [17]

In a lecture Steiner gave on Christmas Eve 1912 he describes the night of the birth of the Jesus Child as being that in which — spiritually, in our hearts — we have before us that which may be called the Birth of the Earthly Light, of the light which is to be born out of the darkness of the Night of Initiation (the German word for Christmas Eve is 'Weihnacht') and which so radiates within and through human hearts and souls that the way upwards to the spiritual heights is illumined and made clear.

On this night of love and peace there should pour into our hearts the fundamental human feeling of love; the fundamental feeling should stir within us that, compared with all other forces and powers and treasures of the world, 'the treasures and the power and the force of love are the greatest, the most intense, the most powerful'. Our hearts should be filled with the certitude that great as wisdom is, love is still greater, that great as might is, love is yet greater. This feeling of the power, the force, the strength of love should pour into our hearts so completely that from this Christmas night, from this night of love and peace, something may overflow into all our feelings throughout the rest of the year that causes us to feel shame should in any hour of the year we do, say, or think, anything that would betray the inner, spiritual vision of the essence of that night in which we endeavour to open our hearts to the inpouring all-power of love. [18]

*   *   *   *

The aspect of the Christ-Impulse that is uniquely set forth in St Luke's Gospel is that which can especially bring home to us how we can feel ourselves united with all that is human, with the whole of humanity, indeed, with the whole of creation. The Christ Jesus who meets us in St Luke's Gospel, the Child who embodies the profoundest love, simplicity, innocence and physical powerlessness — the Child shown to the simple shepherds of the field — finds an immediate 'home' in our hearts. All of us can feel ourselves near and akin to that which so simply, like a child and yet so majestically and mightily, speaks to mankind through the Child of St Luke's Gospel. What an inspiration flows from this Gospel towards those who, again and again in pictures and in other artistic activities, give us scenes that show us the Jesus Child as a being with whom every man, even the simplest, can feel akin. The simplest of us can feel and experience the whole event in Palestine as being a family happening, as being something that unfolds in our own home and in that of our next door neighbour.

All is contained in this childlike picture and experience of a certain aspect of the Christ Impulse, namely, as already stressed, that the most profound and highest element in the world is love — that wisdom is something great, worthy to be striven after, for without wisdom beings cannot exist, but that love is something yet greater; that the might and the power with which the world is fashioned is something great without which the world cannot exist, but that love is something yet greater. He who can feel this higher nature of love over against power and strength and wisdom has a right feeling for the Christ Impulse. For, everywhere where wisdom is, there is a certain twofoldness: wisdom of the gods and wisdom of the Luciferic powers. He who strives after wisdom must inevitably come face to face with the antagonists of the gods, with the throng of the Light-Bearer, with the army of Lucifer. Therefore, says Steiner, there is no godlike all-wisdom, for wisdom is always confronted with an opponent, with Lucifer. Similarly, godlike power is not all-powerful, for it is always confronted with the antagonistic forces of Ahriman.

Pure, true love alone is solely divine. We can speak of the 'all-power' as an ideal, but against it battle the forces of Ahriman; we can speak of 'all-wisdom' as an ideal, but it is opposed by the forces of Lucifer. We cannot speak in the same way of love, for if we love rightly it is capable of no increase. Wisdom can be augmented; power can be augmented, but divine love is unique — it is all-embracing.

We can feel the Jesus Child as He is presented to us in St Luke's Gospel as being the personification of cosmic love, as that love through which we can, in due course, attain to 'ideal wisdom' and 'ideal power', as that love through which, in the distant future, both the Luciferic and Ahrimanic forces are transmuted and no longer act as antagonists to the Divine in the Universe. [19]

It is, then, neither with wisdom nor with power that we can approach the Jesus-Being in St Luke's Gospel. It is through love alone that we can come near to the Child Jesus as He is presented to us in this Gospel. To bring love towards the Child, unlimited love, that is the one thing possible. The power of love is what we can feel so deeply when we let the contents of St Luke's Gospel work on our souls.

Thus, just as it is in the Christmas 'night of initiation' that the birth of the Jesus Child is put before us, so also it is in the same night — as it comes round again and again — that there can be born in our souls, as we lovingly contemplate the birth of the Child, the understanding of true love that resounds above and permeates all life. And if at Christmas an understanding of the feeling of love is rightly awakened in us, if we rightly celebrate the birth of the Child Jesus, the awakening of pure love, then from the moment in which we experience it, there can radiate through and in us that which may bless and warm the wisdom that, throughout the year, we strive to attain. [20]

The beginning of an understanding of the Mystery of Golgotha is a loving comprehension of the World-Christ-Mass. Then into the minds of men pours true love. The warmth of love flows most nobly into man when his soul's attention is directed towards the Child Jesus, Who in the World's Christ-Mass Holy Night appears on earth. [21]

*   *   *   *

On the occasion of a performance of one of the medieval Christmas Plays from Oberufer, Steiner addressed the audience afterwards. In his address he made a significant observation in regard to the love and joy felt by the 'simple' person and that experienced by the spiritual scientist.

It might seem as if the world conception based on spiritual science could impair such simple joy, so full of love: the joy and love that has filled the hearts of many throughout the centuries whenever this old play — Steiner is referring to the *Oberufer Shepherds' Play* — portraying the Heavenly Child and His earthly destiny, was performed. But this should not be the case, though our joy and love may be of another quality. The adult experiences both love and joy, but they are of a different quality from that of a child. Every heart and soul of those striving towards spiritual development will not only experience spontaneous joy, but, in addition, will be filled with a joy that arises out of the realization that such a play has caused countless people to feel themselves drawn to the Heavenly Child. Through spiritual science joy is not diminished, but enriched.

Spontaneous warmth of heart is not impaired by spiritual science, but what it does do, should do, is to lift the experience of joy out of a situation limited to, let us say, a performance of a play, into an integral element of a permanent attitude of soul.

In the past, such plays were performed for people who could, to a greater or lesser degree, experience their content directly, i.e. be immediately drawn to and feel at one with the Jesus Child. 'Our complicated age needs another kind of soul impulse that will enable us to look up again to the Heavenly Child who brought the greatest of all impulses into man's evolution.' [22] What was once 'instinctive' must today become conscious. However, although we must gain spiritual insight and knowledge concerning the life of Jesus and the mission of Christ, it is essential that we connect such knowledge with our most sacred feelings — for instance, love, devotion and reverence — and our strongest hopes. [23]

*   *   *   *

Each of the four Gospels 'speaks' its own language and has its special effect and influence upon us, gives us different insights and experiences.

The Gospel of St Luke, as we have seen, reveals to us the power of Christ Jesus' *love*; the Gospel of St John the magnitude of the *wisdom* of Christ; that of St Mark presents to us a picture that is primarily one of *might*. It speaks to us of the creative Powers permeating the universe. The Gospel of St Matthew is different again: all three elements just mentioned are present — the warmth of feeling and love, the knowledge full of hope and promise, and the majesty of the universe. They are present in a modified form, we might say, and for this reason seem to be more humanly akin to us than in the other Gospels. It is the most human of the four records and describes Christ Jesus as a man in such a way that in all His deeds He is near us in a human sense.

For instance, at the beginning of the Gospel of St John, Christ is referred to as the Creative Logos. In other words, the highest spiritual conception our minds and hearts can attain is presented in the very first sentence of this Gospel. Quite different is the beginning of the Gospel of St Matthew. It begins by giving us the lineage of the man Jesus of Nazareth within a definite people and from a definite point of time. St Mark's Gospel presents us, on the other hand, with an aspect of the Christ-Impulse that may be described as being that of the Spirit-King who brings into human evolution an infinite fount of goodness and an infinite fount of *mighty* love.

Whereas the *Love*, the *Wisdom*, and the *Mighty Splendour* might well overwhelm us, we 'feel able to stand erect before the picture presented in the Gospel of St Matthew'. [24] In it the picture is drawn for us of Christ as man, of His Life as a man during His sojourn on earth. The contents of this Gospel present us with a harmonized human portrait. In St John's Gospel we see a Divine and Cosmic Man, in St Luke's a Being Who is the embodiment of self-giving Love, and in St Mark's Gospel the Cosmic Will operating in a single Individuality. 'In St Matthew's Gospel we have the portrait of the Man who, during his life on earth united in His own Being Supreme Love, Wisdom and Power.' [25]

In endeavouring to comprehend the 'cosmic' communications given in the Gospel of St John, we can sense our weakness and inadequacy before their sublimity and spiritual grandeur. We feel that this Gospel shows us the highest goal to which human wisdom can aspire and human understanding gradually fathom. Of this Gospel Steiner says that 'there is no wisdom accessible to man that is not in some way contained in it. All the Wisdom of the Universe is there'. [26]

However insignificant we may sense ourselves to be, this Gospel, Steiner continues, enables us to divine that some element with which we ourselves are akin descends into our souls and imbues us with the feeling of infinitude. 'The spiritual magnitude of the cosmic life to which man is related is experienced by the soul when contemplating the Gospel of St John.' [27]

'In contemplating the Gospel of St John it is paramountly the spiritual greatness — even though divined but dimly — that pervades the soul like a magic breath, whereas in the Gospel of St Luke the influence is more inward, causing in the soul an intensification of all that the powers of cosmic love and sacrifice can effect in the world when we are able to share in them.' 'St Luke gives us an inkling of what this power of sacrificing love has brought about in the evolution of the world and of mankind — this love that pulsates and weaves throughout the universe.' [28] The Gospel of St Luke makes us feel as if all the human love that ever existed in the evolution of mankind poured into the Being who lived as Christ Jesus.

Whereas the Gospel of St John speaks more to our understanding as a faculty of cognition, more to our heads, the Gospel of St Luke speaks more to our heart, to our feeling, to our power of love as a faculty of cognition.

We have already seen that Steiner is concerned to show Christ as the Being of Love and Compassion, and what we have been saying now serves merely to emphasize this. In his lectures on the Gospel of St John, Steiner's main theme centres on the words uttered by Christ: 'I am the Light of the World'. Light and Love made manifest in the Being of Christ are the aspects presented by Steiner in great detail in some forty or so lectures.

In glimpsing the sublime ideas that the Gospel of St John contains we can sense ourselves being carried far above the occurrences in the life of the individual human soul. All-embracing, eternal Ideas are the concern of that Divine Wisdom that flows to us as we steep ourselves in this Gospel. What streams from it seems itself to be circling, like the eagle, in heights high above every happening in the daily, hourly, and momentary destiny of man. [29]

As was often his wont, Steiner, after having given his hearers a glimpse of a great cosmic happening, then related this happening to ordinary human life. He does so here. He bids us descend from those cosmic heights and to contemplate individual human life, to observe, in this instance, the forces expressed in what we call 'human love'. 'We can perceive love surging and weaving in the hearts of men through the ages. On the one side we see how this love gives birth to deeds of supreme heroism, but we also see that, although great deeds are born of this love in human hearts, it is, at the same time, like a two-edged sword.' [30] Steiner then gives the example of a mother who loves her child deeply: the child commits some misdeed, but so intense is the mother's love that she cannot force herself to punish the child. A second misdeed follows and again the loving mother fails to punish the child. And so it continues. The child grows into adulthood and becomes a criminal and a liability to the community. 'Such was the outcome of the *lack of wisdom* in the mother's love. If love is permeated with wisdom, it is capable of deeds of untold greatness.'

'The significance of the Love that streamed into the world from Golgotha lies precisely in the fact that it was united, in a single Being, with the Light of the World, with true Wisdom.' [31] When we contemplate these two qualities in Christ we relaise that 'Love is the crowning of the World', but also that Love and Light, Love and Wisdom, belong together. This is the great message of the Gospels of St Luke and St John, together.

Steiner relates the cosmic forces streaming into mankind through Christ to the three highest Spiritual Beings: Seraphim, Cherubim and Thrones. As we have already seen, the Christ presented in the Gospel of St John is, in Himself, a Being of the utmost sublimity, but in His Works He draws upon the powers pertaining to the realm of the wisdom-filled Cherubim. In the Gospel of St Luke, the keynote is the warmth-bringing fire of love springing from the Heart of Christ. This indicates, Steiner tells us, that He worked at those sublime heights that are the realm of the Seraphim. The fiery love of the Seraphim, the Spirits of Love, streams through the universe and is brought to the earth through Christ.

But Christ is not only the 'embodiment' of the Supreme Warmth of Love and the Supreme Light of Wisdom. He is not only the channel for Cosmic Wisdom and Cosmic Love to stream down into earth existence from the Heights of the Cherubim and the Seraphim, but also for the Supreme Power of the Thrones (Steiner also calls these Spirits the 'Spirits of Will'). Christ worked, too, in the realm of the Thrones, the realm whence comes all Strength and Power into the world and, in so doing, brings Love and Wisdom to actual fulfilment. In the Gospel of St Mark we are presented with a picture of the Forces through which Christ brings Love and Wisdom, Love and Light, to actual fulfilment.

The Seraphim with their Love lead us into the depths of the human heart. Self-surrendering Love is symbolized in the sacrificial Bull — the symbol of St Luke. The Cherubim, with their Light-filled Wisdom, their Wisdom-filled Light, lead us upwards to the Heights of the Eagle — the symbol of St John. Strength pulsing through the world, making all things possible of fulfilment. Strength, the creative power surging through the world, ordering and directing all happenings, is symbolized by the Lion — the symbol of St Mark. This Power is infused into earth existence through Christ. Through Him we are given the strength, the will, to attain wisdom in and through self-less love. [32]

8.

THE MYSTERY OF GOLGOTHA

All that was poured into human evolution
through Christ's coming, worked in it like a
seed. Slowly the seed must ripen. Only a
little part of the depth and content of the
new Wisdom has flowed into physical existence
up to the present. We are only at the
beginning of Christian evolution. [1]

8.

In the final lecture of the series on the Gospel of St Luke [2] Steiner clarifies the distinction between Christ's Teaching and that of the Ancient Mystery Centres and also elucidates the meaning for the whole of humanity of the Deed on Golgotha.

To his contemporaries, Steiner suggests, particularly to those with some learning and knowledge of the Ancient Law, it must have been incomprehensible that Christ, bringing an entirely new impulse into the world of humanity, should claim as disciples those whom no initiate would formerly have considered suitable for any form of spiritual teaching and initiation. They would have assumed that He would impart His teachings to those who were practitioners of the old form of disciplinary schooling. Hence the Pharisees and the lawyers of their sect could not understand why Christ sat, ate and drank 'with tax-gatherers and sinners' (Luke 5: 30). Christ's response may be paraphrased like this: If I were to impart in the old way the entirely new impulse I have come to give to mankind, if a new form of teaching were not to replace the old, it would be like pouring new wine into old wine-skins. What is now to be given to mankind must be put into a new form, into new wine-skins — into souls not weighed down by the old, traditional teachings. (Luke, 5: 36-39).

Those who were to understand, says Steiner, must now do so through the powerful influence of the Ego, through that which was 'poured into them' by the Christ-Being Himself — not, in other words, through what they had learned from the Ancient Mystery streams. Hence the chosen ones were not men who, according to the old doctrines, were properly prepared, but men who were simple human beings, able to comprehend through the power of Faith [3] what streamed into them from the Christ (cf. Luke 10: 21-24). A 'sign' was to be placed before them, too. A sign was to be enacted before the eyes of all mankind, not (in short) in the secrecy of a mystery centre as had always been the custom up to then. The Mystical Death that had been a ceremonial act in the mystery temples of initiation for thousands of years was to be presented openly before all mankind.

Everything that had previously taken place in the secrecy of the temples was brought into the open as a single event on Golgotha. A process hitherto witnessed solely by the initiates during the three-and-a-half days of the old form of initiation was to take place before mankind in concrete reality. In the ancient mystery centres the three-and-a-half days spent in a kind of deathlike sleep brought to the few initiates who experienced it the conviction that the spiritual will, at all times, be victorious over the physical, over the bodily nature, and that man's soul and spirit belong to the spiritual world. This was, through Christ, to be a reality enacted before the whole world.

In other words, we see, states Steiner, that the Event on Golgotha was an initiation undergone on the outer plane of world history. Hence 'this Initiation was not consummated only for those who witnessed the actual Event, but for all mankind', for the present as well as the future. 'What issued from the Death on the Cross streamed into the whole of humanity; a stream of spiritual life flowed into mankind from the drops of blood which fell to the Earth from the wounds of Christ Jesus on Golgotha.' What had been imparted by other teachers as 'wisdom' was now to flow into humanity as inner strength, as inner power of creative love. 'That is the essential difference between the Event of Golgotha and the teachings given by all other founders of religion.' [4]

Let us look again at what came to pass on Golgotha. When Earth evolution began, the human Ego was connected physically with the blood. [5] This blood-bound Ego force grew stronger and stronger as time went by, and, if Christ had not appeared, men would have become entirely engrossed in the development of egoism and, in the process, the force of selfless love would have atrophied. The turning point occurred on Golgotha. Steiner poses the following question: 'What was it that had to flow?' His answer to this is: 'The blood that is the surplus substantiality of the Ego! The process that began on the Mount of Olives when the drops of sweat fell from the Redeemer's brow like clots of blood (Luke 22: 44) was carried further when the blood flowed from the wounds on the Cross. This flowing blood was the "Sign" of the surplus egoism in man's nature that had to be sacrificed.' [6]

Steiner pre-empts the obvious criticism here by stating that, of course, if the blood that flowed on Golgotha had been analysed it would have been found to contain the same substances as the blood of other human beings. It is quite clear that to anyone endowed solely with the power of intellectual perception the significance of the flowing blood of Christ would be lost; but spiritual science would discover it to have been quite different blood from that of any ordinary human being. Through what Steiner calls the 'surplus blood' in humanity, men would have been submerged in egoism if infinite Love had not enabled this special blood to flow; infinite Love is intermingled with the blood that flowed from Golgotha.

This Deed has to be met by man with his heart, not merely with his head. He can then recognize that in the 'sign' of the flowing of blood is placed before him the reality that, through Christ, there came into the stream of evolution the infinite Love that would gradually drive out egoism.

In the past, man made real contact with the spirit, with the divine essence, only through the Mysteries. But, with the Advent of Christ, with the descent of the Spirit of the Cosmos into Jesus at the Baptism in the Jordan, something quite new entered into earth and human evolution. The spiritual-divine essence — Christ — entered the stream of earthly existence for a period of three years. Then, at the Mystery of Golgotha — when Divine Love replaced the Wisdom of the Father Principle [7] — a force that until then had lived *outside* the Earth poured itself *into* the earthly world, into the earthly part of the Cosmos. Ever since the Deed on Golgotha this spiritual-divine power has lived and worked in the same 'atmosphere' in which our souls live.

In pre-Christian initiation man had to 'go outside', 'reach beyond' his own being to experience the divine-spiritual. He had, Steiner says, 'to abandon his human essence to make contact with the divine essence'. [8] From the moment of the Baptism in the river Jordan something streamed from the Christ-Jesus into the spiritual atmosphere of the earth that enabled every human soul that so willed to live and be immersed in it. Since the Mystery of Golgotha man lives *in* a spiritual environment. This environment can establish an inner connection with the Christ Being and, thereby, man can grow beyond, can overcome, the forces of death that he bears within him, for within him, too, are the love forces of the Resurrection.

Steiner states quite categorically that the spiritual source of man's origin can no longer be found on the old paths of initiation. This source must be found on a new path; on the path that seeks a living connection with the Christ within the spiritual atmosphere of the Earth.

The Christ Impulse thus appears to us as the Spiritual Essence given to man — through a Deed of Selfless Love — at a time when the ancient inheritance was no longer fruitful for human spiritual evolution. 'Humanity would have lost its connection with the Divine-Spiritual World had not a superearthly Being, a Being who descended to the Earth from the Cosmos, poured out his Essence — in Selfless Love — into the stream of human, earth evolution.' [9]

With Christianity, says Steiner, something entered human evolution that enabled man to say to himself: You must remain man in your inmost self. As a human being you will find within yourself that element in which your soul is immersed ever since the Mystery of Golgotha. 'You need not, as in pre-Christian times, abandon your human essence by either descending into egoism or by rising into pride.'

'Ever since the Mystery of Golgotha the quality that the human soul needs to develop is love.' [10] Man in his spiritual development must no longer follow the course of strengthening his soul on the mystery path that leads to egoism, nor fall prey to pride on the path that leads to union with the soul-spiritual esence of the world. Since this Earth-Cosmic Mystery it is essential that man acquire the capacity of transcending egoism and of conquering pride: 'A path must now be followed that is founded on the element of love.' This truth, Steiner confirms, lies at the foundation of St Paul's significant words, 'Not I, but Christ in me.'

It is true, Steiner says, that a pupil of the ancient mysteries may have 'anticipated' St Paul's words, but he could not have experienced their fulfilment. Only after the Mystery of Golgotha — and because of it — did it become possible for man objectively to experience Divine Love — the Christ — as that element that enables him to unite himself with the Divine Essence. Whereas in the ancient mysteries man sought love *outside* his own being, since the Mystery of Golgotha this love can only be found through the experience of 'Not I, but Christ in me'.

Man remains fully human even when he goes 'beyond himself' and discovers Christ *within* himself. 'The soul remains within the human sphere when it attains that experience expressed by St Paul. We then go through the mystical experience of feeling and knowing that a higher human-divine essence *lives* in us. This is the mystical experience of Christ that we can have only through a training in love.'

'The human soul could never comprehend Christ were it not able to transform itself — through the power of love — so that it could inwardly experience the words;"Not I, but Christ in me."'[11]

In one of his many Christmas lectures [12] Steiner makes the point that our whole understanding of the Cosmos makes it impossible for us to believe that Christ has only been 'known' since the Mystery of Golgotha. The initiates and their pupils — there are many indications of this in the Old Testament — also knew Him in pre-Christian times as that Spirit Who was to come. [13] The initiates always pointed to Him whom they saw as the Sun-Spirit descending from the Heights, who was approaching the earth in order to take up His abode on it.

'Then the Mystery of Golgotha took place. That Spirit through Whom the earth has gained its meaning drew into a human body. We know that since then this Sun-Spirit is connected with the Earth.' [14]

Ancient clairvoyant perception, continues Steiner, had to diminish in power and eventually to be lost altogether. With this loss went the power to look 'into' the spiritual spheres to behold the Sun-Spirit. But, with the descent of the Christ-Being, of the Sun-Spirit, into a physical body those who had lost the atavistic, ancient power of clairvoyance could see and experience his physical presence, could also — through the Golgotha and the Whitsuntide Mysteries — experience that He was permeated with Divine Love and that He was that which they were always to possess as the highest treasure. Thus men were able to feel, for the first time in human evolution, that they were to receive within themselves, in their daily lives, in their 'earthly habitation', the great gift of Cosmic Love, the Christ. 'They were to learn to know Him fully in His life, from the first respiration as a Child to His spiritual Deed on Golgotha. They were to know him fully in their hearts.' [15] They were to learn to know — we have to learn to know — the Fire of the Love that can ray forth from the Mystery of Golgotha, a Love that knows no boundaries, no differences between peoples, that is boundless and embraces all men who seek It.

John the Baptist prepared the way for the Christ Event. Steiner states that, through Baptism, John evoked in man — who had become increasingly attached to the physical world and believed this world to be *the* reality — the consciousness that there is a

spiritual world to which, with the higher essence, they belong.
John's exhortations could be expressed: Change your hearts that
are directed to the physical world! 'And indeed their hearts were
changed when they were baptized. They then knew: "I have spirit
in me; my Ego belongs to the spiritual world".' [16] In other words,
Man, through his Ego, was now prepared to seek love, spiritualized love.

This gives us the keynote of the Christ-Event. Christ represents the descent to our Earth of the force of spiritual love — 'that
is today but at the beginning of its work'. If we pursue this thought
inwardly, with the help of the Gospels of St John and St Luke, we
shall see that spiritual love is the very keynote of the Christ-
Impulse; we shall see how the Egos that have been sundered
through the Luciferic influence (see Chapter 14) now search, in
freedom, for reunion with one another in love.

'If harmony and a life steeped in love are to be realized, the
Christ-Impulse [the meaning and content of the Mystery of
Golgotha] must penetrate to the utmost depths of human nature,
so that human love becomes something entirely different from
what it is at present — even among the most noble spirits.' [17]

'Through spiritual science the forces of love are especially
aroused in the whole human soul' — and the ground is prepared
for a gradual understanding of the Mystery of Golgotha. 'The
deepest lesson yet to be grasped fully is the mission of earthly love
in its connection with this Mystery.' [18] Full understanding of this,
says Steiner, will only be possible in what he calls the sixth
culture-epoch (beginning round about 3500). We can, however,
already now prepare ourselves for this later period in human
evolution by trying 'to kindle in ourselves love for everything in
existence'. Fundamental to this preparation is the realization
that, through the Mystery of Golgotha, the foundations of it are
actually already laid within us. Part of this foundation, says
Steiner, may be described in Goethe's words: 'Duty — when one
loves the commands one gives to oneself '. [19] When we have
reached this stage in our spiritual development the guidance of
the Commandments will be obsolete. When selfless love
becomes the source and impulse for our deeds, then we will
experience in our hearts the dawn of a fuller understanding of
Christ's Deed on Golgotha.

9.

LUCIFER AND AHRIMAN AND THE LOVE OF CHRIST

(Address to Lucifer):

O Bearer of that Light, which would confine
Love only to the service of the self;
Thou hast from Earth's beginning granted men
Knowledge, when they, still guided by the gods,
Obeyed the spirit, knowing nought of self.
But since that time each soul of man hath been
The place in which thou fightest 'gainst the gods
Yet now the times are coming, which must bring
Destruction on thyself and on thy realms. . . .
Once thou wert listened to, when Earth began,
And there didst show forth signs of Wisdom's fruit;
The fruits of Love can only come to man
When they are brought to him from realms divine. [1]

Love does not weigh by judgment's rote or rule
The forces that the Universe reveals;
She treasures them for what they may bring forth
And asks how she can mould and use the life
Which is created out of cosmic depths.
'Tis true that Lucifer doth show himself
As bearer of the light to man's soul-sight
When it would seek to gaze on spirit-space.
But then the human soul will always wish
To waken also in its inmost depth
What it should only gaze on and admire.
Although upon his beauty it must look
Ne'er may it fall 'neath Lucifer's fell sway
Lest he should gain the power to work within.
When he, the bearer of the light, sends forth
His rays of wisdom and the worlds are filled

With haughty sense of self, and with full light
Each creature's personality shines forth
A pattern of his own imperious self,
Then may the inmost being of the soul
Build up on this appearance, and rejoice
In all its senses, whilst it radiates
The joy of wisdom, all around, that lives
In its own self and loves to feel alive.
But, more than any other spirit, man
Requires a god who doth not only ask
For admiration when his outward form
Reveals itself in glory to the soul,
But One who radiates His highest power
When He Himself doth dwell within man's soul,
And loving unto death fortelleth life.
A man may turn to Lucifer and feel
Inspired by beauty, or some splendour bright,
And yet so live his life within himself
That Lucifer can ne'er find entrance there.
But to that other Spirit man doth cry,
When he can fathom his own self aright:
'The goal of love for earthly souls - 'tis this
Not I, but Christ, doth live within me now.'[2]

9.

During the course of evolution man, loosed from his tie with the Divine Spirit, has the possibility of realizing within himself free intelligence and free will.

Now, the world-process in which man is interwoven is manifested under the joint action of the spiritual and the corporeal.

Against this order established between the spiritual and the physical by the Divine Spiritual Beings who have been associated with Man since the beginning of all things stands the joint opposition of the Luciferic and Ahrimanic Beings (see Appendix).

Lucifer cannot combine anything corporeal with his own form of being. His ideal is the unbounded, unconditioned action of intelligence and will. As we have already seen, without Lucifer's intervention freedom would never have become a possibility for man. In view of this fact, we can consider Lucifer as being a spiritual helper of man in his evolution. However, Lucifer would wish to extend this tendency of freedom of will and intelligence to the exclusion of all else. That is, Lucifer would have man completely ignore and neglect the physical aspect of existence, that aspect which forms the very basis of man's independence. Here, then, Lucifer's activity becomes a 'war' against the divine order of harmony between the spiritual and the physical in which man's destiny is interwoven.

The Ahrimanic Powers are the complete opposite of the Divine Spiritual Beings with whom man has been connected since the beginning of time. 'These latter are, at the present day, purely spiritual beings, who bear within themselves perfectly free intelligence and perfectly free will, but who create, in this their free intelligence and will, a wise insight into the necessity of the "corporeal" and "unfree", as a World-Thought from whose sheltering lap man may grow up into a free being.' With the corporeal these spiritual Beings are united in love. 'This Love streams from them throughout all the universe.'[3]

In complete opposition to this is the grasping greed of

Ahriman, in whom lives hatred of everything evolving towards spiritual freedom. His aim is to create a cosmic machine. His ideal is, quite simply, to subject everything to the calculable, to measure, number and weight.

The comprehension that the world is *everywhere* spirit-in-matter must form the core of our approach to the world of nature. There we can perceive the activity of both the Divine Spiritual Powers who work in Love and the Ahrimanic Powers who work in Hate of all that is spiritually striving towards freedom.

In perceptive, imaginative consciousness, says Steiner, we can see these opposing powers at work in the seasons. In the universal warmth — as it sets in with the spring and grows in strength in the summer — we can perceive the activity and love of the Divine Spiritual Beings; in the freezing cold of winter we can perceive the contracting, hardening, 'antipathetic' workings of Ahriman.

In the height of summer, Lucifer mingles his power with the warmth, with the love of Nature. At Christmastide, the Divine Spirit-Beings, with whom man has always been united, turn their power of love against the cold hate of Ahriman. Increasingly, towards the springtime, Natural Divine Love is gently at work, mitigating Natural Ahrimanic Hate.

'The yearly sign of this Divine Love, new-manifested as it is year by year, is the time of Remembrance, when we recall how with the Christ the free element of God, Love, entered into the calculable, physical element of Earth. Christ works in perfect freedom within the calculable, the physical. In so doing, He balances, renders harmless that which craves the physical only — Ahriman and his forces. The unique Event of Golgotha is the free, cosmic act of Love within Earth's history.'[4] This Event can only be comprehended by us through the power of love.

In the chapter, 'Light — Love — Illness and Health' we shall speak of Luciferic and Ahrimanic forces in relation to illness and healing. In the same lecture to which reference is made in this connection Steiner has also the following to say: 'After we have enlightened ourselves in regard to Lucifer and Ahriman we can gain a different relation to these powers. We can, as it were, take over the work of Lucifer and Ahriman.'[5] Then, however, the deeds of these two Powers must be transformed into their opposite when they are performed by us. The deeds of Lucifer, for instance, always lead to illusions; of necessity they arouse desires and passions and can easily lead us into what can result in evil. If we ourselves are to counteract Lucifer, if we are to 'regulate his affairs in future', it will only be the love living and creating within us that can take the place of the alluring acts of Lucifer.

In the same way when we gradually remove the 'darkness' (see Chapter 13) which is interwoven into material existence, then we also overcome the Ahrimanic influences, [6] and we shall be able to recognize the world as it really is; we shall be able to penetrate to that of which matter really consists — to the nature of light. Many believe that we see light with our physical eyes. That is not so. That is an Ahrimanic deception perpetrated upon us. 'We do not see light, but only illuminant bodies. We do not see light, but we see by means of light, through light.' [7] All Ahrimanic deceptions regarding the world of nature will be swept away so that the picture of the world will be transformed, for under the influence of Ahriman it is interwoven with error; henceforth, however, our conception of the world will be permeated with wisdom. Man, in evolving a true experience of light, will also develop the counterpart, the soul-spiritual counterpart, of light, and that is wisdom.

Love and Wisdom will become the twofold practical force, the vital impulse that results from a Christocentric spiritual science. Wisdom, which is the inner counterpart of Light, will unite with Love, and Love will be permeated by Wisdom. 'If we are to partake in the spiritual side of evolution, if we are to overcome Lucifer and Ahriman — and in overcoming redeem them — we must permeate ourselves with Wisdom and Love. These two soul-spiritual elements must flow from our souls as our offering to those spiritual beings who, as the Luciferic and Ahrimanic powers in the first stages of evolution, sacrificed themselves to give us what we need for the attainment of spiritual freedom.' [8] We thus repay these higher beings for the services they have done us and, by this repayment, we redeem them.

Here we see ourselves involved in the karma of higher beings. We need to develop a Love and a Wisdom that do not remain in the realm of mankind but penetrate right into the cosmos. 'Love will stream into beings who are higher than we are and they will feel it as a sacrifice on our part. This sacrifice will "rise" to those who once poured their gifts upon us. This Love will rise just as in bygone ages the smoke of sacrifice ascended to the Spirits. Then men were only able to send up the symbolical smoke of sacrifice of spiritual possessions, but in the future they will send up streams of love.' [9] In response to this love- and wisdom-filled sacrifice the spiritual hierarchies will pour down spiritual forces to men that will work within them with ever-increasing power, and assist them in their spiritual striving towards the spiritualization of matter and the transformation of the earth into the Planet of Love.

Steiner illustrates our redemptive role *vis-à-vis* Lucifer from quite a different angle in a lecture dealing with this great spiritual being's sacrifice.

Christianity, he says, is only really at its beginning and man is, as yet, far from being a perfect Christian. However, let us assume the ideal. Let us assume that man's Ego has voluntarily, with complete free will, allowed the Christ forces of love to flow into and fill him. When the Ego has progressed so far that it has filled itself with the Christ, then this Christ force will irradiate the astral body * of man also. In that same astral body into which the Luciferic powers implanted their activity the Christ power will 'radiate from within outwards'.

> What will happen in the future? Because we have overcome with the help of Christ, and only with His help, all those human qualities that emanate from the influence of Lucifer, we, as love-filled and wisdom-filled men, gradually release the Luciferic powers. A time will come when the Luciferic powers will experience the Christ force through men, and through Christ they will be released. Man will save Lucifer, when he takes the Christ force fully into himself. [10]

On repeated occasions Steiner spoke of the necessity of taking an objective view of the two powers usually condemned as being pure evil. We must not forget, he says, that Lucifer, besides being the original bringer of evil forces into the world, the inner evil that arises through the lower passions, is also the bringer of freedom, that Lucifer plays an important role in the development of man towards true inner freedom. [11] In a different context (see Chapter 22) we note that the Luciferic powers directed their 'attacks' principally against all that unites human beings by the blood-tie. [12] The Luciferic element has the effect, among other things, of emancipation upon the soul; that is, it raises the soul above mere entanglement in the physical world. Now 'events and beings of supersensible worlds must be loved by the human soul in the manner of the Luciferic elements'. [13] In other words, the divine

* See Chapter 13, note 14

order of the universe is not transgressed until the kind of love by which man ought to feel himself drawn to the supersensible is directed to physical things. In his tendency to turn man's attention towards the non-earthly, Lucifer cannot be said to be 'evil' under all circumstances, for in this tendency we could say that our attention is drawn towards the true Bearer of Light, the Christ. The Luciferic element, however, by separating human beings one from the other and 'teaching' them to stand on their own two feet, as it were, would lead to lovelessness if in the Heights to which it directs our attention we did not perceive the Christ Impulse of spiritualized love. The Christ turns to 'good' the tendency which otherwise would result in pure 'evil', if the Luciferic influence were carried to its extreme. Lucifer, in his positive role, brought freedom and independence; the Christ transforms this freedom into love. By union with Christ men are led to spiritual love. [14] Lucifer, in spite of himself, in turning our attention towards the non-physical, also 'opens' our gaze to the Mystery of Golgotha. In spite of himself Lucifer participates in his own overcoming in that, if we unite ourselves with the Christ Impulse, we establish a spiritual bond of brotherhood from man to man in spite of the individuality of the Ego which was his gift to mankind.

We have previously stated, with Steiner, that the divine order of the universe is not transgressed unless the love that ought to be directed towards the supersensible is wholly immersed in love for the physical — in which case we have played right into the hands of Ahriman. [15] Everything that develops as intellectual life without being suffused by warmth and love of soul, without being quickened by genuine interest and enthusiasm, directly furthers the incarnation of Ahriman in a way that is after his own heart. [16]

Now, love for the supersensible rightly calls forth in the one loving it an enhanced feeling of self (see Chapter 20) — or, perhaps more clearly expressed in this context, a feeling of the emancipation of the soul from physical entanglement; but love that, in the physical world, is sought for the sake of such an inflated feeling of self is a primary Luciferic temptation. In short, love of the spiritual when it is sought for the sake of the purification of self has the effect of emancipation, of freedom; however, love for the physical when it is sought on account of the self does not have this effect, but, through the gratification gained by this means, only serves to put the self in fetters.

'The Luciferic influence is always present when in our

sympathies for others something is present other than that love which is based on selfless interest in the life of a fellow-man.' This statement by Steiner may be understood as follows: someone may be loved because he is endowed with certain qualities; in such a case there is no intermingling of a Luciferic element with the love felt. Love that has its basis in qualities possessed by the one loved is immune to Luciferic interference. But love whose source is not in the loved one but in him who loves is prone to Luciferic influences. A being loved because it has qualities to which, as lovers, *we incline by nature* is loved with that 'part of the soul which is accessible to the Luciferic element'. [17]

We have previously seen that Lucifer, besides being the bringer of evil into the world, is also the bringer of freedom; that he plays an important role in the universe. [18] Of Ahriman also it must be said that he plays an important part. But whereas Lucifer 'attacks' the soul from within, Ahriman does so from without; that is, through sense perceptions, through the senses. [19] It is to the Ahrimanic influence that we owe, for instance, the wonderful progress that man has made in the field of the exact sciences during the past few centuries. Both Lucifer and Ahriman are opponents of what we might call the 'good, progressive gods'; they both cross the plan of these gods, and yet, at the same time, they are essential to the free development of man.

This dual role, says Steiner, poses a question: What attitude should I, as man, adopt towards Lucifer and Ahriman? What is the right attitude? Am I to love them or hate them? In answering these questions, Steiner bids us consider the following. It is to be borne in mind that both Lucifer and Ahriman are beings who, by their whole nature, do not belong to the physical plane, but have their mission and task in the spiritual world; disharmony and disruption only appear when they bring down their activities into the physical world and arrogate to themselves rights that are not theirs. This is one important aspect of an answer to the question posed. A further equally important aspect is this: our ordinary judgment holds good only for events occurring on the physical plane, it cannot be simply transferred to happenings in the spiritual world. If, therefore, we say 'one power is hostile to another', or 'enmity is not right, it should not exist', we can readily accept and recognize the validity of such judgements for our daily lives on earth; but Steiner makes the point that the same 'rule' does not hold good for the higher planes, for the spiritual world. In regard to these planes, our judgement must be widened, as it were. Just as in the field of electricity both positive and negative poles are necessary, so also in the spiritual world it is necessary that spiritual beings should oppose one another. [20] Steiner reminds us here of the truth of the saying of Herakleitos that strife as well as love constitutes the universe. It is only when, for instance, Lucifer, working through the medium of the human soul, brings conflict into the physical world, that conflict and strife may be called wrong. 'But this does not hold good for the higher worlds — there the hostility of the spirits is an element that belongs to the whole structure, to the needs of the whole evolution of the universe.' [21]

To reiterate: 'As soon as we come into the higher worlds, we must employ other standards for our judgements. That is why there is often a feeling of shock when Lucifer and Ahriman are spoken of as being the opponents of the progressive gods, on the one side, and on the other, as being necessary to the whole course of the universal order' [22] — and to the evolution, spiritual evolution of man.

*　　*　　*　　*

Steiner speaks, on many occasions, in very strong terms of a soul-attitude, widely spread in our present time, that he describes as 'love of ease'. Relating this attitude of soul to life after death, Steiner states that there are people who, during a certain period between death and rebirth, are made to fulfil most unpleasant tasks. 'The seer finds that there are souls who are forced to serve a being such as Ahriman after death.' [23]

As soon as we enter the realm beyond the physical, Ahriman appears quite clearly to us. Now, he has a number of tasks to perform and he needs 'servants' to help him accomplish them.

Why, we could ask, have some souls been condemned to serve Ahriman during certain phases of their spiritual existence between death and re-birth? The exact clairvoyant, states Steiner, investigates how such people lived between birth and death, considers the principal characteristics of such souls, and discovers that they all suffered from one common evil, the love of ease. 'Love of ease and comfort are among the most widespread characteristics of contemporary humanity.' [24]

Should we enquire the reason why most people fail to do something, we find that the answer invariably is: love of ease. Whether we consider the most important things of life or mere trifles , we find that love of ease is ubiquitous. To hold on to the old and outdated, not being able to shake it off, is a form of love of ease. Steiner mentions in this connection that people are not always as wicked as they may appear. For instance, those who were responsible for the burning at the stake of Giordano Bruno, or the maltreatment of Galileo, did not necessarily act out of wickedness, but rather out of love of ease. They could not accept the new. It often takes a long time for people to be able to think and feel along new lines and the reason for this tardiness is love of ease! It is those who were prone on earth to love of ease who have to serve Ahriman in the life after death. For Ahriman, apart from his many other functions, is the 'spirit of obstacles'. Wherever obstacles arise to true progress there Ahriman is to be found. He applies the brakes to life and to the spiritual development of human beings. 'Those who are subject to love of ease on earth will become agents to the slowing down process of everything that comes into the world from the supersensible. So love of ease fetters human souls between death and rebirth to spirits who, under Ahriman, are compelled to serve the powers of opposition and hindrance.' [25]

*   *   *   *

Let us now look a little more closely at the evolution of man and the role that Lucifer played — and continues to play — in the process.

Steiner tells us that when one follows the Akasha Chronicle it does indeed appear that in an early stage of earth evolution man was a totally different being from what he is today. Man was still a being we could describe as male-female, for the differentiation into separate sexes had not yet occurred. [26] Individualization had not occurred and, in consequence, man's life was one of impulses — he did not think in our intellectual sense. His consciousness was *dreamlike*; he lived in '*dullness*'. He had not the ability to connect any thoughts with sensory perceptions. To do this requires a state of 'separateness' from the outer sense-perceptible world. Only then is clarity of thought, intellectual thought, possible.

But there were other beings, Steiner recounts, who did acquire knowledge and wisdom in spite of the lack of differentiation into subject and object as just described. This was possible because they had gone through a different development in a still more remote past. It was possible for the soul of such a being to be fructified by the spirit without first awaiting the development of the physical body as we know it today, without awaiting the development of the inner organs, above all of the physical brain. The human soul had to wait until a brain could be evolved that could become the mediator with the spirit. Without this 'detour' in the physical, this soul would have remained spiritless — it would have remained arrested at the stage of dreamlike consciousness. This was different for the superhuman beings mentioned above. In previous stages their souls had developed organs that needed no physical embodiment in order to enter into contact with the spirit. Whereas our knowledge and wisdom had to be attained in the sense-world, these beings could acquire both *super*sensibly. Knowledge acquired supersensibly is called intuitive knowledge. Contemporary man attains such intuition only at a later stage of his development. This intuition makes it possible for him to enter into contact with the spirit, with the spiritual world, without sensory mediation. We, as human beings, had to make a 'detour' through the world of sensory substance. This 'detour' is called the descent of the human soul into matter, or, popularly, the fall of man. This 'descent', this incarnation into a physical body, went hand in hand with the separation of an androgynous being into the distinct sexes, [27] male and female, and, at the same time, the formation of a physical brain that brought about the condition we know today, namely that the soul of man can think only that which it receives from the outside through the physical senses, unless the intuitive faculties are developed.

Because of their different earlier development, the superhuman beings did not have to take part in this descent. Their acquisition of knowledge and wisdom was a form of clairvoyance that had no need of senses and organ of thought. They were the bearers of a 'primeval wisdom', to the understanding of which mankind is only now beginning to attain. Whereas the superhuman beings had wisdom — according to which the world is created — as a free gift 'from above', as it were, man did not have it given to him; he had to *desire* it (Tree of the Knowledge of Good and Evil).

The longing for knowledge arises through the fact that inner organs are developed, the brain and so forth. Steiner describes this development as being caused by the soul-spiritual in the human being. This longing is a consequence of the intervention of the Luciferic influence (the Devil [28] in Paradise) and could be described as a division of spiritual forces within the human being.

In other words, whereas before the 'temptation' all the energy of the soul was directed 'outward', after this cosmic event a part of this energy was directed 'inward'.

Now, the force by means of which one human being turns 'outward' in order to act together with another human being is *love*. The superhuman beings directed *all* their love 'outward' in order to let universal wisdom flow into their souls. Man, however, owing to the separation just outlined and the formation of inner organs, etc., can only direct part of this love 'outward'. He draws away from the 'outside' world, one might say, that part of his nature which he directs toward his inner development. And thus there arises what we call selfishness. When he became man or woman in the physical body, when he became sensual (and when, thereby, his love became sensual), Man could surrender himself with only a part of his being. With the other part he separated himself from the world around him. He became egoistic. His action toward the 'outside' world became selfish. His striving after inner development also became selfish. He loved because he *desired*, and likewise he thought because he *desired* wisdom.

The soul that, among the selfless, all-loving beings, the superhuman beings, the leaders, does not reside in a male or a female body is itself male-female. It loves, therefore, without *desire*. It surrenders itself completely to others. Thus, too, the soul of man loved before the division into sexes: but at that time the human soul could not consciously understand itself or the world around it, because at that stage in our development as Man we still lived in a kind of dream consciousness. However, the superhuman beings, Steiner informs us, though 'living' in a state of total self-surrender, of total love towards the 'outside' and others and not needing a physical body in order to come to self-consciousness (and, thereby, clarity of intellectual understanding) were, just because of their 'openness', fructified and endowed with wisdom from above, that is, by the creative spirits of the universe. Man, during his 'detour' through the repeated experiences of physical existences, has consciously to develop the selflessness and love and intuitive, wisdom-filled understanding in order to attain the level of spirituality that was (that *is*) 'natural' to these superhuman beings. 'Man must pass through selfishness in order to attain selflessness again at a higher stage, where, however, it will be combined with completely clear consciousness.' [29]

The task of the 'progressive' superhuman beings in the evolution of Man was to impress upon primeval Man something of their own character — love. But they could do this only for that part of the spiritual energy that was directed 'outward'. 'Thus *sensual* love came into being. Sensual love became the force of physical human development. This love brings man and woman together in so far as they are physical beings. Upon this love rests the progress of physical humanity.' [30]

It was only over this love that the progressive superhuman beings, the Spirits of Love (Seraphim), [31] had power. That part of the human soul-energy that is directed 'inward' and is to bring about conscious cognition by the 'detour' through the senses is inaccessible to the power of *those* superhuman beings, because, as mentioned above, they never 'descended' to the development of inner, physical organs of cognition. But they could clothe the impulse toward the 'outside' in love because such love was of the very essence of their nature. Part of Man's soul, then, they could reach, they could touch; part was inaccessible to them. Because of this inaccessibility a gulf opened up between them and primeval mankind. Love, at first in sensual form, they could implant in Man; knowledge they could not give, however, for their own knowledge had never made the 'detour' through the inner organs that Man was developing. 'They could speak no language that a creature with a physical brain could have understood.' [32]

But there were other spiritual beings, not so far advanced as the Spirits of Love, the Seraphim. They were in a special position; they were too far advanced to pass through the stage of incarnating into a physical body, male or female, but they were not so far advanced as to become Spirits of Love. However, they could speak to creatures with a brain in a language that the latter would understand (The Tempter in the Garden of Paradise, [33] for instance). Through this soul-spiritual intercourse between the human soul and these less advanced, but highly spiritual beings, the Luciferic beings, the human soul-energy, inward turning and inaccessible to the Spirits of Love, was stimulated and could 'open' itself to receive knowledge and wisdom. It was thus that knowledge and 'wisdom' of a human kind appeared on earth. These 'half superhuman beings' became the stimulators of human wisdom. One can therefore justifiably call them *bringers of light*. They are the Luciferic beings. Primeval mankind therefore had two kinds of leaders: Beings of Love and Beings of Wisdom.

'Human nature was balanced between Love and Wisdom when it assumed its present form on this earth. By the Beings of Love Man was stimulated to physical development, by the Beings of Wisdom, the Luciferic Beings, he was stimulated to the development of the inner nature,' [34] to an independent soul-spiritual life. 'These Beings brought Man the power to unfold a free activity in his own consciousness, but brought him at the same time the possibility of error and of evil.' [35]

If, says Steiner, we wish to make a graphic picture of what happened at this primeval stage of Man's evolution we can say that Man descended from Divine Heights. It was ordained, by high spiritual beings, that he should develop in a certain way, but through the Luciferic influence he was cast down more deeply into matter than would have been the case without that influence.

> When man had gone downwards to the lowest step, a mighty impetus was needed upwards. This impetus could only come because that Being from the higher Hierarchies whom we designate as the Christ-Being had, in the higher worlds, formed a resolution which He would not have needed to have made if he had been concerned with his own evolution alone. He could have 'ignored' the evolution of humanity. But, if the upward impulse had not been given, human evolution would have been such that — in the hands of Lucifer and Ahriman — the downward path must have continued. The Christ would have had an *ascent*, but humanity an irrevocable *downfall*. [36]

It was only through the fact that Christ took the resolution to unite Himself, physically, with mankind, only through the act of embodying Himself in an earthly existence, as a man, that the upward path was made possible for humanity. It was only through this act, born of selfless love, that the Redemption of man (in which he must also be consciously active) from that impulse which emanated from the Luciferic forces — designated symbolically as 'Original Sin' — was made possible. 'Christ accomplished something that was not necessary for His own evolution.' 'What,' asks Steiner, 'what kind of Act was this?'

It was an Act of Divine Love. There is no human feeling capable of fully realizing the intensity of Love required by the Christ-Spirit to make the decision to work upon earth in a human body. 'Thereby, through an Act of Love, that Event was brought about which is the *most important* in human evolution.' Without this Act, Man would have sunk ever deeper into the sensory, and the goal of mankind, the mission of spiritualizing love, would have been rendered impossible. 'When we grasp the Love-Act of God, when we try to grasp it as a great Ideal in comparison with which every human act of love can be but small, then, through the feeling of utter disproportion between human love and that Divine Love needed for the Mystery of Golgotha, we may draw near to the building up, to the giving birth within our souls of those Imaginations which place before our spiritual gaze that momentous Event of Golgotha.' [37] It is possible, Steiner tells us, to attain an Imagination of the Mount on which the Cross was raised, that Cross on which hung a God in human body, a God who out of His own Free Will, that is, out of Love, accomplished the Act (cf. St John's Gospel, 20: 30) whereby the earth and humanity could attain their goal. If the God who is designated by the name of Father had not at one time permitted the Luciferic influence to come to Man, Man would not have developed the condition for the free Ego. With the Luciferic influence the foundation for the free Ego was developed. That had to be permitted by the Father-God. But just as the Ego for the sake of freedom had to become entangled in matter, so now, to be set free from this entanglement, the whole Love of the *Son* had to lead to the Act of Golgotha. Through this alone the freedom of Man, the compete dignity of Man, first became possible. *We have to thank a Divine Act of Love* that we can be free beings. As men we may feel free beings, but we may never forget that for this freedom we have to thank Christ's Act of Love. [38]

In several lectures Steiner refers to a carved wooden 'Group' on which he worked for many years. This is a majestic statue of the Representative of Man, of Christ, between Lucifer and Ahriman. We cannot go into detail regarding the meaning and purpose of this great work and the reader is referred to Steiner's own commentaries. [39] But the following statement by him is very relevant to our main theme: 'The whole group is so designed that the central figure [the Christ] is in no way aggressive, but intended by its gesture to express only love. The Christ does not fight against Ahriman, but radiates Love. However, neither Lucifer nor Ahriman can endure this Love — it brings about the destruction of their very beings.' [40] It is their experience of the proximity of spiritualized love that causes them to give up their power. The Love of Christ creates a balance between these two great Spirit-Beings. [41] Our understanding of the Mystery of Golgotha is all the deeper if we hold in our hearts this attitude of the Christ towards the two great adversaries Lucifer and Ahriman. Not in judgement does He act, but in love.

10.

LOVE AND FREEDOM: THE ESSENTIAL NATURE OF THINKING

> *Philosophy, in its very name, love of wisdom, shows that it is not merely an affair of the intellect, but of the entire human being.* [1]

10.

In a remarkable lecture given in 1920, with the title 'The Path of Freedom and Love and their Significance in World Events', [2] Steiner clarifies the relationship that exists between spiritual freedom and spiritualized love. He begins by posing the question: How do we in reality become inwardly more and more spiritual? It is certainly not by harbouring as many thoughts as possible of the surrounding world, for instance, for such thoughts merely reproduce the outer world, which is a material world. No, we become more spiritual through the inner, *will-permeated* work we carry out in our thoughts. This is why, Steiner continues, meditation consists not in indulging in haphazard thoughts, but in holding certain easily envisaged thoughts in our consciousness, drawing them to the centre of our consciousness with a concentrated effort of will. 'The greater the strength and intensity of this inner radiation of will into the sphere of thinking, the more spiritual we become.' [3]

Now we can go a step further in this process of meditation and thereby attain complete freedom in our inner life if we increasingly efface the actual thought-content, in so far as this content has its origin in the world about us, and then proceed to animate into ever greater activity the element of will which streams through our thoughts whenever, in everyday life, we form judgements, draw conclusions, make decisions, and so forth. Our thinking then becomes what Steiner calls in his basic book, *Philosophy of Freedom*, *pure* thinking. We think, but our thinking is filled with will — indeed, *pure thinking* could equally well be called *pure will*.

We become inwardly free when our thinking is permeated through and through with will, for then it is no longer under the dominion of the laws of necessity that prevail in the material world. In such will-kindled thinking we raise ourselves above, free ourselves from, this 'necessity' and permeate ourselves with a force that is inherently our own and that we ourselves have activated. *Freedom* becomes a reality when we allow the will to become an ever increasingly active force in our thinking.

It is relevant, both in the present context and to our main theme, to consider the will somewhat more closely. When, we could ask, does the will show itself with particular clarity and purity in what we do? Certainly not when we perform such involuntary actions as sneezing or coughing. We are, of course, doing something in such cases, but we cannot ascribe to ourselves any definite conscious impulse when we sneeze or cough. The matter is somewhat different when we speak. Here we are doing something in which our will is undoubtedly present. But in the act of speaking, volition and the absence of volition intermingle. Once we have learnt to speak we no longer need to formulate each word by dint of an effort of will — an element of instinct enters into speech. But the more our activity is free of organic processes, the more do we penetrate our deeds with the activity of thinking. To illustrate the point, Steiner gives the example of a portrait painter who is not merely concerned to paint a physical likeness, but endeavours to reveal something of the essence of the human being he is portraying. We can imbue our actions to a greater or lesser degree with our thinking. The more our conscious actions evolve towards perfection, the more our thoughts penetrate, 'fill' them.

Now how do we achieve inner perfection in our actions? We achieve this, Steiner states, by nurturing and developing in ourselves *devotion to the outer world*. At first sight this may appear to be a paradoxical statement. What Steiner means is this: the more our devotion to the world around us deepens and intensifies, the more does this world stir us to action. And it is just through developing devotion to the world around us that we succeed in imbuing our actions with thoughts. 'What is devotion to the outer world? Devotion to this world, which pervades our actions with thoughts, is nothing other than *love*.' [4]

We can now say: just as we attain inner *freedom* by irradiating the life of thought with will, so do we attain *love* by permeating the life of will with thoughts. We unfold love in our actions by letting thoughts radiate into the realm of the will; we develop freedom in our thinking by letting what is of the nature of the will radiate into our thoughts. And because each one of us is a unified whole, when we reach the stage in our spiritual development where we achieve freedom in the life of thought and love in the life of will, there will also be freedom in our actions and love in our thinking. There is a living process of mutual irradiation. 'Action filled with thought is wrought in love; thinking that is permeated with will gives rise to actions that are truly free.' [5]

Freedom and Love grow and develop together. We can bring them to realization within ourselves in such a way that, through us, the one unites with the other for the good of the whole of humanity, both present and future. [6]

Our deeds do not remain confined in us, they detach themselves from us, as it were. They become world-happenings — and, if they are permeated by love, then love radiates out from us into the world. An egotistical action has quite a different effect on the world from one permeated by love. The former constitutes a hindrance to the process of human and world evolution, whereas the latter contributes to and furthers this process. [7]

*　　*　　*　　*

In his work *The Philosophy of Freedom*, [8] to which brief reference has just been made and which bears the sub-title 'The Basis for a Modern World Conception' and is described as being 'some results of introspective observation following the methods of Natural Science', Steiner elaborates upon the theme of freedom and love. The present writer is well aware that only many years of working with and assimilating the contents can do anything like justice to this work, of which Steiner wrote: 'The way it should be read is with attention to the fact that it brings one to a wholly different way of thinking and willing and looking at things. If this were done, one would realize that such an approach lifts one's consciousness out of the earth into another world, and that one derives from it the kind of inner assurance that makes it possible to speak with conviction about the results of spiritual research.' [9]

In the first chapter of *The Philosophy of Freedom* Steiner makes reference to two forms of love. The distinction is made between *instinctive love*, i.e. sexual desire, and what he calls *human love*. Whenever love is not merely the expression of instinct it depends on the mental picture (Vorstellung) [10] we form of the loved one — 'And the more idealistic these mental pictures are, just so much the more blessed is our love'. We often hear that love makes us blind to the failings of the one we love. But the reverse is also true: love opens the eyes for the good qualities of the loved one. These good qualities remain unnoticed by many. Someone, however, sees them and, just because he does, love awakens in his soul. He makes a mental picture of what others have failed to see. [11]

In our ordinary everyday life it is true to say that, in general, our feelings of love are closely linked to our instincts, to our life of desires. But it is possible — as shown in several places in these pages — to free love from the human body. Whereas in our 'normal' life the original impetus for love comes from 'within' us, it is possible to develop this love through being immersed in outer objects, things and people, so that we are able to forget ourselves and become one with that which is 'outside' us. If we perform an action in such a way that it does not arise out of the impulses which have their origin in our desires and instincts, but out of love for what is around us, then we have the kind of love which is at the same time the power of human freedom. That is why Steiner says in *The Philosophy of Freedom*, that, in a higher sense, the saying 'love makes us blind' is not true, but that, on the contrary, 'love makes one see'. Those who live and act through love make themselves free, for they free themselves from the instincts and desires which otherwise so easily enslave them. They can act as free human beings in the sense that they do what they know should be done and not what they would be led to do under the dictate of their instincts and desires. [12]

Human love is called forth, not by *physical* perception, but by the forming of thoughts about the spiritual, inner, invisible qualities of a person — or object — and these thoughts kindle our love. In this form of love we are confronted with feelings which do not rise up without our active and conscious participation from our instinctive bodily life, but are born of our thinking — without which they would not come into being. In contrast to this we can say that when love is based on instincts — when we merely wish to satisfy cravings arising from desires — thinking is all but non-existent, is very dim. This kind of 'love' is an expression of egoism in one of its basic forms.

In a later chapter, entitled 'The Factors of Life', Steiner speaks of a third, a higher form of love — the capacity of thinking to penetrate into the depths of the phenomena. This power of thinking to 'see' ideas he calls *intuition*. This power, which he also calls 'spiritual love', may penetrate into lesser or greater depths of the phenomena. It may, for instance, 'see' only as much of the idea of a thing as is actually revealed by its physical aspect; on the other hand, it may penetrate the physical veil and 'see' what creates the object — as Goethe did when he 'saw' the archetypal plant, i.e. the Idea which underlies and creates all plants.

Steiner brings this line of thought to a culmination in the following sentence: 'In so far as we sense and feel (and also perceive), we are single beings; in so far as we think we are the

All-One Being that pervades everything.' [13] In other words, in so far as man thinks, or rather, when man attains and 'exercises' the power of intuition, of spiritual love, then he and God are one. When man attains the *reality* of thinking within himself he realizes the divine within himself. [14]

In our present context we can understand the nature of spiritual love in the following way. Though my feelings for a person are on a higher level than mere sexual attraction because I admire some spiritual qualities in that person — and can therefore be described as being human love — they may nevertheless still be limited by my personality. In other words, they depend on what *I* consider worthy of admiration and love. But if I am able to assess the other person solely for his own sake (irrespective of whether he pleases or displeases me), if I am able to understand the other person completely and identify myself with him, then the love that now awakens in me is spiritual. Such love is no longer bound to my personality — with my sympathies and antipathies, likes and dislikes, and so forth — any more than the concept of the person in question. Both my thinking, my knowledge of and my feelings for the person are concerned solely with the other person, not with myself. We could also say that my feelings now partake of the spiritual nature of thinking. I live now not in my 'I', my Ego, which corresponds to my bodily nature, but in the 'I' which is one with the 'World-I'. We can also now say that the power within thinking which enables us to penetrate into the depths of the phenomena — the power which Steiner calls spiritual love — is the divine love-filled power of Christ.

*　　*　　*　　*

A short digression may be justified at this stage.

It is quite clear that Steiner's spiritual science differs from the 'mystical' schools in the extremely high value it accords to *thinking*. To give any kind of full answer regarding the reason for this is neither within the present writer's ability, nor is it the main object of our thesis. A short answer could be that in Steiner's conception, man has his unique place in the cosmos as a thinking being. It is, in particular, in Steiner's *Philosophy of Freedom* that we can find the justification for his view of this 'unique place' and the reader is urged to make a close and sustained study of this work.

In clarification, however, we could say: It is quite clear that when Steiner speaks of the essential nature of thinking he is not concerned with the mere intellect — which is only capable of grasping the material world and formulating the so-called 'laws' of nature. Steiner's own reference, in a course of lectures entitled *Mystery Knowledge and Mystery Centres*, is one of the clearest expositions of what he meant by 'thinking':

> In *The Philosophy of Freedom* the argument is that to experience thinking in the real sense means that a man can come to no other realization than this: If you live in thinking in the real sense, you are living in the Cosmos even if, to begin with, somewhat diffusely. This connection in the most intimate experience of thinking with the secrets of the world-process is the root-nerve of *The Philosophy of Freedom*. Hence the statement is made in the book that in thinking we grasp one corner of the whole world-mystery.
>
> This may be putting it simply, but what is meant is that when a man experiences thinking in the real sense he no longer feels outside the mystery of world-existence, but within it; he no longer feels outside the Divine, but within the Divine. If he comprehends the reality of thinking within himself, he comprehends the Divine within himself. [15]

A passage from *The Philosophy of Freedom* is here quoted at length as it may serve to bring further clarification into Steiner's conception of the essential nature of thinking — it also succinctly sums up some of the points made in this chapter:

> No other activity of the human soul is so easily misunderstood as thinking. Will and feeling still fill the soul with warmth even when we live through the original event again in retrospect. Thinking all too readily leaves us cold in recollection; it is as if the life of the soul had dried out. Yet this is really nothing but the strongly marked shadow of its real nature – *warm, luminous, and penetrating deeply into the phenomena of the world*. This penetration is brought about by a power flowing through the activity of thinking itself — the power of love in its spiritual form. There are no grounds here for the objection that to discern love in the activity of thinking is to project into thinking a feeling, namely, love. For in truth this objection is but a confirmation of what we have been saying. If we turn towards thinking *in its essence*, we find in it both feeling and will, and these in the depths of their reality; if we turn away from thinking towards 'mere' feeling and will, we lose from these their true reality. If we are ready to experience thinking *intuitively*, we can also do justice to the experience of feeling and will; but the mysticism of feeling and the metaphysics of will are

not able to do justice to the penetration of reality by intuitive thinking — they conclude all too readily that they themselves are rooted in reality, but that the intuitive thinker, devoid of feeling and a stranger to reality, forms out of 'abstract thoughts' a shadowy, chilly picture of the world. [16]

Referring again to the capacity of thinking to dive into the depths of the phenomena, to the power of spiritual love within thinking, to intuition, [17] the further point can be made that we only experience 'freedom' when we are able to identify ourselves completely with the being or object confronting us; when we set aside all our own viewpoints and inclinations and see the world exclusively through the eyes of the other. In other words: we need to become completely selfless; to manifest a selflessness which has been achieved through a strong Ego that has taken its development in hand. Selflessness does not imply Egolessness! It is a dynamic state of being which enables us to find our true 'I' — as distinct from subjective 'I' — through the other being who then becomes a gateway to 'The All-One-Being that pervades everything'.

In *The Philosophy of Freedom* Steiner also speaks of what he calls 'moral intuition'. [18] Elsewhere he states that the three most beautiful life fruits nurtured in man when he assimilates what is given to him by spiritual science are: 'Knowledge in human worth, feeling for human dignity, willing in love for humanity'. 'For this spiritual science works through the will, so that it can reach up to ... moral intuition'. When moral intuitions are permeated with love, then we act freely out of love springing from our individuality. This is in deep contrast to Kant's conception of duty, which we shall have occasion to mention in more detail later. 'When we look for where moral intuition is rooted in the human being, when we look for what is the real driving, ethical motive in moral intuition, we find it at its highest in love purified by spirit. There, where this love has become spiritual, there it draws into itself moral intuitions; and a man is moral because he *loves* duty ... ' [19]

Moral human worth blossoms when it is one with human freedom and is rooted in true human love, in spiritualized love — and love of duty can become, in the deepest sense, love for mankind and, in consequence, can become a true ferment for the good in social life.

*   *   *   *

Steiner insists that the great mission of man is to bring Freedom into the world, and with Freedom true Love. For Love without Freedom is impossible. A man who blindly follows an impulse, just follows it, is led willy nilly by it; but for him who can act otherwise there is but one force he would follow, and that is love. Freedom and Love, says Steiner, are two inseparable elements. If Love is to enter into the stream of evolution, it can happen only through Freedom, which means transmuting, out of one's own free will, the freedom given to individual man through the influence of Lucifer into selfless love given to mankind by Christ.

The Earth is the Cosmos of Freedom and Love — and man, the tenth hierarchy, may be called the Spirit of Freedom and Love. [20]

In one reference to his book *The Philosophy of Freedom*, Steiner stresses that, among other things, he had been concerned to clarify the experience of freedom in thought, in pure thinking emancipated from the senses.

In thoughts which consciously arise in the human soul as an ethical, moral ideal, in thoughts which have the strength to influence the human will and to lead it to action, in such thoughts there is freedom. We can speak of human freedom when we speak of human actions shaped by man's own free thinking, when he reaches the point, through a moral self-training, of not allowing his actions to be influenced by instincts, passions, emotions or by his temperament, but only by the devoted love for an action. In this devoted love for an action can develop something which proceeds from the ideal strength of pure ethical thinking. This is a really free action. [21]

Love is the foundation of freedom.

*   *   *   *

In his fundamental work *Theosophy*, Steiner draws our attention to the transitory and the eternal in relation to freedom.

He begins by stating that if we relate ourselves to the world purely out of our personal inclinations, then only the transitory reveals itself to us. But if we 'withdraw ourselves from the transitory nature of ourselves and live with our feeling of self, with our "I", in our permanent nature, then the transitory parts of our nature become intermediaries; and that which reveals itself through them is an Eternal reality in the things. This relationship between his own Eternal nature and the Eternal in the things must be established by the seeker.' [22] Whenever we observe an object of nature, we should seek the Eternal in it, we should seek to perceive the Eternal that expresses itself through the object. We should ask ourselves: what is the permanent that lives in the transitory stone, the transitory human being, that will outlast the sense-perceptible object as it confronts us? It is an error to suppose that directing our inner attention to the Eternal would destroy devoted observation and our feeling for the qualities of everyday affairs, would estrange us from the immediate realities of life. Quite the contrary is the case. Every object, no matter how insignificant, unveils to us innumerable mysteries, when we see not only with our eyes, but when, '*through* the eyes the spirit is directed upon them'. Everything remains vividly perceptible to the senses, nothing is lost; an infinitude is gained. 'Indeed a person who does not understand how to observe with the eye even the tiniest thing will achieve only pale, bloodless thoughts, not spiritual sight.' [23]

He who undertakes such exercises of observation soon notices that a transformation takes place within himself. He arrives at a different valuation and estimate of the world from the one he had previously. His whole feeling takes on a new relationship to the sense-perceptible world. The transitory no longer attracts him merely for its own sake; it becomes for him an image of the Eternal — and this Eternal he learns to love. This new, objective relationship does not cause him to be estranged from life, but he does learn, on the contrary, to value each thing according to its true significance. He is a poor discerner who would go wandering with his head in the clouds and lose sight of actual life. [24]

We can see here that love of nature, in so far as it bears something of a sensuous nature, must be clearly distinguished from that higher loving of nature that is of a more spiritual kind, that seeks for the spirit that reveals itself in the things and events of nature. The latter kind of feeling for nature develops the spirit itself and establishes something permanent in the spirit. We must distinguish between such a feeling for nature and a pleasure in nature that is simply based on the senses. In regard to the latter, the soul requires purification just as much as in regard to other propensities based on mere physical existence and personal inclination. [25]

Thus, says Steiner, there opens out to the seeker, to the spiritual scientist, the possibility of ceasing to be subservient and obedient to the influences of the external world of the senses —

influences which sway his will one way one minute and another the next. Through 'purified' vision he sees the Eternal in things and, moreover, he recognizes that when he acts out of himself, out of his 'I', then he is also conscious that he acts from out of the eternal being of things, for they 'give utterance in him of this eternal being of theirs. He acts, in other words, in harmony with the eternal World Order, when he directs his action from out of the Eternal living within him. He thereby knows himself no longer merely impelled by things of the sense-perceptible world; he knows that he impels them according to the eternal laws implanted in them, laws which he recognizes as being within him, too.' [26] He acts out of this recognition of the Eternal — a recognition that he has attained out of his own free will and out of love for the Eternal.

This ability, Steiner reminds us, to act from out of the Eternal within him, out of his inner being — as distinct from personal, limited inclinations — is as yet only an ideal towards which Man can strive. The attainment of such a goal lies in the distant future. 'But the seeker must have the will clearly to recognize the path. This is his *will for inner freedom*. For freedom is action from out of one's own inner being. And only he can act from out of his inner being who draws his motives from the Eternal — that he has learnt to love.' [27]

On one occasion Steiner stated that in *The Philosophy of Freedom* he wanted to provide a foundation for a new social feeling of freedom which would enable a new form of social life to emerge: 'And now I would like to underline this by saying that we must cultivate love as a power of acquiring knowledge — for example, in developing a sharper faculty of perceiving a person anew each day. For each day are we not fundamentally a different person?' [28]

Fundamentally, we are indeed different every day. Usually we allow ourselves to be driven by outside events and circumstances and allow differences to take place within ourselves without our being aware of them. The scientist of the spirit, however, as part of his training of the will, needs to be conscious of the differences that are taking place within him. This development of the will takes the form of noting what has influenced his inner life during the day, of tracing what has changed his inner life during the past year or so, and so on. This is one aspect of taking one's life consciously into one's own hands. Another, important aspect, is this: we ourselves have to direct quite definite impulses and motives so that we are not always changed from without, but are able to observe and direct our willing and actions consciously and freely.

If we do this consistently, then our approach to our fellow-men also changes, for we recognize that they too should be left free in their life of will and action, that only through such freedom can selfless love develop between man and man. Through such a training of the will indicated above we can begin to recognize the true essence of our own being and when, as a result of our new experience of ourselves, we approach our fellow-man in such a way that his individuality is allowed to express itself rather than the impression we may have made upon him, then his innermost being begins to speak to us. Love and freedom form the living foundation upon which the spirit in man can 'meet' the spirit in man: 'Social life then becomes ennobled by the spirit'. [29]

11.

LOVE AS A COGNITIVE POWER

People will be prepared to admit that the faculty of memory can be developed into a power for acquiring knowledge. But perhaps the more strict scientists will not be able to accept the second faculty for acquiring knowledge which I have to describe. And yet, despite this, it is a real power for acquiring knowledge, though not as it appears in everyday life, but when it is developed. This is the power of love. [1]

When the power of thought and the power of will are developed further than in ordinary life, then the power of feeling, which is the deepest, most essential part of the human soul, will also be transformed. [2]

A power of the soul, which many are unwilling to accept as a means of knowledge, is raised to a higher level. This is the power of love. [3]

11.

In a lecture given in 1923 in Vienna Steiner discusses the force of love as a means of knowledge. He begins by making the point that we are here dealing with something which is generally not considered to be a means of knowledge 'by those who desire to be taken seriously in the realm of cognition'. The reason for the lack of recognition of the force of love as an organ of knowledge is that 'we first become aware that this is a means of knowledge when we enter the supersensible realms' [4] — and modern philosophies, and theories of knowledge, do not concern themselves with such realms.

Steiner prefaces what he has to say regarding his description of the first steps in the process of unfolding a 'higher' love as an organ of cognition with the remark that it may seem 'paradoxical'.

One exercise he suggests to help unfold this organ of higher love is the recollection, in reverse, of the happenings of the day — an exercise to be carried out during a quiet period before going to sleep at night. This consists of bringing the events of the day into our consciousness so that we begin with the last occurrence of the evening first, visualizing it as precisely as possible, then visualizing the next, then the third from last, and so on, thus moving inwardly backwards to the moment we woke up in the morning. What is significant in this exercise is the *reversal* of the customary order of visualization. Through such an exercise we 'reverse' the whole of life, as it were. We think — and feel (if we put our whole soul into the visualization process) — in a direction opposite to the normal course of the day.

If we 'pass through' more and more such inner experiences of the soul in this way, we discover that the inner experience is freed more and more from the external course of nature — from the 'law of necessity'; we could also say that we 'actually become more and more self-directing'. [5] But — and here is the paradoxical element — even though we become in this way more and more individualized and achieve an ever-increasing inner power of self-direction, at the same time we learn to pay attention to the life of our fellow-men, to nature, in more complete consciousness. We also become aware that, the more powerfully we develop this conscious absorption in, say, another human being, the more intense becomes the degree of our selflessness — 'and the greater grows our force of love in compensation'. This experience of not living in oneself but in another being becomes so powerful that we reach the stage where, to Imagination and Inspiration, we can now unite Intuition, that is, the intuitive 'entering' into the other being. We arrive at *Intuition*, [6] so that we no longer experience only our own inner being, but also that of our fellow-man. We do this without losing our individuality, and yet we are, at the same time, in a state of complete selflessness! We find ourselves in that form of existence in which the Pauline words 'Not I, but Christ in me' reverberate and become reality.

Here love becomes a cognitive force, which gradually makes it possible for us not only to become one with the being of the other — and with our own inner being, too — one with the person we confront here and now, but, in 'knowing' the being of that person, the eternal essence of that person — and of ourselves — we are now also given the cognitive organ by means of which we can look back into former earth-lives. Just as we learn in our present life to look back, in reversed order, upon contemporary events, so we also learn through the elevation of love to look back upon pre-earthly spiritual life; we learn to recognize that the 'real' life of a human being consists of a succession of earthly lives, between which longer or shorter periods of *pure spiritual* life intervene (or, we could say that the former intervene between the latter!). 'For this elevated form of love, lifted to the spiritual spheres and transformed into a force of knowledge, teaches us also the true significance of death.' [7] When we are capable of spiritual love, then we actually learn in immediate, exact clairvoyance to know that inner experience which can be described by saying that one experiences oneself *spiritually*, that is, outside the body. If we once experience this spiritual element in our lives *in actual knowledge* 'outside the body', that is, clairvoyantly, then we know too the significance of laying aside the physical body in death, of passing through the Portal of Death to a new spiritual life — a further step in the unfoldment of that which forms the totality of our cosmic life. We thus learn, when we have been able to develop the higher spiritualized form of love as a power of cognition, not only the significance of death, but also the significance and essence of immortality. [8]

In his book *A Road to Self-Knowledge*, Steiner describes a common experience our soul has when we want to find our way about in the supersensible world in exact clairvoyance — outside the physical body. It may happen, he says, that we have before us some supersensible fact or being. We can perceive it, but we do not know what it is; we also find that we are unable to compare it with other beings or facts. If we were able to do this we would be able to form a correct judgement of what it is we are perceiving. We can perceive, but not discern. In other words, our 'sight' in the supersensible world may be limited to the perception of single 'things', of single beings, without the faculty of being able to move freely from one to another.

The reason for this, Steiner tells us, is that the whole nature of perception in the spiritual world is entirely different from what we are accustomed to in the physical world. For instance, in the world of sense perception, provided we have a sound pair of eyes, we can see every visible object that confronts us and, for example, we have no difficulty in distinguishing between a daffodil and a cow. If we can see one thing, we can see another — with the same pair of eyes. This is not the case in the spiritual world. We may have an organ of supersensible perception developed which enables us to perceive and experience this or that fact or being, but if another fact is to be perceived an organ must be specially developed for this purpose — the same, of course, is true if we wish to perceive individual entities, beings, in the supersensible world. [9]

Fundamental to the development of an increasing ability to *cognize* individual entities, facts and beings in the supersensible world is love. Pure love in the spiritual world unites the soul of the 'perceiver' with the beings and facts of that world. Pure love, in the spiritual world, is, in short, a cognitive power. In the world of the senses we have to prepare ourselves for the unfolding of this cognitive power of love in the spiritual world, in clairvoyant vision. This preparation takes place, Steiner says, when we strengthen our capacity for love in the world of sense perception. The greater the selfless love we develop in the physical world, the stronger the cognitive power of love grows in respect of the supersensible world.

In regard to 'individual entities' of the supersensible world the situation is this: we cannot, for instance, cognize those supersensible beings which are connected with the plants of the physical world, if we do not love plants in the world of the senses, and so on. [10]

Out of his insight into the essence and activity of the spiritual world, Steiner speaks on many occasions of what the soul and spirit experience during the state of physical sleep. In the Initiation science of today, he says, the real facts that distinguish sleep from waking come to be known when we advance from Imagination to Inspiration.

Through Inspiration we become conscious of what usually remains unconscious during sleep. We learn to perceive what we do as soul and spirit while asleep, and we become aware that on falling asleep the soul and spirit leave the physical body and the etheric body. We also perceive that everything absorbed in ordinary waking life through our thinking is left behind. When we pass from waking to sleeping we experience what is not usually brought into consciousness; we enter a world where thinking is not as it is here on earth, but where everything is inwardly experienced. To take one example: during sleep we experience light inwardly; in waking life we think, let us say, about the effects of light — how it makes shadows and colours, appears in relation to objects, and so on. Such thoughts we 'leave behind' in sleep. In sleep we enter into what may be described pictorially as being the 'weaving, living light'; we pour ourselves out into light. Each one of us, when asleep, becomes a being, a 'substance', of the living light. We become 'light within the light'. During sleep each one of us lives like a 'cloud of light in Cosmic Light'. This does not mean, Steiner informs us, that in the spiritual world we live simply as the substance of light, but that we live in the forces which in waking life become, for instance, thoughts — are grasped as thoughts. We experience, inwardly, light as being permeated by creative forces, by the forces that work inwardly in the kingdoms of nature and in us, as well as existing 'independently' as spiritual worlds. In clairvoyant inspired knowledge light is not experienced in the same way, nor is it the same as we experience it in the physical world through our ordinary senses, but — to express it figuratively — the living light is the gossamer of spiritual weaving, as it is also the 'body' of each spiritual being. [11] Light, in the spiritual world, is experienced as creative, weaving spirituality.

It is in this sense that the following statement by Rudolf Steiner, relative to our spiritual experience of those who have crossed the Threshold after death, may be understood: 'When, as seers, we seek the Dead we can find them within the Light — if we perceive light not merely in a material way. The light that surrounds us forms the "bodies" of the Dead; they have "bodies" woven out of Light. The light that enfolds the earth is "substance" for the Beings who are living in the spiritual world.' [12]

Now, along with the spiritual experience of our being during sleep there is another that Steiner characterizes by comparing it with our sensation, as physical men here on earth, of heat and cold.

Again, it is not a sensation that is dependent on a physical body, but a purely inner experience of being 'substance' of warmth in the Cosmic Substance of Warmth — just, as previously outlined, we live as light in the Light. Thus, Steiner tells us, we are not only a 'cloud of light', but a 'cloud of light permeated by weaving waves of warmth'. What, then, we experience in sleep also bears warmth within it. Just as when we are asleep, having left our physical and etheric bodies 'behind' us on earth, we, as beings of soul and spirit, experience light not as light but as living spirit and, through Inspiration, realize ourselves and other beings to be living spirit; so also, in the spiritual world, when we experience ourselves as warmth, within the Cosmic Warmth, it is not the sense of warmth that we usually have in the world of sense perception, but the inner, spiritual experience of 'weaving, strength-endowed love'. As beings of love we experience ourselves among Beings who are Beings of Love in the midst of a cosmic existence of love, who radiate forth love out of their own essence. [13]

Hence, if we wish to experience the world in which we live when we are asleep, we must enhance our capacity for loving; we must develop the faculty of love as an organ of spiritual cognition; otherwise, says Steiner, the spiritual world will remain an unknown world to us.

Man cannot find his true self without this capacity for love; for all that he really is during sleep — during a third part of his life on earth — remains a closed book for him unless he can find the key to it through the training of love as an organ of cognition. All that is experienced during sleep would have to remain an unsolved riddle for men on earth if they had no wish to enhance their capacity for love. [14]

*   *   *   *

On many occasions Steiner writes and speaks of four stages of cognition. Before we enter upon the path of higher knowledge, we know, consciously, only the first of these four stages. Perception by the senses of the tangible, physical objects around us may be described as belonging to this stage. The second stage is that of imaginative knowledge, of 'strengthened thinking' gained through meditation, in which we apprehend the living, moving images of the world. [15] The third stage is Inspiration, in which we perceive the spiritual beings that express themselves through these images — 'we hear a kind of music of the spheres that sounds from beyond'. This inspired knowledge is attained by emptying our consciousness *after* we have strengthened our thinking. The fourth stage of cognition Steiner calls Intuition.

We cannot here attempt an adequate explanation of what Steiner means by 'meditation', 'strengthened thinking', 'empty consciousness', Inspiration and Intuition. A thorough study of his works is essential if one wishes to become more than merely theoretically acquainted with these terms. Here we must content ourselves with the few bald statements just made. The same may be said of Steiner's statement that Intuition is attained by making the power of love a cognitive force. [16] We can, however, say here — as in several other instances in these pages — that the kind of love Steiner means is that which enables us to identify ourselves with others, to feel what is happening in our fellow-men just as we feel what is happening in ourselves. When we experience identification with, and coming to life in, another human being, then we learn 'the highest degree of love that consists, not in "forgetting oneself" in a theoretical sense, but in being able to ignore oneself completely and enter into what is not oneself. Only when this love goes hand in hand with ... higher, inspired, cognition are we really able to enter the spiritual with all the warmth of our nature ... with our soul forces. We must do this if we are to progress in knowledge. Love must become a cognitive force in this sense.' [17]

Love must become a cognitive force if we are to be able to take the highest step in spiritual cognition, if we are to achieve Intuition. [18] Only through Intuition can our knowledge of the spiritual world be acquired as real knowledge, that is, derived directly from experience. We have then entered right into the spiritual world, into the Beings of that world.

The process of entering right into the spiritual foundation and essence of the sense-perceptible world, into the spiritual world — through Intuition — brings with it an experience of things quite different from what we normally have by means of ordinary 'sense knowledge'. [19] On one occasion Steiner described the difference referred to here in the following way: When a physical object is *in front of* me, then I stand *here* and the object is *over there*. With my ordinary, everyday consciousness, I can experience it only by looking at it *from outside*. Among other things, then, my relation to the physical object is determined by space. Now, in this way we could never have a real experience of the spiritual essence of another being. In the spiritual world there is no 'here' or 'there', there is no 'in front of' or 'outside of'. There is only a condition of being 'in', of being 'at one with' - though even these terms are not really adequate. In regard to a spiritual Being, in the spiritual world — as also to the spiritual essence permeating a physical manifestation — there is only one way of experience, that is, by entering right into it, intuiting it. And this faculty is only possible if we have first cultivated love towards man and nature. [20]

Intuition, grounded in love as a cognitive force, enables man to enter into his own true spiritual essence. 'When through the capacity for love we are able to enter clairvoyantly into spiritual Beings, there is also revealed to us that which makes man, in his inner experience, a complete being.' [21] Our previous incarnations are revealed to us. Here we need to discriminate between those who have so-called visions and see themselves as Cleopatra, or Alexander the Great, for instance, and those who have attained the highest stage of spiritual cognition, Intuition. The former is most unreliable — personal wishes, selfish love, and so forth, play far too large a part. 'The true Ego, present in all the repeated lives on Earth, can manifest itself only when the faculty of love has been so enhanced that any other being, whether in Nature or in the Spiritual World, has become just as dear to a man as in his self-love he is dear to himself. The true eternal Ego — the Ego that goes on through all repeated births and deaths — is manifest to a man only when he no longer lives egotistically for momentary knowledge but in a love that can *forget self-love* and can live in another being in the way that, in physical existence, he lives in self-love.' [22] Only through Intuition, which cannot be achieved without the cognitive power of selfless spiritualized love, is it possible to achieve the necessary spiritual insight to experience ourselves in our eternal being.

Earlier in this chapter an exercise was mentioned that Steiner suggests as being of assistance to us in developing love as a cognitive force: the recollection of the day's happenings in reverse order. However, he also makes the instructive comment that such an exercise is 'only the negative half of what is needed for enhancing and training spiritually our capacity for loving.' [23] Complementing such an exercise is essential. Steiner instances the need to follow lovingly each stage in the growth of a plant. Usually we only perceive this growth from outside, as it were. We do not, in short, take an active part in the process. We must, exhorts Steiner, learn to enter into, become one with every detail of plant-growth, until in the end, in our soul, we 'become the plant'. The plant becomes as dear to us as we are to ourselves. In the same way we can inwardly picture and live ourselves into the life of an animal, or the processes underlying the formation of a crystal. We need to learn to take inward pleasure in the shaping of a crystal's planes, corners, angles; and to experience a sensation of pain in our being when the mineral is split asunder, and so on. When we can do this then, in our souls, we enter not merely with sympathy but with our whole, love-imbued will into every single event in nature.

This experience, however, Steiner states emphatically, must be preceded by a capacity for love extending to the whole of mankind. 'We shall never be able to love nature in the right way until we have first succeeded in loving our fellow-men.' [24]

12.

DUTY AND LOVE

The attitude of soul — to think and act
not merely from duty, but from love,
prepares the soul to become a servant of
the good powers of health and of all
the health-giving forces sent down from
the supersensible world to our physical world. [1]

12.

In the ninth chapter of his *Philosophy of Freedom* Steiner discusses in a cogent manner the nature of a free and moral deed and the contrast between a deed performed as mere duty and one founded in love.

Steiner's exposition is closely knit and the present author could certainly not improve upon it. The following ten paragraphs are, therefore, lifted more or less verbatim from the chapter referred to — 'The Idea of Freedom'. [2]

If we seek out the conceptual principles underlying human actions we obtain a system of ethics that is not so much a science of moral laws as a natural philosophy, a natural history of morality. It is only the laws thus obtained that are related to human action, as the laws of nature are related to particular phenomena. These laws, however, are by no means identical with the impulses on which we base our actions. If we want to understand how our actions arise from our *moral* will, we need first of all to study the relation of this will to the action. First and foremost, we must keep our eye on those actions in which this relation is the determining factor. If we reflect upon such an action afterwards we can discover what moral principles arise in regard to it. While I am performing the action, however, I am influenced by a moral maxim in so far as it can live in me intuitively; it is bound up with my *love* for the objective I desire to achieve through my action. I ask no man and no rule 'Shall I perform this action?', but carry it out as soon as I have grasped the idea of it. This alone makes it *my* action. If I act only because I accept certain moral standards and codes, I am really little more than a superior automaton. Only when I follow *my* love for my objective is it I myself who act. At this level of morality I do not act because I acknowledge a ruler over me, an external authority, or a so-called inner voice. I acknowledge no external principle for my action, because I have found the source of my conduct within myself, namely, my love of the action, my love for the deed. I do not work out mentally and I do not prove intellectually whether my action is good or bad; I do it because I love it. My action will be 'good', if my intuition, immersed in love, finds its right place within the intuitively experienced relationship between things; the action will be 'bad' if this is not the case. Again, I do not ask myself; 'How would another person act in my place?', but I act as I, as a particular individuality, find my will activated to act. No moral standard, no general accepted usage or custom, no maxim applying to all men, is my immediate guide, but solely my love for the deed. I feel no compulsion — neither the compulsion of nature that rules me through my instincts, nor the compulsion of moral commandments; I simply carry out what lies within me. [3]

An action is felt to be free in so far as the reason for it springs from the 'ideal part' of my individual being; [4] an action carried out under the compulsion of nature or under the obligation of a moral code, is felt to be unfree.

A deed performed out of freedom does not exclude, indeed it includes, moral laws; but it shows itself to be a deed done on a higher level than those actions dictated solely by such laws. Why should my action be of less service to the public good when I do it out of love than when I do it *solely* because I consider serving the public good to be my duty? The mere concept of duty excludes freedom because it does not acknowledge the individual element but demands the subjection of the individual to a general standard. Freedom of action is conceivable only from the standpoint of what Steiner calls ethical individualism. [5]

But how, Steiner continues, forestalling the obvious objection, is a social life possible if each one of us is striving to assert his own individuality? This objection is characteristic of a misunderstanding of 'moralism'. Such a moralist believes that a social community is possible only if all men are united by general, fixed moral rules, by a communally fixed moral order. What he does not understand is the oneness and harmony of the idea-world. He does not see that the world of ideas working in *me* is no other than the one working in my fellow-men. Admittedly, this unity is but an outcome of our experience of life. Indeed, it cannot be otherwise, for if the unity of the world of ideas could be recognized by any means other than by individual observation, then general rules and not personal experience would be valid in its sphere.

I differ from my fellow-man, not because we are living in two entirely different spiritual worlds, but because from the world of ideas that we share, that is common to us both, we receive different intuitions. He wants to live *his* intuitions, I *mine*.

However, if we both really conceive out of the idea, and do not obey any external impulses (physical or spiritual), then we cannot but meet one another in the same striving, in having the same intentions and interests. A moral misunderstanding, a clash between men who are morally free, is impossible. Only the morally unfree, who follow their natural instincts or the accepted commands of duty, come into conflict with their fellow-men, if they do not obey the same instincts and the same commands as themselves. To *live* in love of the action and to *let live*, having understanding for the other person's will, is the fundamental principle of *free human beings*.

From the standpoint of free morality it is not asserted that it is only as free spirit that man can exist. Free spirituality is the ultimate stage of man's development, of man's evolution. Nor is it denied that conduct according to standards and codes has its justification as one stage of development. However, this cannot be acknowledged as the highest level of morality. For the free spirit in man overcomes rules in the sense that he does not just accept commandments as his motives, but regulates his action, his conduct, according to his own impulses, his own intuitions.

When Kant says of duty: 'Duty! You sublime, you mighty name, you encompass nothing lovable, nothing endearing, but you demand submission . . . [you] lay down a law . . . before all inclinations become silent, even though they secretly work against it', [6] then, says Steiner, out of the consciousness of the free spirit, man replies: 'Freedom! You kindly and human name, you encompass all that is morally lovable, all that is most worthy of my humanity, you make me no one's servant, you do not merely lay down the law, but wait for what my moral love of itself recognizes as law, because it feels unfree when faced with any law simply imposed upon it.'

This is the contrast between mere law-abiding morality and morality born of freedom.

The free spirit needs to go beyond the laws of his State as seldom as the philistine, who sees morality embodied in some external code of conduct, and certainly the free spirit is never in any real opposition to such laws. For all the laws of the State, just like all the other laws of morality, have sprung from the intuitions of free spirits. There is no rule enforced by family authority that was not at one time intuitively grasped and laid down as such by an ancestor. Similarly, the conventional laws of morality were first laid down by definite men and so, too, the laws of the State first originate in the head of a statesman. These leading individualities have set up laws over other men, and the only person who feels unfree is the one who forgets his origin and either looks upon these laws as extra-human commandments, that is, as objective moral concepts of duty independent of man, or turns them into the commanding voice within himself that he supposes, in a falsely mystical way, to be compelling him.

He who does not forget the origin of such laws, but seeks man within it, will count such laws as belonging to the same world of ideas as that from which he, too, draws his moral intuitions. If he believes his own intuitions to be better, then he will try to replace those in existence with his own; but if he finds the existing ones justified, he will act in accordance with them as if they were his own.

*   *   *   *

In a cycle of lectures to young people in which Steiner discusses educational and spiritual impulses for life in the present century he also speaks of duty and love. [7] His remarks here supplement and also throw some light on the statements he makes in the chapter of his *Philosophy of Freedom* to which reference has just been made.

Among other things Steiner refers to two moral impulses in the human soul that he describes as being of supreme importance: *moral love*, in man's inner life, and outwardly, in the life of social relationships between human beings, the moral impulse of *confidence*.

'The degree of strength in which moral love will be needed in the immediate [sic] future for all moral life, was not necessary in the past.' [8] It is true, Steiner continues, that in the past it could also be said that it was not only the experience of joy but also the element of love that were the wings that carried men to the heights of great deeds; but it must be added that the joy and love that fired human beings to great deeds were really only a metamorphosis of impulses that grew out of the family, out of the racial stock, out of the blood-tie, out of man's inclinations towards the other sex, out of the necessity to live together in small communities, out of man's pursuit of his own advantage, and so on. [9] In the future, however, great and *pure love, working from within outwards*, will have to give man the wings to fulfil his moral intuitions. 'Those human beings will feel themselves weak and lacking in will, in face of moral intuition, who do not experience

the fire of love for what is moral springing from the depths of their
souls, when through their moral intuitions they confront the deed
to be accomplished.' 10

Here Steiner again reminds us of Kant's words: 'Duty! You
sublime, you mighty name, you encompass nothing lovable,
nothing endearing'. As already indicated, the content of duty
stands here as a moral injunction imparted from outside and the
human being confronts this injunction in such a way that he has to
submit to it. The *moral* experience that emerges from such
submission is that there is no inner satisfaction gained from
obedience to duty. Only the bleak statement: 'I must perform my
duty' remains. As a response to this Steiner reminds us of
Schiller's ironical retort to Kant's definition of duty:

I serve my friends gladly, but unfortunately I do it with inclination,
And so it often worries me that I am not virtuous.
(*Gerne dien' ich den Freunden, doch tu' ich es leider mit Neigung,*
Und so wurmt es mich oft, dass ich nicht tugendhaft bin).

Over against the so-called categorical imperative — as it
comes down to us from former times out of old moral impulses —
stands the summons to us to unfold love for what is to become
action and deed.

With Schiller, we are developing beyond Kant's categorical
imperative. Humanity has now reached the stage of evolution
where love must give the impulse for action. Love born of the
individual, not a commandment from without, must be the
'birthplace' of action.

Here we are again led to Steiner's conception of ethical
individualism, and, at the same time, to 'the necessity of knowing
that this ethical individualism must be borne on the love arising
from perception of the deed to be accomplished'. 11

The objection could be raised here — particularly by those
who are not aware of progressive spiritual evolution — that if we
try to found morality on the individual, then social life will be
disrupted (see p. 152). However, seen in the light of the fact of
progressive spiritual evolution this objection, and others of a
similar kind, make no sense. Humanity is developing toward
individualism and, as Steiner bluntly puts it, 'there is no sense in
saying that ethical individualism would disrupt the community'. 12 It is far more a matter of seeking those forces by means
of which man's evolution can, in fact, progress.

Such a force, says Steiner, is *confidence* — confidence between one human being and another. Confidence is necessary if man is to develop an ethical individualism that will hold social life together, as it were, and fill it with real life.

Just as in our 'inner being' we must call upon *love* for an ethical future, so must we call upon *confidence* in relation to men's dealings with each other. 'Confidence in an absolutely real sense, individual, unique confidence, is hardest to wring from the human soul, but without . . . such confidence civilization can progress no further . . . Ethical impulses will penetrate to depths of the soul where they spring directly from the confidence between man and man.' [13]

Steiner himself is confident that just as love will fire the human hand, the human arm, so that from *within* it draws the strength to do a deed, so from without there will flow the mood of confidence in order that the deed may find its way from one human being to another. 'The morality of the future will have to be grounded on the free moral love arising from the depths of the human soul; future social action will have to be steeped in confidence.' [14]

In a short series of lectures *The Balance in the World and Man: Lucifer and Ahriman* [15] Steiner expounds certain basic conceptions in relation to love and duty, on the one side, and the influences emanating from Lucifer and Ahriman, on the other.

He begins by making a comment we can all take to heart: 'The present age that demands rights will be succeeded by one that asks after duties'. [16]

Whenever we turn our thoughts and attention to duty, Steiner points out, we 'look away from ourselves'. Again he mentions Emmanuel Kant and describes the picture of duty that Kant has as being that of a lofty goddess whom man looks up to. In a religious sense we may feel duty as an impulse laid upon us by the Beings of the higher Hierarchies. We 'look up', away from ourselves. We could say that we surrender ourselves to duty, that we 'go right outside ourselves'. [17]

Now, Steiner pursues this thought further. In this 'going-out-of-himself' in the feeling of duty, man can begin to learn how to reach beyond his ordinary self. There is, however, Steiner warns, a danger to man in all such endeavours to reach out beyond oneself, 'in all such endeavour after spiritualization'. If man were to give himself up entirely to this, he would lose the ground from under his feet, he would lose his feeling of gravity and thereby, also, his balance. He must, therefore, endeavour, when he surrenders himself to duty, to find within himself something that can give him 'weight', so that he may maintain his equilibrium and gravity. Schiller, Steiner reminds us, expressed this very beautifully when he said that man has the best relation to duty when he learns to *love* duty.

'When a man speaks of learning to love duty he no longer merely surrenders himself to duty; he rises out of himself, taking with him the love with which otherwise he loves himself and, with it, he loves duty.' [18] So long as love is self-love — and we speak of 'rights' and not yet of 'duty' — it is a Luciferic force. 'But when man takes this self-love out of himself and loves duty in the way that he otherwise only loves himself, he releases Lucifer. He takes Lucifer into the realm of duty and gives him, so to say, a justified existence in the impulse and feeling of duty.' [19]

If, on the other hand, a man cannot draw forth the love out of himself and offer it to duty, then he will continue to love only himself; and 'since he cannot love duty, he is obliged to subject himself to it. He becomes a slave to duty, he becomes a man who *does* his duty — hard and cold and uninspired. He hardens in an Ahrimanic sense, notwithstanding that he follows duty devotedly'. [20]

Duty stands, as it were, in a midway position between the forces of Lucifer and Ahriman. If we surrender ourselves to it then our freedom is annulled. We become slaves to duty, 'because Ahriman draws near with his impulses'. But if we bring our selves — if we bring all our power of self-love — as an offering to duty, bringing thus to duty the Luciferic warmth of love, then, 'through the state of balance induced in this way between Lucifer and Ahriman, we find a right relation to duty'. [21]

Thus we are truly redeemers of Lucifer. [22] 'When we begin to be able to love our duty, then the moment has come when we can help towards the redemption and release of the Luciferic powers — we set free the Lucifer forces and lead them forth to fight against Ahriman. We release the imprisoned Lucifer, imprisoned in our self-love, when we learn to love duty.' [23]

When we consider what man calls his 'rights' we can readily see that they are united with Lucifer. It is perfectly natural that man should love his rights. It is also natural for Lucifer to be connected with man's feeling that this or that is his right. 'Everywhere that right asserts itself, Lucifer is speaking too. It is very often only too evident how Lucifer makes his voice heard in the demand for some right or other.' [24] Self-love, a Luciferic force, speaks strongly in such demands.

To counteract this aspect of the feeling that this or that is a right, a balance, a polarity, has to be created over against it. This can be achieved by cultivating the polar opposite of the warmth of self-love, the warmth of Lucifer, by calling on the aid of Ahriman.

Love, says Steiner, is inner fire. Self-love is also of such a nature. Its opposite, in our present context, is calmness; that is, the quiet acknowledgement of what happens in the world. As soon as we approach our rights, not with the warmth of self-love but with quiet, controlled and calm interest, we 'call in the forces of Ahriman'. 'Calm and peace of mind have the "coldness" of Ahriman; in the quiet understanding of what is in the world, we unite our warmth and understanding love with this calmness. And then we release Ahriman, when we meet what has come about with understanding, when we not merely demand our rights out of self-love but understand what has come about in the world.' [25]

A balance is created between two trends, between two opposing forces — those of Lucifer and Ahriman. On the one hand, man learns to understand the conditions that already prevail in the world; on the other, he feels the urge to make new conditions possible. This, says Steiner, 'is the revolutionary current in human life'. In this revolutionary stream Lucifer is active; in the prevailing, conservative stream we find Ahriman. And man, in his life of rights, in his endeavour to balance these two streams, lives in the middle, between these two poles. 'Thus we see how "right" and "duty" show each of them a state of equilibrium between Lucifer and Ahriman.' [26]

13.

LIGHT — LOVE — ILLNESS AND HEALTH

The weaving essence of the light streams forth
Through depths of space to fill the world with life;
Love's grace doth warm the centuries of time
To call forth revelation of all worlds.
And spirit-messengers come forth to wed
The weaving essence of creative light
With revelation of the souls of men:
And that man, who can wed to both of these
His very Self, he lives in spirit-heights. [1]

St Francis enlarged his heart to cover
his whole soul. [2]

13.

In one of a series of lectures dealing with manifestations of karma, [3] Steiner makes some far-reaching statements concerning the essence of physical matter, on the one hand, and of the soul, on the other.

'Every substance upon the earth is condensed light.' [4] Wherever we perceive physical substance, including our own physical bodies, we perceive condensed light, we touch condensed light. Light is the foundation of all material existence. On the first day of Creation God said, 'Let there be light', and there was light. Inasmuch as man is a material being, his substance is woven out of light, condensed light. [5]

The *fundamental* essence of the soul, however, is love. 'All the different phenomena of the soul are modifications, are manifold transformations of love. Every stirring of the soul is in some way a modification of love.' [6] Our soul is woven spiritually out of love.

Love and Light are the two fundamental elements of all earthly existence; they are, in various ways, interwoven in all phenomena.

Steiner now refers to a Power, essential to the evolution of man — and hence also of the earth — to which reference is made elsewhere in these pages on several occasions — namely the Luciferic Power, the Luciferic element. This element is a mediating force between Light and Love. It weaves the one into the other. Without this third element the powers of Light and Love would merely exist side by side, as it were, without being able to interfuse with one another. The Luciferic forces, i.e. the light-bearing forces, as such, have no particular interest in love, on the contrary. * But they are concerned to spread the element of light abroad as much as possible.

The Luciferic Beings, Steiner tells us, are always active when our soul, woven out of love, comes into any sort of relation to light. In other words, the startling realization that dawns on us is that the Luciferic influence is always woven into love. † Love

* See also Chapter 22.
† See, however, Ch. 9.

always bears the impress of Lucifer. [7] Stated thus baldly the reader may be forgiven for thinking, 'How grotesque! How absurd!' But he is once again urged to accept that in this essay only bare indications of such matters can be given and that to acquire a fuller picture and better understanding Steiner's numerous statements and descriptions of the essence and activity of Lucifer — and Ahriman — need to be carefully assimilated and made into personal experience.

We owe it, in the first instance, to this Luciferic influence that love does not perpetually manifest itself as mere self-abandonment, but is permeated with wisdom. [8] Without this influence, without this wisdom streaming into love from the Luciferic Beings, love would be an impersonal force in man for which he himself could not bear any responsibility. But, through this influence, 'love becomes the essential force of the Ego' (see Chapter 22).

We see then that our physical bodies, woven out of light, are not interwoven with love alone, but with love that is permeated by Lucifer. Love, we now learn from Steiner, that is permeated with the Luciferic element, and that then, interwoven with this Luciferic element, impregnates the physical body, is the cause of many illnesses. [9]

Now, a serious illness is in some way or other connected with our karma and we could ask the question: Have we the right to interfere, as healers, with what is working out of karmic consequences? Speaking particularly of illnesses caused by the Luciferic influence, Steiner's answer is this: We have the right to do so provided we find the remedy to expel the Luciferic element in the right way. [10]

We have to remember that, in speaking of illnesses caused by the Luciferic element we are specifically speaking of those which, in one way or another, are the result of man's yielding to the allurements of the Luciferic Principle in a previous incarnation — the degree to which he succumbed to these allurements has become an integral part of his karma. [11] Lucifer's influence would have penetrated in particular into his astral body; or, differently expressed, would have given him the tendency to act and judge more from his emotions, passions and desires than he would have done if the Luciferic influence had not 'entered' his soul so strongly, had not 'tempted' him. [12] We could also say that his 'I' was not strong enough to resist the temptation. Since the Advent of Christ, however, we, as men, have the power within us to withstand the Luciferic allurements. Indeed, in the course of evolution the Christ experience within us can not merely get rid of, but can also redeem the Luciferic Powers. [13]

If, as a result of the Luciferic influence, man sins against morality between birth and death, he experiences the 'repercussions' in the life after physical death. All the things which in the life between birth and death were submitted to moral judgement penetrate down into the foundation of the human being; that is, into that which organizes the next existence on earth and imprints itself into the spiritual plastic forces which then construct the threefold human 'body' — the physical body, the etheric 'body', and the astral 'body'. [14] Faults that were the object of a moral judgement between birth and death develop into causes of disease that work more from the astral realm. [15]

The purpose of this digression into the nature of the influence of the Luciferic element in respect of man's astral body was to give a background to Steiner's answer to the question: Have we the right to interfere with an illness that is a part of man's karma? Steiner's answer, as we have seen, is 'Yes'. We have the right to do this, if we find the means to expel, for instance, the Luciferic element in the right way. And what is the remedy that exerts a stronger action so that the Luciferic element is balanced — even driven out? This question is intimately linked with the further question — and the answer to both questions is the same: What is it which has been 'sullied', 'defiled', by the Luciferic element? It is love. Hence the remedy that exerts a stronger action is *pure* love. Only by means of pure, Christened love, can we give real help for karma to work out in the right way: 'We must pour in Love'. All those acts of healing dependent upon what we may call a 'soul-spiritual healing process' must have the characteristic that selfless love is part of the process. 'In some form or other all soul-spiritual healing depends on a stream of love — which we pour into another person like a balsam.' [16] All that we do in this sphere must be founded in love. All should stream forth from the impulse of love.

Steiner gives a stimulating answer to the question: What does the healer 'communicate' to the person to be healed? It is 'an interchange of tensions'. What Steiner means by this he describes as follows: 'Certain processes in the etheric body of the healer create with the person to be healed a sort of polarity. Polarity arises just as it would arise in an abstract sense. For instance, when one kind of electricity, say positive, is produced, then the corresponding, negative electricity appears. Thus polarities are created, and this act must be conceived as emanating from an act of sacrifice.' [17] In other words: one evokes in oneself a process which induces a polarity in another person, and this induced polarity is the sacrifice of a force which is no other than the 'transmuted power of love'. [18] This fundamental love force is essential to the right kind of healing. The healer and the healed may not always be conscious of these processes of love — but they are present in the region of the subconscious. In the technique of the healing process, even, says Steiner, in the way in which the hands are moved in certain forms of healing, we could say that we have 'the reflection of a sacrificial act'. 'Therefore even where we do not see the direct connection in a process of healing ... we have, nevertheless, before us an act of love, although the action may be completely transformed to a mere technique.' [19]

Since the soul is woven, fundamentally, of love, we can, as healers, assist the sick person in certain illnesses by psychic means. By such means, what in its essence consists of love is enriched and strengthened by what it receives in the way of love. We can help the sufferer, who has been caught in the toils of Lucifer, to free himself again.

Let us now look at illness from another viewpoint, suggests Steiner — from the viewpoint of the substance woven from light in which the soul dwells.

If a pure 'love substance', that is, not permeated by either Lucifer or Ahriman, were to flow into matter, flow into 'condensed' light, it would then so flow into the human physical body that the latter could not be damaged. It is only because a love that has 'absorbed' Luciferic or Ahrimanic forces can penetrate the substance woven out of light, the physical body, that the latter becomes less perfect than it would otherwise have been, if these forces were not active. The purer the love substance, the healthier the body of woven light, the physical body.

How can we counteract these forces that have flowed into the physical organism from an imperfect soul, that is, from a 'sullied' love substance? What happens to the physical body by this influx of something impure? One way in which Steiner describes what happens is this: 'Everything presenting itself — strange as it may sound — as the defilement of that which is woven out of light, is a *darkness* woven out of a Luciferic or Ahrimanic influence.' [20] The 'darkness' of which Steiner is speaking here is to be understood as relative, relative to the Light of the Sun Spirit, the Light of Christ. Thus we see 'darkness' woven into the human substance. But — and this is the significant point — 'this *darkness* can only be thus interwoven into the human substance because this substance, the human body, has become the bearer of the Ego that lives on from one incarnation to the next.'[21] Only a *human* body can be subject to this corruption. Only man undergoes on Earth the unfolding process of individual karma.

Now, man draws what he needs for his physical life from the mineral, plant, and animal kingdoms. As already stated, these kingdoms also contain the various substances woven out of light. *But* in none of these substances are there any of the Luciferic or Ahrimanic influences that in the course of human karma have acted on the physical organism through the soul. In the three kingdoms of nature that which in man has been defiled remains pure.

Let us consider a mineral substance, a salt or any other substance to be found in nature and that man also has within him. In him this substance is interwoven with love defiled by Lucifer or Ahriman. Outside, in nature, it is pure. Indeed for everything of a physical nature that can be found in the human organism, and which is more or less defiled in man, there is a corresponding substance in nature that can be found in its pure condition. 'That which exists in the world of nature in its purity', Steiner states, 'is the external cure for the corresponding substance in man in its damaged, diseased state.'[22] In the human body the disease or injury is characterized by Steiner as a form of 'darkness'. As healers we are often able to remove the 'darkness' in man if we counterbalance it, treat it by the introduction of a corresponding substance found in nature, say, a mineral. The substance woven of pure light can make whole, can heal, the substance woven of defiled light.

Though quite obviously the issues involved here have been over-simplified in this short study — Steiner goes into great detail regarding these matters in many lectures he gave to medical doctors — we may nevertheless now say that man can be helped from two different sides: on the one hand by soul-spiritual methods of healing or transmuted love, and on the other by 'external' methods of healing, by medication or transmuted light. The healing process is therefore attained either by inner soul-spiritual means — by love — or by the external method, by the introduction into the human physical body of densified light. [23] We either draw the required remedy from our surroundings, from condensed light, or from our own soul by the healing loving act, the sacrificial act, and we then heal with the soul-forces given to us by love.

'All healthy earth conditions are in some way conditions of balance between Light and Love, and everything unhealthy is a disturbance of this balance.' [24] If the disturbance is in the soul, in the element of love, we can then help by unfolding the forces of selfless love; if the disturbance is more within the body, in the light, we can then help by providing the ill person with unsullied light that is able to dissolve the darkness.

The relation of man's life on earth to his life in the spiritual, is illustrated by Steiner, in respect of the power of healing, in the following way: 'Everything we are able to accomplish on earth with devotion, with love for the task at hand, so that we are completely involved in what we do, and realize that what we do is worthy of man, contributes to making us, after death, servants of the spiritual beings of the higher Hierarchies, who send healing, constructive forces from the spiritual into the physical world.' This and the following statement show most forcibly the importance of loving enthusiasm in man's deeds here on earth. 'If enthusiasm were to fade away in the physical world, if love were to die, mankind in the future would enter a physical existence with less healthy and constructive forces from supersensible realms than at present' [25] — a wonderful illustration of the connections between the physical and supersensible worlds.

*   *   *   *

In a short cycle of three lectures Steiner gives us a most penetrating and loving insight into the being of St Francis of Assisi. [26] Those readers who are already familiar with Steiner's work will have been stirred, when reading his lectures on the Gospel of St Luke and the first two of the short cycle concerned with St Francis of Assisi, by the warmth of heart with which he imbues these lectures.

Our present interest in the lectures on St Francis is Steiner's emphasis on the healing power of love.

Before entering upon his characterization of St Francis' life and deeds, Steiner illustrates what is meant by the healing power of love by referring to the work of a poet who lived at the end of the twelfth and beginning of the thirteenth century, Hartmann von Aue.

Hartmann's most important poem was *Armer Heinrich* ('Poor Henry'). The substance of this poem is this: Poor Henry was once a rich knight, but he did not take into account the transitoriness of earthly things. He lived only for the day, squandered his wealth thoughtlessly, and thereby rapidly produced 'bad karma'. He was thus stricken with a form of leprosy. The most skilful physicians could not help him. His disease prevented him from mixing with his fellow-men, and he lived on an isolated farm, well taken care of however by an old farmer and his daughter. One day the farmer's daughter heard that the knight could be cured. If a virgin out of pure love sacrificed her life for him his health would be restored. She went with Henry to the most celebrated school of medicine of the day, and to the physicians there declared her willingness to sacrifice her life to save the knight. At the last minute however Henry refused to allow this to happen, and they both returned to the farm. We are then told that very soon after returning home Henry made a complete recovery from his incurable illness, and that he spent a happy old age together with the woman who had been ready to sacrifice her life to save his.

Selfless love on the part of both of them led to health.

This can, of course, as Steiner points out, be dismissed as mere wishful thinking expressed in poetic form. However, such a sceptical attitude cannot be maintained when it is realized that what is expressed here in poetic form was actually lived by one of Hartmann von Aue's most famous contemporaries, Francis of Assisi.

The story of the life of St Francis is so well known that all we need do here is to pinpoint a few relevant life-situations.

In his youth, Francis was filled with the ideal of winning honour and fame with the weapons of war. He was also a spendthrift, squandered his father's possessions, and was generous towards his friends.

This kind of chivalrous but rather superficial mode of life came to an abrupt end through an inner experience that came about like this: Francis had heard of an expedition to be undertaken in the service of chivalry against Naples. One night he dreamt that he saw a great palace and everywhere weapons, swords and spears, and shields. On waking he said to himself that this dream was a sign for him to join the expedition. Shortly after joining this expedition he had some very clear 'spiritual impressions'. It was as though an inner voice said to him: 'You have interpreted the dream wrongly; go back to Assisi and you shall hear the correct interpretation.'

Francis obeyed and shortly after his return home he had an inner dialogue with a spiritual being, who said: 'Not in external service have you to seek your knighthood. You are destined to transform all the forces at your disposal into powers of the soul. All the weapons you saw in your dream signify the spiritual weapons of mercy, compassion and love. The shields signify the reasoning powers you need to exercise in order to stand firmly in the trials of a life spent in performing deeds of mercy, compassion and love.' [27]

Shortly after this Francis suffered a severe illness — so often the turning point in human life and the beginning of a process of inner transformation.

'The young knight who had longed only to become a great warrior was transformed into a man who now most earnestly sought all the impulses of mercy, compassion and love. All the forces he had thought to use in the service of the physical world were transformed into moral impulses of the inner life.' [28]

Francis found a remarkable use for what now unfolded within him. At that time leprosy had invaded many parts of Europe. There was no cure, and the lepers were simply banished to places remote from their fellow-men. No better way of dealing with this illness was known. But Francis knew of a better one. The moral impulses developing within him led him to search out lepers everywhere — and in many cases this 'incurable' disease was cured by him, because he went to the afflicted with the healing power he possessed through the spiritual weapons he bore within him: mercy, compassion and love. This power rendered him fearless; 'it gave him courage not only carefully to cleanse their wounds, but to live with the lepers, to nurse them conscientiously, to kiss them and permeate them with love'. [29]

The healing of poor Henry by the daughter of his faithful servant is not merely a poetic story, it expresses what actually occurred in a number of cases through the love of the historical personality of Francis of Assisi. 'He was full to overflowing with moral force, and this actually passed over to those to whom he turned his love.' [30]

In his concluding remarks, in the lecture from which the substance of what has been outlined about St Francis has been drawn, Steiner asks the question: 'How did this love develop in St Francis?' His answer is a revealing one. 'We have seen that in him appeared the knightly virtues of the medieval European spirit. He was a valiant youth. His valour, permeated by the Christ Impulse, was transformed into active, practical love.' We see, in short, the old valour resurrected, transmuted into love. 'Valour transposed into the spiritual is love.' [31] It is courageous love imbued with healing power.

Elsewhere Steiner goes so far as to say that, if a loving attitude of soul, if selflessness and courageous love were to prevail among men, then an illness, an epidemic, would find no 'soil' in which to spread. [32]

14.

THE POWER OF LOVE IN THE EVOLUTION OF EARTH AND MAN

At the turning-point of Time
The Spirit-Light of the World
Entered the stream of Earthly Being.
Darkness of Night
Had held its sway;
Day-radiant Light
Poured into the souls of men:
Light that gives Warmth
To simple Shepherds' Hearts,
Light that enlightens
The wise Heads of Kings.

O Light Divine,
O Sun of Christ!
Warm Thou our Hearts,
Enlighten Thou our Heads,
That good may become
What from our Hearts we would found
And from our Heads direct
With single purpose. [1]

14.

Steiner points to a significant time in the evolution of humanity when the concept of love — and that of compassion — came into being (see also Chapter 7). He reminds us of the remarkable fact that six or seven centuries before the inpouring of the Christ Impulse into humanity, founders of religion and systems of thought appeared in many different parts of the earth. [2] It is true that there are great differences between these various teachings, but in one respect they are similar: they all teach that compassion and love must reign among men. The point of significance is this: six or seven centuries before the dawn of the Christian era, 'there begins to stir the consciousness that love and compassion are to be received into the stream of human evolution'. [3] Thus whether we are thinking of the 'birth' of wonder, or of conscience, [4] or of love and compassion in the stream of evolution, all signs suggest that at that moment in history something permeated mankind which we may recognize as the 'meaning and purpose of Earth evolution'. [5]

In emphasizing the point of the 'meaning and purpose of Earth evolution' Steiner answers the question: Why was it necessary for man to leave the worlds of Divine Spirit, to be expelled from the Garden of Paradise, only to have to reattain them? His answer is: Man could not remain in the Divine World because only by incarnating into the physical world could he, as a spiritual being, develop the forces of wonder, conscience, or moral obligation, love and compassion. And we could add, in accordance with our discussion elsewhere [6] on love in relation to the forces of redemption: only by man's entering into physical existence could the Earth itself be redeemed through the power of love.

From the sixth or seventh century before the birth of Christ and onwards into our own time we can perceive the dawn of impulses which spread more and more widely among mankind. It is, of course, Steiner continues, very easy to state that humanity is seldom ruled by compassion and love — seldom, too, by conscience. It is true for instance that in ancient Greece slavery was still an accepted form of human life, but we must likewise remember that since those days love has so far gained ground that, even if today inequalities still persist among men, there is already present in an ever-growing number of people's hearts something like a feeling of shame that certain deplorable conditions still exist in the world. Nobody would suggest the reintroduction of slavery as it was in Greece or in the New World in the nineteenth century. In spite of man's cruelty to man it is nevertheless universally felt that 'the greatest of all forces in the human soul is that of love and compassion'. [7]

If we hold firmly in our minds that the unfolding of love and compassion constitutes the meaning and purpose of Earth evolution, and then turn to the greatest of all impulses — the Christ Impulse — we can perceive that even outer circumstances alone indicate that this impulse was given to mankind as a gift of the Spiritual Worlds at the time when the Earth was ready, as it were, for the development of these soul qualities.

Now let us look a little more closely at some aspects of earth and human evolution from the standpoint of spiritual science.

During earlier incarnations of the Earth [8] man in his as yet non-physical manifestation was endowed by high Spiritual Beings with the forces, the 'inner life', of Will, Feeling and Thought.

The mission of man's earth existence, through a series of incarnations, is to bring about a perfect harmony between these three elements. In occult symbolism this Earth mission has been expressed by means of an equilateral triangle. The centre of such a triangle is a complete symbol of a balance of these three forces. Through this balance, or harmony of forces by the inner being of man, by the deeds of the 'I', of the 'Ego', in man something quite new on earth is created: a fourth element emerges, the element of Love. This fourth element is 'added' to the three forces of willing, feeling and thinking with which man was endowed by spiritual beings, and it is through the Christ in Man, the very Essence of Love, that this force of Love can be realized.

Love, says Steiner, can only develop in the busy work-a-day world when a complete harmony exists between the three forces that in earlier epochs of earth existence were each in turn — in the order just stated — the dominating influence.

Thus, continues Steiner, 'our planet is the Planet of Love and therefore the result of the balance or harmony, that is reflected in the cooperation of the three forces, is the active spirit of Love, and this spirit of Love is to be woven into the whole of evolution in the future . . . .' [9]

This harmony between the elements of willing, feeling and thinking is such that the inner being of man becomes the substance of Love. This Love is what we may describe as the really creative element in earth existence. [10]

To the previous incarnation of the earth Steiner gives the name 'Ancient Moon'. This Ancient Moon and the spiritual beings inhabiting it had also a mission. It had the task of developing not love, but wisdom. Before it reached its present earthly mineral condition our planet 'passed through the stage of Wisdom'. [11] A simple, and one might say logical, observation will illustrate the point Steiner is making here. If we look about us at all the creatures of nature, if we observe them not merely with our intellect but with the forces of our heart and soul, with our intuitive faculty, then we can find wisdom everywhere stamped upon Nature. The Wisdom of which Steiner is speaking here is a kind of 'spiritual substance lying at the foundation of all things'. [12]

Just as Wisdom was evolved on Ancient Moon, and is now found in all things, so in like manner is Love evolving. 'The Cosmos of Wisdom is evolving into a Cosmos of Love'. [13]

The new force that Earthly evolution is implanting in the pristine Wisdom is the power of Love. 'In man on Earth it has to have its beginning. All that the *I*, the *Ego*, of man brings to development within him will grow into Love.' [14] Love came into existence, says Steiner, in its most sensuous form, [15] but during the course of life upon the earth it will become ever more spiritualized, until at last , when the earth has reached the end of its evolution, the whole of existence will have become pervaded with Love, as today it is pervaded with Wisdom. And this must be accomplished, not by higher spiritual beings, but by man.

'You will understand Esoteric Christianity,' states Steiner, 'when it says: Just as other forces, of which Wisdom is the last, streamed down from divine beings during the Ancient Moon period, so now Love streams into the Earth and the bearer of Love can only be the independent Ego which develops by degrees in the course of the evolution of the Earth.' [16]

On one occasion Steiner expressed the following thought: 'The Possessor of the Love-Mystery is the Sun-Spirit Whom we call the Christ.' [17]

The power of Love gained through the Christ Impulse will spiritualize the whole of the Earth. The more the human soul is warmed by love, the more powerfully will it be able to work on the transmutation of matter. Christ brings the impulse of love in its most spiritual form to the earth.

It is the sublime Sun-Being, the Christ, [18] Who at His revelation stands forth as the all-embracing prototype of Love. Into the innermost depth of man's being the seed of Love is planted by Him. Thence it shall grow until it fills the whole of cosmic evolution. Just as the pristine Wisdom now reveals its presence in all the forces of Nature, so in the future will Love be revealed — Love as a new force of Nature, living in all the phenomena which man will have around him. This is the secret of all future evolution. The spiritual knowledge man acquires and also every deed man does with true understanding is like the sowing of the seed that will eventually ripen into Love. Only inasmuch as Love arises in mankind, is true creative work being done for the cosmic future. For it is Love itself which will grow into the potent forces leading mankind on towards the final goal — the goal of spiritualization. [19]

'To the extent that spiritual knowledge flows into the evolution of mankind and of the Earth, there will be viable and fertile seeds for the cosmic future. For it is the very nature of true spiritual knowledge to be transmuted into love.' [20]

The Wisdom, Steiner tells us, that was prepared through an earlier stage of the Earth's evolution (as Ancient Moon) manifests outwardly as Wisdom of the World. In our present stage of development this Cosmic Wisdom is in the Ego of man turned inward. From our present stage of evolution onward the Wisdom manifest in the outer world, in Nature, becomes inner Wisdom, Wisdom in man himself. When thus resurrected, thus transformed, in the inner life, in the 'I' of man, it grows into the seed of Love.

'Wisdom is the premiss, the forerunner of Love; Love is the outcome of Wisdom re-born in the "I" of man.' [21]

The materialistic mind does not, of course, take the notion seriously that there is such a thing as Cosmic Wisdom; for such a mind all that can exist is human knowledge. If however, Steiner suggests, men were to consider the course of evolution with an unbiased mind, they would not fail to recognize that 'all cosmic wisdom in the beginning of the Earth's evolution was advanced as far as human wisdom will be at the end of it'. 'The human being, in fact, always follows along groping his way behind the Cosmic

Wisdom. All that men will discover in the course of the Earth's evolution is already present in Nature. But what the human being will really give to the Earth is love, a love that will evolve from the most sensuous to the most spiritualized form of love.' [22]

In terms of Esoteric Christianity the question, 'Of what does the Earth consist?' may be answered by saying: it is a manifestation of divine powers, an outer material manifestation of inner spirituality. This divine spirituality is called, in Esoteric Christianity, the 'Logos', or the 'Word'. Everything visible has issued forth from the Logos. In its purest form, the *external* body of the Logos appears especially in the outer sunlight. But sunlight is not merely material light. To spiritual perception, says Steiner, it is just as much the vesture of the Logos, as our outer physical body is the vesture of our soul. [23]

If we were to confront a fellow human being in the same way as the majority of people today confront the sun, we would clearly never learn to know him. Our relation to him would be such that instead of pre-supposing a soul-spiritual element within him, we would simply consider his physical body as constituting his total being. The sunlight has the same relationship to the Logos as the body has to the soul. *In* the sunlight spirituality radiates down to the Earth. 'If we are able to conceive not only the sun-body, but also the sun-spirit, we find that this spiritual part is the love that streams down upon the Earth. Human beings exist in order that they may take into themselves the warm love of the Divine, develop it and return it again to the Divine. But they can only do this by becoming self-conscious ego-beings.' [24]

Before turning our attention to the next planetary existence, that which is to succeed our Earth and which Steiner calls the Jupiter epoch, we need to consider two principles which in pre-Christian times were continually active.

If we look back to ancient times we find gods and folk spirits, or group spirits, working within groups of people — such as, for instance, the Hebrews — through the ordinances of the Law. There we find that love is governed by the blood-tie. The further back we go in the history of mankind the more we find that all those related by blood considered themselves as 'belonging' to one another. Jehovah [25] worked in the forces of blood relationship. He produced order and harmony through this relationship. Working against Jehovah, against the Father Principle, were the Luciferic Beings. They directed their strongest attacks against the principle of blood relationship. They always worked, up to the time of Christ, towards the centering of man within his own individuality. Then the Christ appears and centres man entirely within his own being by giving him His inward power. The Luciferic Beings had worked prematurely towards this individualizing process for a very long period of time, but it was only at the time of Christ's Coming that man was ready for what these Beings desired.

In short, two principles were continually at work in those olden times: there was a binding, uniting principle, which worked through blood relationships, and a sundering principle, which sought to centre man in his own individuality. 'We can see', says Steiner, 'how the whole of humanity has been fashioned under the influence of these two principles.' [26]

Let us now turn our attention to the future, to the fifth stage in the evolution of our planet, the Jupiter stage. The inhabitants of Jupiter, a transmuted human kingdom, [27] will recognize all entities in their environment with their spiritual powers of perception, and just as with our intelligence we admire the wisdom contained in stones, plants, animals, and our fellow-men, just 'as we draw wisdom from them that we also may have it', so the Jupiter beings will direct their forces to all that surrounds them, and the love implanted in them during the Earth evolution will, as Steiner puts it, 'be wafted to those who now surround them.' [28] Conversely, just as we on earth learn from the wisdom contained in the world of Nature around us, so also will the Jupiter beings 'edify themselves with the outpourings of love that radiate from the beings about them'. [29] To restate: this love which is to develop on Earth can only unfold through human Egos being related to one another in freedom, that is, not by means of blood relationships. Development of this kind can only take place through men being 'torn away' from group-soul, group-spirit tendencies. [30] True love can only develop between one free individual and another. Where beings are united within a group-soul we cannot speak of true love. As stated elsewhere, we as human beings must be 'separated' from each other in order that love may be offered as a free gift (see Chapter 22). It is only through the separation that has come about during the course of evolution, where individual Ego meets individual Ego, that love 'as a free gift' has become possible. 'This is why an increasing individualism had to come about on earth.' [31] The group-soul directs the various elements united within it as to how they shall act. 'Can it be said that the heart loves the stomach? No, the heart

is *united* to the stomach by the being who holds them together.' [32]
In the same way several animals in a group are united within the
group-soul nature and their responses are regulated by the wise
group-soul. Individual, freely-given love can be offered only
when the group-soul nature has been overcome.

Man could only be prepared for the development of self-less love
gradually, and we can see how, before he possessed a 'complete'
Ego of his own, he was part of a group under the direction of a
group-soul, and that members of the group loved each other *because
of* the blood-tie. This was a kind of 'preparatory school for love' [33]
man had to pass through before he became fully individualized.
We have also seen how Luciferic beings opposed with their
strong liberating forces all relationships based on the blood-tie,
how they strove, albeit prematurely, to make man independent.

Gradually, we might say, man matured so that he might
eventually receive 'the highest potency of love — the Christ
Principle'. [34] The Christ Principle, as distinct from the Father
Principle, has given the impulse by which a free individual can
love a free individual. 'Through being Christened, human love
may become more and more spiritual ... and man will thus
transform the earth.' [35] He will 'draw along' with him the lower
creations, he will 'redeem' the lower kingdoms of nature.

It will be remembered that Angelus Silesius was aware that the
gods are dependent on their creation, even as their creation is
dependent on them. Steiner on one occasion said. 'Through their
participating in mankind the gods will learn to know love, though,
in another sense, it is they who bestow it.' [36] This is not easy for us
to comprehend. Steiner asks us to look at it this way: It is entirely
possible for someone to bestow a gift upon a friend and only come
to *know* his gift through this friend. For instance, a very rich
person helps a poor friend with a gift of money. This gift gives rise
to a feeling and expression of deep gratitude in the soul of the
needy one. The feeling of gratitude is at the same time a gift; it
would not have come into being if the rich person had not first
given. He is the originator of the feeling of gratitude, although he
does not feel it and is only acquainted with it through its
reflection, which streams back to him from the person in whom
he rouses it. It is somewhat in this way that the gift of love is
imparted by man to the gods. They kindle love in man so that he
feels it, but they only learn to know it as a reality through man.
Through man the gods feel the warmth of love. They lack
something when man does not feel love. [37]

After this digression from our consideration of love in the stream of earth and human evolution, let us look for a moment at the last few centuries leading up to the manifestation of Christ.

Steiner reminds us that when the Greeks and Romans were the leading peoples in the western world, man had reached that stage in evolution when he established a kind of balance between his understanding of the physical world, on the one hand, and the spiritual world on the other. He had to come to terms with the material world, we could say. He had learned to understand and to love it. [38] However, as the Graeco-Roman age progressed, man had also progressed so far in the conquest of the physical world, had become so deeply engrossed in it, that he could only recognize the spiritual when it manifested itself in a physical form. He had to have a god in human form before he could recognize Him, for he could no longer penetrate to the spiritual world and perceive Him there. [39]

We have previously seen that the human being was destined for self-conscious love upon the earth, was destined for 'clear day-consciousness', as distinct from the atavistic, dreamlike consciousness characteristic of ancient civilizations; [40] we have also seen that as the Graeco-Roman epoch progressed man became more and more enmeshed in the physical world and lost his direct vision of the spiritual world. The consequence of these two strands in his spiritual evolution was that in order to be able to 'recognize' the divine essence of what was gradually unfolding, individual human love, he needed to be able to perceive this essence in a physical form. And this is actually what came about, in that the Being of Divine Love, the Being of the Logos, became a man of flesh, whom men could perceive with their physical senses. The Being of the Logos, of the Spiritual Sun, appeared in a physical body, in Christ-Jesus. The historical appearance of Christ means that the forces of the Logos were incarnated in Jesus of Nazareth and were actually present in Him in the sense-perceptible world at that culminating point of time when man had lost the inner spiritual vision of the Spiritual Sun. 'The force of the Logos-Love assumed a physical human form in the body of Jesus of Nazareth . . . The Logos became flesh.' [41] The Being of Divine Love became a man of flesh. The Universal Light of Warmth and Universal Warmth of Love flowed in the Christ-Being. [42]

*   *   *   *

Inherent in Christ's Mission on earth was, as already indicated, the infusing into mankind of the full force of the Ego, an inner independence of the soul, through the development of which spiritualized love, given in freedom, could be born. The Christ gave to mankind the impulse to spiritualize love, to loosen the bonds in which love had been entangled through the blood-relationship. [43]

Steiner often spoke of the manifestation of Christ as a 'turning-point of history'. [44] One aspect of this 'turning-point' is the impulse given by Christ to overcome the blood-tie and thus spiritualize love. As we have also already seen, closely interwoven in the evolution of humanity up to the birth of Christ two streams are in operation: the Father Principle, striving to unite humanity, and the Luciferic Principle, striving to make every human being independent, to endow the single individual with the greatest possible power. These opposing powers were always active and, as a result, the Ego of man was perpetually being 'pulled' to this or that side, 'towards human love on the one side and towards inner self-sufficiency on the other'. [45]

Now, Steiner says, at a particular point of time in the history of mankind the interworking of these two streams reached a kind of crisis. This crisis set in when, during the period of the Roman Empire, widespread intermingling among the people in many territories of the earth took place. This was a most crucial 'moment' in the evolution of mankind. The issue at stake, on both an earthly and on a cosmic spiritual level, was this: Men were facing a Janus-like danger; either they would fail to develop the Ego or they would lose all connection with humanity as such and become one-sidedly self-sufficient, self-loving, egotistic individuals.

This was the crucial point that had been reached. Something quite specific had to happen if the evolution of humanity was to progress. What had to happen was this (though I have referred to this several times already, it will bear reiteration): the human Ego had to become sufficiently 'mature' to develop within itself what may for the first time be called *freedom*, inner spiritual activity, as distinct from 'pressure' from without being exerted by the group-spirit. The spiritual essence in man, the Ego, was facing this decisive issue and to meet it, it had to be completely liberated, had, in other words, to acquire full consciousness of itself. Thus mankind, with the exception of the peoples of the Orient and of the New World, was confronting a 'birth of the Ego through which it could know the love that springs from its own inmost being in freedom. Out of freedom the Ego was to unfold love, and out of love, freedom. Only a being who develops an Ego of this nature is in the real sense *man*.' [46] It was at this point of history that, for the first time, full manhood became a possibility. At this point in time the Christ Impulse, the Impulse that was to make man truly man, streamed over the earth.

In the words spoken by John the Baptist and by Christ Himself, 'The kingdom of Heaven is at hand', is indicated the essential quality of this 'turning-point in time'.

With his fully-developed Ego, man can transcend the kind of love he has in common with the animals — a love which, Steiner states, has its seat in the astral body. 'In the *"I"*, the Ego, the Godhead speaks — earthly conditions have no voice here. In the *"I"* the kingdom of the Spirit speaks.' [47]

We could say, states Steiner, that until the Incarnation of the Christ there were three kingdoms — mineral, plant, animal — and a kingdom which had, indeed, risen to a higher level than these, but had not yet reached completion, 'had not yet been imbued with its full super-earthly reality of being'. [48] This 'new' kingdom, the kingdom of man, 'exists by virtue of the fact that into an Egohood there enters that which is otherwise nowhere to be found on earth, namely, the clear consciousness of the spiritual world, the kingdom of God'. [49] Through the spirit-imbued Ego man is enabled to develop spiritualized love. The words of St Paul, 'Not I, but Christ in me', then become a reality.

In one of his lectures on the Gospel of St John [50] Steiner asks us to imagine that Christ had not become Man on earth and had not poured fresh power into men enabling them to replace the old ties of blood-love by a new, spiritual love. [51] What would have happened? Love, the power that draws men together, would have gradually disappeared from the earth. Without Christ, love would have died out, and men would have grown more and more isolated in their own individualities. All men would have become victims of the strife of all against all — 'The strife which indeed will come', says Steiner, 'but only for those who have not become penetrated by the Christ Principle'. [52]

It is true that today, in spite of the Christ Event, we still see discord and strife everywhere; we are still far removed from any true realization of Christian Love. But, as Steiner repeatedly points out, we are but at the beginning of Christian evolution.

Once we have fully realized the intensity and power of the

Christ Impulse we need also to recognize the following: 'Without the Christ Impulse, and through the isolation, separation, and mutual antagonism which largely prevail among men, something resembling a struggle for survival will ensue.' This struggle for existence, a tenet of Darwinism, is falsely applied to the human race as the explanation of human evolution. Applied to the animal world the Darwinian theory is right, 'because in that kingdom there is no impulse able to turn strife into love'. 'Christ as a Spiritual Power in humanity will refute all Darwinism', indeed, all materialistic theories, by His Deed on Golgotha. Nevertheless, it is incumbent upon us to realize that we 'cannot ward off the *war* of opinions, feelings and actions, unless we combat in ourselves and settle inwardly the antagonism which would otherwise flow into the world'. Whoever combats what is to be overcome and harmonized within himself (see above, in connection with willing, feeling and thinking) will not combat the opinion and the action of a fellow-man. He will confront his fellow-men, not in a polemical and bellicose spirit, but in a spirit of love. The point is that the 'combat' is diverted from the outside world to man's inner being. 'The forces governing human nature must combat each other inwardly.' [53]

'We could even describe the progress of human evolution as the diversion of the strife in the "outside world" to the work of harmonizing the "inner" forces of man. Through Christ, man was endowed with the possibility of establishing harmony within himself, of harmonizing the antagonistic forces in his own being.' [54]

In our present context we could say that the mission of Christianity in the process of evolution is to kindle in man the impulse to find pure love, where the well-being of the one cannot possibly be conceived without the well-being of the other. All divisions must fall away under the influence of Christianity, and the next stage, the Jupiter stage, of our planet must be prepared under the influence of this principle.

Religion in pre-Christian eras was founded in and rested on faith. Christianity must imbue such faith with the fire of clear spiritual knowledge. 'Whereas formerly man had to believe before he could come to knowledge, in the future full knowledge will shine with light and man will . . . ascend to the recognition of the highest spiritual worlds.'

From instinctive faith mankind evolves 'to wisdom, glowed through by love'. [55]

15.

REINCARNATION AND KARMA

Maria (turning to Lucifer):

In human nature there are springs of love
To which thy power can never penetrate.
They are unsealed when faults of former lives —
A load unwittingly assumed by man —
Are in a later life by spirit seen,
And by the free-will of self-sacrifice
Transformed to earthly action, which shall tend
To bear fruit for the real good of man. [1]

Studies that are concerned with Karma of human
beings must be undertaken with deep earnestness
and inwardly assimilated. For it is not the mere
knowledge of some particular karmic connection that
is important. What is really important is that
such studies should quicken the whole of man's
nature, enabling him to find his bearings in life.
Such studies will never be fruitful if they lead
to greater indifference towards human beings than is
otherwise the case; they will be fruitful
only if they kindle deeper love and understanding
than are possible when account is taken merely of
the impressions of a single life. [2]

15.

In his book *Theosophy*, [3] which first appeared in 1904, Steiner shows us how, before birth, the soul-spiritual unites with the life-germ coming from the line of the 'generations' and is subjected to the laws of heredity. This binds man's spiritual nucleus to certain qualities, advantages and deficiencies of the body; it enters a given chosen family, a chosen nation and race. This fact in itself determines human destiny from many aspects. The soul's endeavour to follow the laws of truth and goodness will be checked or aided in one way or another.

Why does one eternal nucleus — the higher spiritual essence of every human being, which comes to expression in the soul when it surrenders, by incessant striving, to the laws of eternal truth — why does one eternal nucleus unite with a more perfect bodily sheath, whereas another unites with an unfavourable sheath?

A further question we might ask is this: why do certain gifts or, in particular, blows of destiny, come to a person who appears to be striving to live a good life? Does it not frequently appear as if 'evil' were recompensed and 'goodness' punished? Does it not often seem that undeserved advantages or disadvantages are placed in a man's cradle at birth?

To these, and many other questions, Steiner gives detailed and far-reaching answers in *Theosophy* and in many lectures concerned with reincarnation and karmic relationships.

Summarizing his answers to those questions that are of relevance to our present theme we could say: the whole acquires a meaning only if, for instance, such undeserved capacities or deficiencies, such 'undeserved' gifts or disadvantages, are viewed as effects, the causes of which were predisposed by the human being before birth; in other words, in a former earthly incarnation.

From many different angles throughout his lectures Rudolf Steiner shows that the effects of characteristic faults and virtues appear in the following or second or third earthly life, the effects, for example, of benevolence and envy, love and hatred, love of truth and mendacity, and so forth. He traces the lines of karma, too, in the predispositions to health and illness.

Admittedly these aspects just mentioned are but the first steps towards an understanding of these things. Steiner's contribution, given to the world out of his exact clairvoyant insight into these matters, goes far beyond these elementary steps. [4]

The depth and width of Steiner's insight can only be touched upon here. For instance, he clearly saw, experienced, and stated, the relation of the Beings of the Higher Worlds in the formative processes of man's karma; he clearly and uniquely stated the role of man's free will in these processes, and, again uniquely, has vividly explained, with countless examples, the role that metamorphosis plays in the process of reincarnation.

We can see in Steiner's dynamic conception of reincarnation and karma the human being, endowed with free will and imbued with pure love, as a being who is intimately woven into the invisible cooperation of the spiritual Hierarchies with the visible world of sense perception. We can see in his conception of man a being without whose cooperation the world would lose its direction; a being in whom the impulse towards the spiritualiz-ation of matter, the redemption of the created world, lives and works; a being in whom the Deed of Christ, the Love of Christ, can reach its fulfilment.

We could perhaps say that for Steiner the process of reincarnation of man is at one and the same time a highly individual process on the one hand, and a subtle weaving into and with the cosmic acts of the Beings of the Higher Hierarchies on the other. Through Steiner's conception of reincarnation we can truly see man as a microcosmic counterpart and revelation of macrocosmic happenings. [5]

*   *   *   *

Now let us look at a few of the many instances of practical living and its relationship to the shaping of future lives — limiting ourselves in the main to our theme of the power of love.

For example, what appears in one life as urge or impulse, desire and ideation, emerges in a later life as habit. Good habits, good traits of character prepare a healthy physical body for the next life. A bad habit, on the other hand, makes its appearance in a later life in the form of an illness or as a tendency to illness. Thus, the causes of good health and of illnesses can be sought in the inclinations and habits of a previous life.

The actual *destiny* of an individual, on the other hand, is the result of his former *deeds*. Here the quality that has a clearly recognizable influence upon the karmic formation of a following life is love. There are people who act towards their environment lovingly and sympathetically; they love nature and mankind in a way that leads to active, sympathetic deeds. The more strongly this sense of all-embracing love and sympathy has developed and becomes 'habit' in the soul — and, therefore, rooted in the etheric body — the greater becomes the capacity of the individual concerned to retain the qualities of youth for a long time in a subsequent incarnation. A person who radiates much love in one life will, in another, be able to stay young, inwardly as well as outwardly, for a long time in the next life. On the other hand, an individual prone to show antipathy, who harbours many feelings of hatred in one life, will age prematurely in a later life. [6] Interestingly, Steiner mentions that a body that shows the signs of age at a physically early age stems from the former life of a harsh critic. Individuals who lead a life of aversion and ill-will, who 'become harsh critics at an early age will in the next life be people who are almost born with the wrinkles of old age'. [7]

Steiner warns us, however, that in dealing with reincarnation and karma we cannot simply apply a rigid, simple formula: for example, hatred in this life, therefore ill-health in the next. We need to have a spiritual insight of a person's calibre before we could justify such a statement. To make his point, Steiner gives a different picture of metamorphosis in the following statement. Let us suppose, he says, that we do not endeavour to overcome our lack of loving interest, or even our feelings of hatred, towards someone. 'Lack of love and lack of interest appear in a following life as a kind of timidity or fear.' [8] We could speak of a dis-ease of the soul in this instance. Similarly, a glad, open and loving attitude toward others in one life will manifest itself in the next in the ability of soul 'to stand firmly in life', to be capable of meeting crises with equanimity and courage. Not to suffer from feelings of inadequacy and hopelessness can be the consequence in a later life of an earlier one imbued with loving interest for the world and humanity.

On one occasion Steiner mentions that envy strengthens the Luciferic power and untruthfulness that of Ahriman. [9] Both qualities show a lack of love in the soul of him who envies, who tells lies. 'Those who experience envy develop in such a way that (in their next earthly life) they cannot find a connection with other people. They cannot begin or conclude anything. Untruthfulness gives rise to a kind of shyness, so that it will be impossible for them to look another person in the eyes.' [10]

Steiner then shows how these soul-effects reach right down into the physical constitution in a third earthly life. In both the case of him who envies and of him who is untruthful, we perceive that the following life manifests different forms of 'a weak soul and unstable character'. Now, the soul is the architect of the physical body, and as a consequence not only of the previous life of soul instability but also of the life prior to that, in which envy and untruthfulness were characteristic traits of the soul, in the third earthly life a soul may well incarnate in the form of an awkward, helpless child, unable to cope with itself, unable to come into contact with others. 'This will have a physical foundation, for even with regard to their physical constitution they will be weak and, as a result, handicapped in their social connections.' [11]

But Steiner does not stop here. Destiny, he says, calls for the application of therapeutic measures. For instance, he says: 'Just those to whom we have told lies, whom we have envied' — to whom we have shown a lack of love — 'they are the people we shall find in our environment when we are born again.' [12]

Now the therapeutic measures could be somewhat like this. We could ask ourselves: What is the right thing to do, in a higher moral sense, when I know that someone is adopting an unloving attitude towards me, is envying me, for example, or is spreading untruthful rumours about me? What attitude of soul is the right one for me to harbour towards such a person? 'Never should I avenge myself, but rather help him; this will be the right thing to do. The best thing we can do for another person is to forgive him; to shame him by being specially good to him . . . For in that case he will not come back in his next life as a helpless, weak person. Forgiveness alone can bring this about.' [13] Inherent in any act of forgiveness is a strong element of true love.

In a lecture with the title 'Examples of the Working of Karma Between Two Incarnations', [14] Steiner goes into some detail regarding the question of alternating sexes in successive incarnations and, similarly alternating qualities of soul, complementary qualities of soul. Those of particular relevance to us here are 'the two qualities of soul we will call the *capacity for love and inner strength*'.

The outstanding stamp of the one personality is loving devotion to his fellow-men, forgetfulness of self, surrender to what is around him. Such an incarnation will alternate with one in which the individual feels the urge not to lose himself in the outer world but to strengthen himself inwardly — applying this strength, for instance, to bring about his own progress. This latter urge must not, of course, degenerate into lack of love, any more than the former inclination should degenerate, as it might well do, into a complete loss of one's self. [15]

These two qualities need to complement each other. As Steiner well reminds us, there are many people who have the desire to sacrifice themselves. But such a desire is not enough. Before anyone can make a sacrifice of real value to the world, he must have the strength required for it, and, in addition, he must first 'be something before he can usefully sacrifice himself; otherwise the sacrifice of self is of little value. Moreover, in a certain respect a kind of egoism — although it is repressed — a kind of laziness, is present when a man makes no effort to develop, to persevere in his strivings, so that what he can achieve — and sacrifice — is of real value'. [16]

During the months of February to September 1924, Steiner gave some eighty lectures, in various cities in Europe, including Torquay and London, dealing with esoteric aspects of karmic relationships. [17] In one of these, given in Dornach, Switzerland, [18] he speaks, in particular, of the impulses of love and hatred. In connection with the former, as so often on other occasions, he stresses the difference between a deed performed out of genuine love and one done out of a mere sense of duty, convention, respectability, and so on.

If we, in one earthly life, are able to perform actions sustained by genuine human love, warmed through and through by love, then this love remains a real, active force in our souls beyond this earthly life. What we take with us through the Portal of Death, as an outcome of our loving deeds, what is then 'mirrored' in the other souls we come into contact with in the spiritual world, comes back to us as a 'reflected image; and as we form from this our astral body, with which we "descend" on to the earth again for a new earth-life, we find that the love which we developed and "poured out" in our former earth-life, and which finally was "returned" to us in the spiritual worlds by other souls, we find that this force of love, in our new earth-life, is transformed into joy and happiness'. [19] Such is the metamorphosis. A man does something, out of love, for his fellow-men. In the passage through life between death and a new birth this 'outpoured love of the one life on earth is transmuted, metamorphosed, into joy that streams in towards him'. [20]

If, says Steiner, you experience joy through a fellow-man in one earthly life, you may be sure it is the outcome of the love you unfolded towards him in a former life on earth together. Joy which comes from other human beings towards one 'warms and sustains life — it gives life wings, as it were. It is the karmic result of love that has been given out'. [21]

Then, in the next period between death and a new birth, what we thus experienced in joy in the earth-life we have left is reflected back again to us in the many souls with whom we were together on earth and with whom we 'live' together again in the spiritual world. As is the case with love, so also the reflected image of the warmth of joy is instilled, imprinted into our astral body, and in the next life on earth, the third in succession, becomes the basis, the impulse for a quick and ready understanding of man and the world. If we take an active interest in the lives and actions of other men, Steiner states, it is a sure sign of the presence of joy in our last incarnation and of the love we poured out in our incarnation prior to that.

Steiner contrasts the different form of metamorphosis the soul undergoes if, instead of acting out of love, a man acts out of a sense of duty. Necessary as the latter may often be in social life, there is all the difference between acting out of a rigid sense of duty and acting out of love. Deeds done out of a sense of duty do not call forth joy in the next life on earth. They, too, undergo that mirroring in other souls in the spiritual world, and, having done so, set their imprint upon the astral body. One consequence of this is that in the next life such a person has the feeling that people are indifferent to him. What a person thus suffers is due, in whole or in part, to the lack of love flowing from him in a former life on earth. What man experiences as indifference towards him makes him in the next, in the third successive life, the kind of person who does not know what to do with himself, who drifts aimlessly through life. It is a matter of indifference to him whether, for instance, a piece of music, or a poem or painting, is good or bad. But there is always something which prompts in him the question: What is the good of it anyhow? [22]

Steiner also develops the sequence of metamorphoses which,

in one life, have their root in antipathy or hatred. [23] In the next
earthly life is born what meets us as distress, unhappiness, pain
— in other words, the opposite of joy. [24] A 'portion of what we
experience as suffering that is inflicted upon us by others in one
earthly life may very well be due to our own feelings of antipathy,
hatred, in former lives on earth'. [25] A portion, says Steiner,
because there are, of course, other karmic connections, too. [26]
The outcome of this suffering, which comes to us as a result of
our own antipathy in the previous life, is a kind of mental dullness
in the third life, in contrast to the quick, open-minded insight into
the world which has its root in joy and love. 'Stupidity in any one
life is always the outcome of hatred in a preceding life.' [27]

'What we develop as the content of our soul in our present life
will have its outcome and effect in the next life. If anyone wants to
be extra stupid in his next earthly life but one, he need only
indulge in hatred in this life. But the converse is also true: if he
wants to have a free and open insight into life in his next
incarnation but one, he need only develop the power of love in his
present life.' [28]

It is thus possible to affect the course of the karmic stream. As
educators of children, Steiner exhorts us, we should not lose
sight of this fact. If, for instance, a child shows a tendency to
dullness and stupidity — and we 'perceive the karmic connections' — we can assist the child to develop love in its heart, and if
we discover which are the other children in his environment to
whom he is karmically connected — 'with a delicate and open
observation of life this is possible' — then we can encourage the
dull and stupid child to perform deeds of love for these other
children. If we succeed in doing this, then we help 'to create, in
this life of the child, a *counter-weight*, a balance to the antipathy,
possibly hatred, which was a characteristic feature of his soul in
his last life but one. And in the next earthly life a greater degree of
intelligence and perception will manifest itself.'

In such ways as this, says Steiner, 'our insight into karmic
relationships becomes a real service to life'. [29]

To help a child — or any human being, no matter of what age
— to develop an especial love towards those for whom antipathy
or hatred was felt in a former life, or former lives, soon shows
beneficial results in the present life. Sympathy and love specifically aroused and directed by an understanding teacher
results in the lighting up of the whole life of soul, including,
particularly in a child, a brightening of the intelligence.

Needless to say the transformation of antipathy into sympathy, hatred into love, in the present life, shows itself too in a betterment in the inner soul life.

*   *   *   *

In a lecture entitled, 'Karma and the Animal Kingdom', [30] Steiner gives a brief but illuminating sketch of our relationship to the animal kingdom. He begins by reminding us that we, as human beings, have an astral body, that the animals also have such a body and that therefore they are also able to feel pain, just as we do. 'But they do not possess the power to evolve spiritually through the experience of pain and through the conquest of pain; for they have no individuality', [31] they have no *individual ego*. The animals are, Steiner continues, much more to be pitied than we are. We have to bear pain, it is true, but each experience of pain is for us a means, an opportunity to evolve. Through mastering pain we evolve spiritually.

During the course of evolution we have left behind us the animal. We could indeed say that the animals sacrificed themselves in order that we should be able to evolve spiritually. [32] The animals 'manifest to us our own former organizations when we were capable of feeling pain, but could not yet transform it into something beneficial' for ourselves and for the rest of humanity. We could say that the animals surround us 'as *tokens* of how we ourselves came to our present state of perfection'. [33]

We should learn to consider such matters, says Steiner, not as mere theories, but rather with a cosmic feeling. When we look upon the animals we should feel, for instance: When you animals suffer, you suffer something from which we human beings reap the benefit. We have the power to overcome, to transform suffering, but you must endure it. Because of your sacrifice, we are able to overcome suffering.

'If we develop this cosmic feeling . . . we can then experience an all-embracing feeling of sympathy, of love for the animal kingdom.' [34]

The liberation of our astral bodies from all the grosser characteristics we owe to the animals. These grosser characteristics — from which, admittedly, we have not yet completely liberated ourselves — may be seen for instance in the slyness of the fox, the stubbornness of the mule, the passionate ferocity of the snake, and so on. Such characteristics have withdrawn from us to a greater or lesser extent during the course of evolution, and in their fullness lead an independent existence outside us — in the animals. [35]

When we begin to realize that we, as human beings, have become what we are, individuals whose karma compensates for what is experienced as suffering, when we realize that we owe this to the animals, whose karma does not allow of such compensation, when we have through spiritual striving attained freedom and selflessness — then we will also consciously comprehend our karmic relationship to the animals, and out of love and understanding make good the sacrifice the animals have made for us by our own loving treatment of them.

Through the consciousness of karma a better relationship between man and the animal kingdom than exists at present will be born, especially in the West. Man's treatment of the animals will be such that through selfless love and understanding he will 'lift up' those who are unable to strive on their own account. As the Tenth Hierarchy, the Hierarchy of Love, it is part of man's task to redeem the animal kingdom. [36]

16.

THE POWER OF LOVE IN THE PROCESS OF INCARNATION

*In many respects the purpose of incarnation
on earth is to forge bonds of ever greater
warmth and love.* [1]

16.

Steiner speaks on several occasions of the spiritual reality underlying the process of procreation. Of particular relevance to our present theme are some statements he made in a course of lectures on *Rosicrucian Esotericism*. [2]

Amongst other pronouncements, he makes the easily comprehensible statement that, in any healthy relationship between man and woman, the process of procreation is preceded by impulses of love.

This process, imbued with loving sympathy, is perceived by the clairvoyant as a streaming to and fro of astral forces between the man and the woman. 'The companionship between the souls themselves is expressed in the *play* of the astral forces.' [3] Now, before the physical act of love takes place there is already 'reflected' in this 'play' of astral forces the individuality, the being who in the spiritual world, is in the process of incarnating. This, Steiner states quite unequivocally, is the essential reality in the procreative act. In other words, the soul that is descending from the spiritual world is already beginning to be active in the incarnation process before actual physical fertilization takes place. 'The spiritual world is in fact also instrumental in bringing about the meeting of the man and woman' [4] in the first place. We can see here that a wonderfully intimate interplay is taking place between forces from the spiritual world and the sympathy born of love that precedes physical fertilization.

The individual, the Ego, who is in the process of incarnating brings together those who love one another. The archetype wishing to incarnate draws to itself, as it were, the astral 'substance' that now has an effect upon the feeling of love, the passion. The astral passion, surging to and fro between man and woman, mirrors the astral substance of the descending, incarnating individuality; the astral substance descending from the world of the spirit is encountered by the astral feeling of those who love one another — and this feeling is itself influenced by the substance of the incarnating entity. [5]

We see, in brief, that the incarnating individual participates in the choice of parents, and we can also see that, in a certain sense, the child loves the parents even before conception and is guided to them. 'The parents' love is the responsive love to the child's love.' [6] Parental love, seen in this light, may be regarded as being the 'reproduction' of the child's love that precedes actual physical birth.

Life between death and rebirth usually goes on for many hundreds of years and descent into a physical body may also have been prepared for over several centuries. All through this time, moreover, the individuality wishing to incarnate has been 'working down' into the earthly conditions and events.

'A great-great . . . grandfather of yours fell in love with a great-great . . . grandmother. They felt the urge to come together, and in this urge you were already working in the spiritual worlds. And when a rather less distant great-great . . . grandfather and great-great . . . grandmother loved each other, you once again were, in a sense, the mediator. So did you summon all the generations to the end that at long last those should emerge who could become your mother and your father.'

'In that mysterious and intangible quality that pervades the relationships of earthly love, forces are indeed at work, proceeding from human souls who look for future incarnations.' [7] Therefore, we cannot speak of complete freedom in the *external* conditions and circumstances that bring men and women on Earth together as parents of a child. Such affairs of earthly love between man and woman are guided to a greater or lesser degree by spiritual beings seeking to incarnate into physical bodies.

Steiner elaborates upon this theme in regard to incarnation into a gifted family, e.g. the Bach family, or the Bernoulli family, a mathematically gifted family. [8] It is clear from what has been said in the previous paragraphs that in the matter of generations of gifted musicians, or gifted mathematicians, and so on, we are not dealing with the generally accepted scientific concepts of heredity. 'Development in the human realm is a matter of *self-heredity*. Each man can say that he has not received his traits from any ancestor or parent, because these had their own individuality as well as he. Therefore, no matter how paradoxical it may seem, he has received them from himself. In each succeeding life he is a further developed *repetition* of what he was in earlier incarnations.' 'The activity of the incarnating ego is largely a sorting out and rejection of the hereditary materials presented by nature.'

'A gifted man of high moral principles also needs parents who transmit a physical body suitable for the functioning of his moral gifts. And he has these parents and no others because he is this or that particular individuality.' [9]

As we have said, the individuality himself seeks his parents. He does this with the assistance of higher spiritual beings called, by Steiner, the Spirits of Wisdom.

This conception of incarnation often meets with resistance from parents. They are fearful, for instance that they might lose something if the child were not to inherit certain qualities from them, certain talents and so forth. True knowledge, however, says Steiner, reveals that not only was the love of parents present in the incarnating individual, in the child, before it was born — in the spiritual world — but also that the incarnating eternal kernel, the Ego, chose a particular couple of parents just because they are what they are. In particular, continues Steiner, spiritual science shows that it is love that is the force guiding the child to the mother. The child has a very close relationship to the mother before birth, even before conception. 'Mother love', as indicated already, 'is a reciprocal force. Spiritually regarded, therefore, mother love extends to the time before birth; it is rooted in *mutual* feelings of love'. [10]

*   *   *   *

Steiner puts the question before us: Why do we incarnate? His answer is far-reaching and illustrative of his Christocentric conception of human life. [11] The best way, he states, of answering the question is to consider the essential difference between incarnations in the pre-Christian era and those that have taken place since the Advent of Christ. In pre-Christian incarnations all souls still preserved something they had possessed when incarnations began, namely, a 'natural' vision of the spiritual world. Progress in the course of successive incarnations actually brings with it the fact that this instinctive clairvoyant relationship is gradually lost. The more the physical world has become the sole arena of human life, the more completely has the spiritual world 'vanished' from the vision of man.

Now, the vital significance of the Christ Impulse is that if we selflessly surrender ourselves to the Christ, and thereby unite our Ego with him, we take into ourselves the spiritualizing power of Love and are then able to ascend gradually, but now in full consciousness, to where we were at the beginning of our evolution. Moreover, owing to the process of successive incarnations, we will have become immeasurably richer than we ever were. 'Herein lies the great difference between pre-Christian incarnations and those that have taken place in the Christian era.' [12] In the pre-Christian era such an ascent was not possible; on the contrary, mankind was in process of descending in increasing measure into the world of matter.

At the present time we are still living in a period of transition; normal human cognition is deeply bound up with the physical world and largely restricted to purely physical perception. 'It must be remembered that the Christ Impulse is still in its initial stages of activity in man; it is in future incarnations, when men have taken that Impulse fully into themselves, that they will begin to love their incarnations.' We will love our incarnations because they give us the opportunity of experiencing what can only be experienced through earthly existence: 'The receiving of the Christ Impulse into the soul'. [13]

17.

LOVE — THE ROOT OF EDUCATION

Pedagogy is love for man resulting from knowledge of man. [1]

From my head to my feet
In the image of God,
From my heart to my hands
His own breath do I feel.
When I speak with my mouth,
I shall follow God's will.
When I see and know God
In my father and mother,
In all loving people,
In flowers and in trees,
In birds, beasts and stones,
Then no fear shall I feel;
Only love can then fill me
For all that is round me. [2a]

Proper imitation develops freedom;
Authority develops the rights life;
Brotherliness, love, develops the economic life. [2b]

17.

The full devotion of a teacher to his task is not instilled by the learning of rules and theories; [3] it will only be brought forth if he is able to penetrate into the whole being of man as body, soul and spirit. When we, as teachers, begin to know the full being of man, of the growing human being, we find a spontaneous love for him springing up, ever fresh, in our hearts. Love, resulting from a spiritual scientific knowledge of man is the surest foundation upon which the art of education can be built.

Such a love for the being of man will never permit us as educators, or as parents, to bring any form of coercion to bear on what human nature itself, the true human spirit, wills to do. We must understand how to leave this nature to unfold itself in freedom and learn to act only as helpers in the process. The younger the child the more important is it to allow this development to take place freely. If, for instance, we impatiently coax the little child to walk or to stand, we may harm the organism of the child for the whole of its later life. We must learn to look at a child, not as it is at any given moment, but always in relation to its whole journey through life.

Steiner gives a practical example of a 'wrong' and a 'right' kind of help to give to a young child.

If a child is coerced to stand and to walk, to orientate himself in a vertical position in space, we often find that in later life, particularly between the 50s and 60s, the adult suffers from all manner of metabolic ailments.

If on the other hand as parents we observe — with selfless love — how the child's organism adjusts itself without outside help to attain the upright position and then in due course to walk; if, out of a religious feeling, we approach the child with reverence for the creative, divine spiritual forces which are 'orientating' him rightly into three-dimensional space, then we generate health-forming forces which express themselves in later life in, for instance, healthy metabolic activities between the ages just mentioned — a time of life, Steiner adds, when we especially need health-sustaining forces to permeate the processes of metabolism. [4] A child who is allowed to stand and walk in his own good time is given a sound foundation upon which to develop into a healthy man.

In the early years, say between six and ten, a child's environment should be so introduced to him that the feeling is aroused in him that all things have a divine origin, that everything is a manifestation of God. Our aim in so doing is to awaken in the child, first of all, a sense of gratitude for everything that, born of love, takes place in the world, gratitude for what others do for us, and also for the gifts bestowed on us by Nature. The awakening of such a sense of gratitude will guide religious feeling in the child along the right path. [5] Love for all creation, for all that has issued forth from the divine Father, should then accompany the sense of gratitude. Such love will deepen and enrich the child's perception of the world in a religious sense. 'If gratitude and love have been unfolded in the child before the age of ten, then we can proceed to assist in the development of a true sense and understanding of duty. Premature development of a sense of duty by dint of injunctions will never lead to a religious inwardness.' [6] We could add here that we cannot instil moral concepts into young children by appealing to their intellect; we have to appeal to their feeling and their will. [7]

Before the age of nine or ten it is not possible to convey to the child's soul an understanding of the Mystery of Golgotha, or of all that which is connected with the divinity of Christ. A feeling, an inner understanding of the principle of universal divinity, of the Father, should always precede the introduction to the child of the Mystery of the Christ. The basis for a right understanding of the Mystery of Golgotha is laid down if the child is first led to feel how divinity is immanent in all Nature — not only in the Kingdoms of Nature, but also in his own heart, in the heart of his teacher, in the hearts of all men. If this is brought to the child by a teacher who inwardly feels this, too, then it will be by the 'authority' of the love dwelling in the teacher's heart that the child will be 'taught' to feel gratitude and love for this universal divinity — and for the teacher himself. Rudolf Steiner, in his many addresses to the children of the first Waldorf (Rudolf Steiner) School [8] always asked the children, 'Do you love your teachers?' and the spontaneous response, 'Yes', was a source of delight to him. [9]

'The capacities of love, devotion and unselfishness are the real foundation of the art of teaching.' [10] Again and again Steiner stresses in his lectures and seminars concerning the education of children that the life of feeling requires careful tending. Real social life is not possible without love. 'We must do all we can to see that the children entrusted to our care love one another and love their teachers also. That sensitivity to authority which children need between the seventh and fourteenth year should gradually be transformed into a love that is allied to the highest respect. In this way we lay the foundation of the teaching: "Love thy neighbour as thyself". And since we are developing at the same time that gratitude which leads the way to a knowledge of the supersensible world, to "Love thy neighbour as thyself" is added "Love God above all things." '[11]

In a booklet Steiner wrote during the first decade of this century, *The Education of the Child*, [12] he dwells at some length on the need to nurture the quality of reverence in the soul of the seven- to fourteen-year-old child. Among other things he writes: 'Veneration and reverence are forces whereby the etheric body grows in the right way. If it were impossible during these years to look up to another person in unbounded reverence, one would have to suffer for the loss throughout the whole of one's life. Where loving reverence is lacking, the living forces of the etheric body are stunted in their growth.' [13]

On many occasions Steiner stressed the point that he who developed a feeling of reverence in childhood would have the power to bless in old age. [14] The feeling of reverence in early life, stengthening the etheric body, the body of life-formative forces, forms the foundation not only of the power of blessing, but also of healing.

Whatever makes the strongest impression on the etheric body, works also most powerfully into the processes of forming and consolidating the physical body. The strongest impressions are those that are born of religious experience. Unless a child, particularly between the ages of seven and fourteen, receives religious impulses deep into his soul, his will-forces, and consequently his character, will never develop healthily. The more a man can feel his place and role in the Universal All, the more unified will be his life of will. If he does not feel himself strongly linked to the Divine-Spiritual, his will-life, and therefore his character, will remain 'uncertain, divided and unsound'. [15]

The life of feeling is further strengthened and developed in a healthy way during this second seven-year period of childhood through the parables and pictures, especially the 'pictures' of great personalities that we, as teachers, present to children; [16] similarly a loving and reverent study of the marvels of Nature is vital for the right formation of the life of feeling. Important too is the cultivation of the sense of beauty and the awakening of the artistic feeling through the arts. 'Joy and happiness in living, a love of all existence, a power and energy for work — such are among the lifelong results of a right cultivation of the feeling for beauty and for art.' [17] Again, the moral sense, which is also being developed during these years, through the pictures of life presented to the child, through the 'authorities' to whom he looks up, this moral sense becomes well established if the child out of his sense of beauty feels the good to be at the same time beautiful, the bad to be ugly. Love and joy and beauty should permeate the surroundings of the growing child. [18]

In the second seven-year period of a child's education, the teacher needs to work artistically; that is, he needs to 'add' to the religious attitude out of which he has particularly been active during the first seven years of the child's life a deep love for his work. This does not imply, of course, that such love need not be present in the earlier, or, for that matter, in any later period of education; but particular emphasis on love in his attitude to his activity needs to be cultivated in the middle period of a child's school life. Steiner even goes so far as to state that during the second seven-year period only that which is 'born of Love for the Educational Deed will have any real effect on the child'. [19]

If we, as teachers and parents, can acquire the right love for education, we shall be able to assist in the child's development in such a way up to the age of, say, fourteen, that we can then 'hand him over to freedom', that is, to the free use of his own intellectual and spiritual powers.

If we have approached the young child in an attitude of religious reverence and educated him in love up to the time of puberty, the right course for us to take from then on is to leave the youth's spirit free, and our relationship with him should be founded in mutual respect for the living freedom of thought. This freedom should not be endangered, for it is just the attainment of such freedom, founded in gratitude and love, that we, as educators and parents, should have striven to assist the growing human being to achieve. [20]

If gratitude has been developed in the child during the first seven-year period of life, 'it will be easy, between the ages of seven and fourteen, to develop what must be the activating impulse in everything man does in life. This is love'. Only if the virtue of love has been especially nurtured during the second seven-year period of life will it be possible for that 'most inward of human impulses, the impulse of duty', [21] to develop in a natural and harmonious way in the third seven-year period. What Goethe once expressed can then become a guiding line for life. Goethe asks: 'What is duty?' and his answer is: 'It is when one loves what one commands oneself' (see Chapter 12). This is the goal which we all must attain. However, we shall only reach it when we grow towards it by stages: Gratitude — Love — Duty. [22]

In a course of lectures for the teachers of the first Waldorf School in Stuttgart, Steiner, apropos of the right preparation for the age of puberty and a loving sense of duty, refers, from a somewhat different angle, to some of the matters just discussed. We shall be giving the right preparation for the attainment of puberty, he states, if in that period of life which begins about the ninth or tenth year, we encourage *wonder* in the child — awakening in him, among other qualities, a feeling for beauty. His feeling for beauty once awakened and gradually made more conscious will be a right preparation for him, when he reaches puberty, to learn to love the world in a healthy way. 'Love will have its right and true development in him.' Steiner is not, of course, merely concerned here with love for the other sex. That is only one special form of it. [23] 'Love reaches out to include all things, all humanity. It is the very deepest and innermost of all the impulses that lead men to deed and action. We ought to do what we love to do. Duty should grow to be one with love; we ought to love doing what we ought to do.' [24]

In relation to the adult's approach to children who are in need of 'special care', some of whom, in fact, may be bordering on conditions of insanity, Steiner emphasizes very strongly the need to cultivate within oneself, as curative pedagogue, the quality of love. 'There is a real call to us to look with love upon the soul-spiritual nature that descends from the spiritual world, to look with love upon it, even when it comes to expression in so-called insanity — yes, to look with love upon the very details of the insanity. And then we shall feel impelled to go beyond the symptomatology that can furnish a psychography of the case, and look rather at the karmic connections into which this insane human being comes.' [25]

The need for constant self-education, self-observation, is

fundamental to all those who have a position of responsibility towards the growing human being. 'Observe the difference — first when you approach a child with more or less indifference, and then again when you approach him with real love. As soon as you appproach him with love, and cease to believe that you can do more with technical dodges than you can with love, at once your educating becomes effective, becomes a thing of power. And this is more than ever true when you are dealing with abnormal children.' [26]

Speaking about educational methods — and techniques — Steiner draws our attention to a fundamental aspect of the teacher's approach to the child entrusted to his care, namely, the kind of knowledge of man, of the growing child, which the teacher needs as a foundation for a true art of education. It is beyond the scope of our present theme to go into any sort of detail in this regard and the reader is referred to, among others, a series of lectures Steiner gave to teachers, which in English has the title, *Human Values in Education*. [27] For our present purpose we shall confine ourselves to a short consideration of the following question and Steiner's answer to it: What sort of a person must one be if one wishes to pursue a vocation based on a knowledge of *life*? On a knowledge of man? Among the answers there is one that will crop up more persistently, perhaps, than any other: One must be objective! True. 'But the question is whether or not this objectivity is based on a lack of paying heed to what is *essential* in any particular situation.' [28]

For the most part, Steiner points out, people are of the view that love is far more subjective than all else in life, and that it would be impossible for anyone who loves to be objective. [29] For this reason, when knowledge is spoken about, love is never mentioned as an organ of cognition. 'Nevertheless for *real* life love is the greatest power in the acquiring of knowledge. * Without love it is impossible to attain to a knowledge of man which could form the foundation of a true art of education.' [30]

As teachers we need a science of man which will enable us to love man. Implicit is also that we can love our own knowledge. There is much wisdom, Steiner reminds us, behind the fact that formerly men did not speak simply of acquiring knowledge, but of philo-sophia, of a love of knowledge. [31]

* See Chapter 11.

* * * *

In other connections we have noted the emphasis Steiner lays on the recognition of the spiritual-divine in man, of the fact that before entering through physical birth into earth existence every man is a spiritual being among spiritual, divine beings. In the child, in every man, we see the divine made manifest. As teacher and parent we should see in every growing child the unfolding of cosmic laws of a divine-spiritual nature. Hence every child becomes for us a 'sacred riddle', for every child embodies the question, not how shall I educate him so that he conforms to some abstract picture of man according to this or that theory, but how shall we foster what the spiritual world is manifesting in earth-existence? [32] If we look upon every human life as a sacred riddle, we cannot help contemplating every human being with great inward attention. Through the contemplation of the manifestations of the Divine, through a spiritual-scientific cognition of man, our love of mankind is deepened within us. With this human love, enriched by a study of man which gives 'profundity to the most inward, sacred riddles of life', with this love the teacher and the parent can embark rightly upon the task of education. Then the educator's task is transformed from mere adherence to some abstract ideology (thought out in the head and devoid of life-feeling) or dreamlike mysticism (out of touch with the realities of earth-existence) into a priestly calling. [33]

The essential thing about spiritual science — as we have had occasion to emphasize already — is that it is not mere theoretical teaching. People can be very lucid and know everything 'in their heads', but they are not spiritual-scientists when they merely know things in an ordinary intellectual way. [34] 'Head-knowledge' has no access to Life. It must be transformed into 'Heart-knowledge'. [35] In order that this transformation should be able to take place we must keep inwardly alive and flexible. Or, differently expressed, we need 'to remain young in growing old'. If we do not, 'our hearts grow cold', [36] and heart-warmth, love, cannot then stream into and fructify the head. Head-knowledge can do no other than remain cold theory. But such knowledge need not remain so. 'All head-knowledge can be transformed into heart-knowledge'. [37]

Head-knowledge is transformed into heart-knowledge through heart-warmth, through love. Head-knowledge, theory, fructified by love, is transformed into *heart-wisdom*.

Such knowledge can never be acquired by adopting theories quite unrelated and alien to *life*, which they inevitably must be, if they are based on a 'mechanical', materialistic mode of thought. [38] It can only be attained 'if we have a feeling, a sense for every expression of life and can lovingly enter into all its manifestations'. [39] A living knowledge of man must form the foundation of a true art of education. The following statement by Steiner could well be seen as a guiding principle for such an education: 'Knowledge of man can only be won if love for mankind — in this case love for the child — becomes the mainspring of our work.' [40]

*   *   *   *

On more than one occasion Steiner speaks of the teachers' staff meetings as being the heart of a school. (In the particular instance to which reference is being made here, Steiner's concern was with the teachers of the first Waldorf School founded in 1919 in Stuttgart, but what he says here is relevant to any of the 250 or so Waldorf Schools that have been established throughout the world during the past 62 years.) [41] In these staff meetings every teacher throughout the school shares experiences he has with this or that group of children, or with a particular child, with his colleagues. These meetings, held once a week during term time, contribute greatly towards making the school into a living organism. They function in a similar way, one might say, to the heart in the human body.

It is of paramount importance in these meetings that any observation, any suggestion, made by one teacher to another should be imbued with love for the child under discussion — and with love for the colleague to whom the observation is addressed. Steiner describes the kind of love meant here as being 'the love which belongs to the artistic teacher'. To clarify what he means Steiner characterizes it in the following way: If a man is ill, we feel sympathy for him, sympathy which arises out of a love for humanity. But our love must extend even further than this. If we are to treat a sick man we must also be able to 'love the illness; one must be able to speak of a beautiful illness'. [42] Steiner asks that he should not be misunderstood. We recognize, of course, that for the patient it can be a very serious illness, but for the healer whose task it is to enter into it and treat it lovingly it can be a 'magnificent' illness. We could say that we have here an example of the 'objectivity' of the power of love. Similarly, a boy who, let us say, is being discussed at a teachers' meeting, may be a right ne'er-do-well. But the important thing to recognize is that such a lad, by his very roguery, can sometimes be so extraordinarily interesting that one can but love him deeply. There can be something very 'lovable about a boy who is an exceptional rascal'. [43]

If we can develop a love for what constitutes the totality of the object — including the illness a man is suffering, the roguery of a lad, and so forth — then we approach it from an experience of the whole, not from that of a multiplicity of parts. We approach it, in other words, as a creative artist, not as an analytical scientist. The creative artist in the teacher (and the priest in him) approaches the child in a 'whole-some', in a whole-making, healing way. [44]

*   *   *   *

Before bringing these pages on education to a conclusion let us consider briefly some of Steiner's salient remarks regarding the growing child in relation to the socio-economic life.

If we are in earnest in regard to the creation of a truly social organism, a truly social community, then we need to realize that such an organism can never arise through socialistic programmes for education (e.g. where pupils are given a say in the direction), because if socialism is introduced into schools, its existence in later life, in the community, is preempted. What Steiner means is this. People only become mature enough for a socially just life together in adulthood, if in their childhood — up to the age of about fourteen — their life has been built on true authority rooted in love. To treat children between the ages of seven and fourteen as though they were adults, as though they were 'equals' in the sense that they are capable of independent judgement, of objective discrimination, and so on, is to ignore the manifestations of the spiritual needs of children of that age. Loving authority needs to precede freedom of thought and independent judgement. To treat children of this age as equals in a socialistic sense is to defeat the purpose of the exercise. Such treatment is based on an ideology remote from the realities of life. [45]

There is in this connection a phenomenon to which a teacher should pay careful attention. A young person, in his early and middle teens, is not fully able to judge a social injustice that may take place in his environment. His reasoning power is not mature enough. However, feelings in such matters often help us to judge truly well before our reason is mature enough to do so. 'A noble nature will, already in childhood, be moved to a righteous, noble anger by anything like injustice, although it may be only in his feelings that his soul can sense the injustice.' 'When this noble sense of indignation is to be found in the character of a child, we ought to take particular note of it, because the judgement of feeling aroused by the injustice remains in the soul. This noble anger in early youth permeates the soul and, as life goes on, becomes transformed. In the second half it reappears in a differnt form as the quality of loving kindness and goodness. We do not often find such loving goodness in the latter part of a person's life without finding that, in his early years, it found expression in a noble anger' — aroused by some form of social injustice. We, as teachers and parents, should endeavour lovingly to understand and appreciate this noble anger. In such understanding the 'soil' is nourished which later will allow loving kindness to manifest itself in the grown man. 'The hand that never clenched its fist in noble anger in the first half of life will not easily be stretched forth in blessing in the latter half.' [46]

The nature of freedom — freedom in the spiritual sphere — is touched upon elsewhere in these pages and we need not dwell on it further here, but the point to bear in mind in our present context is this: it is not only spiritual freedom which should develop in the human being after puberty — between the ages of, say, fourteen and twenty-one, but also universal human love. [47] Now, it is clear from all that we have been considering hitherto that this power of universal human love should be specially fostered. For, if it is not developed during the third seven-year period, the economic life will never be warmed through by brotherly love as it should be. Brotherliness is only possible in the economic sphere — the sphere of greatest conflict in our modern world — on the foundation of true universal human love.

Brotherliness, fraternity in economic life — towards the realization of which it is essential we strive — 'can only arise in human souls if education after the fifteenth year works consciously towards universal human love. That is, if all concepts concerning the world and education itself are based on human love.' [48]

If from the fourteenth year onwards we do not infuse all education with the power of universal love a sound economic life will never emerge. And, of paramount importance too, only if love is developed in the right way, will freedom in the spiritual sphere be possible. [49]

18.

CLAIRVOYANCE, OUR EGO AND LOVE

In all thy ways on earth
Thou must not lose thyself;
Mankind doth not attain
To sun-kissed distances
If he would rob himself of personality.
So then prepare thyself,
Press on through earthly love
To utmost depths of heart
Which ripens cosmic love. [1]

18.

In regard to our Ego and the development of clairvoyance, Steiner makes the following significant comments.

When, through *rightly* developed clairvoyance, [2] an awakening to the supersensible worlds takes place, the 'inner link' with the physical world is not lost. The memory of the soul's experiences in this world remains. If this were not the case, then other beings and events would be present in clairvoyant consciousness, but not our own being. We would be 'possessed'. We would have no knowledge of ourselves in relation to beings and events in the supersensible worlds.

In the light of this, it is clear that rightly developed clairvoyance must at the same time entail the cultivation of a strong Ego-feeling. [3] However, the strong Ego-feeling we are here visualizing is not one in which egoism dominates. That is not the kind of strong Ego-feeling that is meant. Let us look at this a little more closely.

As Steiner points out, an over-developed Ego-feeling, in earth-existence, works against morality. An Ego-feeling too weakly developed causes the soul to be lacking in inner firmness and stability. In order that the Ego-feeling should be strong in a living, creative way it must be permeated by feelings of 'good-fellowship, sympathy, and love'. [4]

It is, then, essential that the soul's feeling of self, its experience of the Ego, should be modified by the power of love. It is then possible for the soul to undergo a training to attain 'the noblest of moral forces, that of feeling with another'. [5] If, on the other hand, a strong Ego-feeling, or rather a strong Egocentric feeling, projects itself into the soul's conscious experiences within the physical world, then moral impulses and ideas cannot develop in the right way, they would be quite unable to bring forth such fruits of love as, for instance, the experiencing of another being in one's own soul. [6] Love, 'the most important result for man of his experience in the physical world' [7] would be lacking.

'We may say that on becoming clairvoyantly conscious the human soul awakes in the spiritual world; but we must also say that, in love, the spiritual awakes in the physical world. Where love and fellow-feeling are stirring in human life, we sense the magic breath of the spirit interpenetrating the physical world.' Rightly developed clairvoyance can never weaken sympathy and love, for such clairvoyance is rooted in a love-imbued sense of self. Without such roots the individuality must inevitably lose itself. 'The more the soul feels itself at home in spiritual worlds' — and if the individuality is lost this feeling cannot arise — 'the more it feels lovelessness and lack of fellow-feeling to be a denial of spirit itself.' [8]

'True love and real kindness of heart are experiences of the soul which strengthen the forces of consciousness in the way necessary for acquiring exact clairvoyance' [9] — a form of clairvoyance in which a strong Ego-feeling in the sense outlined is lacking is diffuse, subject to constant error and often unbalancing for the soul. A basic requirement in the process of preparation of the soul for the spiritual faculty of clairvoyance is the capacity for selfless love with its inherent disposition towards genuine human kindness and fellow-feeling; and selfless love, in its turn, is both dependent on and instrumental in the cultivation of the strong Ego-feeling needed to 'find one's way' in and investigate in full consciousness, spiritual worlds, their beings and events. 'The life of feeling has great significance for Ego power. Love heightens the power of the Ego; envy and hate cause it to wither. If a man hates his fellow-man, if he disparages his worth by speaking falsely of him, he weakens thereby his own Ego power; he diminishes health and vitality within himself.' [10]

In the first of a series of lectures published under the title, *Between Death and Rebirth*, Steiner makes the following poignant remark: 'A human being feels that his Ego has a certain value in the great household of the world, but he can lessen this value. How do we diminish the value of our Ego? If, for example, we hurt someone whom we perhaps ought to love, at that moment we have actually diminished the value of our Ego. We are of less value in our Ego after we have done someone an undeserved injury'. [11]

If we wish to understand the relationship between our Ego and love we could begin by asking the questions: What then is essential for love to manifest itself? What is essential in order that one person should love another? Steiner gives an answer which, at first sight — as so often in such delicate matters — appears paradoxical. We have touched on this already, but the point cannot be too often emphasized. His answer is quite simply: In order that one person may truly love another he must be in possession of his full Ego-consciousness. Expressed differently we could say: that he must be wholly independent. 'No one can love another in the full sense of the word if this love be not a *free* gift from one person to another. Only he who is independent, who is not *bound* to the other person, can love him. To this end the human being had to become an Ego-being.' [12]

Ego-consciousness, Egoism, has a good and a bad side. [13] It is the foundation of human independence and freedom, on the one side, but, on the other, also of all that is bad and evil. But in the course of evolution we had to go through the development of egoism, if we were to be given the seed of doing good out of our own free will. Through the divine forces which had guided him before the 'descent' from the Garden of Eden man 'would always have been impelled to do the good'. [14] If we had remained under the sole influences of these forces, we would always do the good without any conscious thought, feeling or act of will. If spiritual development were to take place, however, we had to be given the possibility of going our own way. Just as we have descended so must we ascend again to spirituality; and just as the 'descent' was linked with the increasing predominance of egoism, so does the 'ascent' depend on our selflessness, on our feeling of love and sympathy for one another growing stronger and stronger. [15]

We can see — to elaborate further on the two-fold aspect of the Ego — what a sharp two-edged sword the Ego of man is. On the one hand, as already indicated, this Ego is the cause that we harden within ourselves, that we desire to draw into the service of ourselves not only all our inner capacities, but also all the outer objects of the world — including our fellow-men. It is this aspect of the Ego that causes us to direct all our wishes and activities towards satisfying it at the cost of all others; which causes us to draw to ourselves as our own possession a part of the earth, which belongs to all, to drive away all the other Egos from its realm, to fight them, and be constantly at variance with them. On the other hand, it must be stressed again, we must not forget that the Ego is also that which gives us our independence and our inner freedom, that 'elevates' us above all other creatures on the earth. The 'dignity of man is founded in this Ego, it is the basis of the Divine in man'. [16]

This conception of the Ego — which has been put forward here only in barest outline — offers difficulty to many people today, particularly among those who suggest, without discriminating between the two aspects just discussed, that the Ego should be overcome, 'cast out', so to speak. [17]

If we consider spiritual evolution we can see, says Steiner, that this Ego of man has developed from a group-soul nature, [18] from a kind of all-inclusive universal Ego out of which the individual Ego has been differentiated. It would be a retrogressive step if we were to crave to dissolve our individual Egos into some sort of universal consciousness, into some sort of communal consciousness. 'Everything', says Steiner, 'which causes man to strive to lose his Ego and dissolve it into a universal consciousness, is the result of weakness.' [19]

He alone, states Steiner, understands the Ego who knows that after he has gained it in the course of cosmic evolution it cannot be lost; and above all man must strive for the strength — if he understands the mission of the earth — to make the Ego more and more inward, spiritualized and divine. True spiritual science cannot agree that the Ego should be dissolved into a universal self, should be 'melted' 'into a sort of primeval sea'. It sees the need to correct this erroneous thinking and to stress that the final goal is a community of free, independent Egos, [20] of Egos which have reached an intense degree of individualization — for, as already emphasized several times, only thus is selfless love, spiritualized love, love born of freedom, possible. It is the mission of Earth-life, of the Earth stage of evolution as a whole, to develop love, to attain to spiritualized love. And, it cannot be repeated often enough, this can only be achieved if Egos face one another freely. 'Love is not perfect if it proceeds from coercion.' 'It is the divine plan to make this Ego so independent that as an individual being in all freedom man can offer love — even to God.' It would amount to man being like a marionette if he could, even in the slightest degree, be 'forced' to love. 'Thus,' says Steiner, 'the Ego will be the pledge for the highest goal of man. But at the same time, if it does not discover love, if it hardens within itself, it is the tempter that plunges man into the abyss.' For it is that which separates men from one another, which brings them to war against one another, to compete against each other — instead of emulating each other — in every branch of life. 'Thus in every field of life the Ego can become the apple of discord. Hence we may say that the Ego can lead, on the one hand, to the highest and, on the other, to the lowest. For this reason, it is a sharp two-edged sword. And because He brought the full Ego-consciousness to man, Christ Jesus, is . . . symbolically represented in the Apocalypse as one who has the sharp two-edged sword in his mouth.' [21]

Commenting on the picture of the abyss in which is found a humanity unable to receive the Christ Impulse, which has remained 'stuck' in matter, excluding itself, so to speak, from the spiritualizing process leading into the future; commenting on this abyss in which the Beast of the Apocalypse, with the seven heads and ten horns, glowers at us, Steiner says: 'Many might ask: Is it not hard and unwise on the part of Providence to lead a number of men to such a frightful fate, and in a way, to condemn them to the abyss of evil? Would it not have been more fitting for a wise Providence to have averted this frightful fate from the very beginning?' [22]

Steiner's answer may be summed up as follows. If it were impossible for us to sink into the abyss of evil, we would also not have been given the possibility of attaining 'love' and 'freedom'. A man unable to choose good or evil, of his own free will, would be a being who would merely be directed to an unavoidable good and who would have no inner power to choose the good of his own purified will and out of a love which springs from freedom. If, in other words, it were impossible for man to succumb to the enticements of the apocalyptic monster, it would also be impossible for him to follow Christ out of his own individual, spiritualized love. 'It was in accordance with a wise Providence to give the possibility of freedom to humanity . . . and this possibility of freedom could be given on no other condition than that man himself has to make the free choice between good and evil.' [23]

In the early centuries of Christianity there was a saying which ran: 'Christus verus Luciferus', i.e. Christ is the true Light-bearer. Why, asks Steiner, is Christ called the true Light-bearer? Because through Him that was born into evolution which, prior to his coming, was 'premature', namely, spiritual independence. Through the Ego-impulse which streamed into humanity through Christ, men, as individuals, were given the possibility of unfolding selfless love for one another. Thus what Lucifer — as the Tempter in the Garden of Eden — wished to give to humanity in anticipation, prematurely, before humanity was sufficiently mature to receive it, was brought to humanity 'at the turning-point of time' by the true Light-bearer, Christ. He brought the impulse to independence, but he also brought the spiritual love which unites. The Love principle of Christ brings Egos together, makes communities of individuals, communities founded in conscious, selfless love and freedom. [24]

*   *   *   *

On several occasions Steiner discusses the question of immortality in relation to the individuality, to the Ego and to the power of Love.

There is, says Steiner, a certain amount of confusion among people when they speak of the immortality of the soul. If immortality is admitted at all, what is often meant is that the being of the human soul passes through the Gates of Death and then finds some place or other in the Universal All. But every created thing does that, even the mineral passes over into the Universal All when it dissolves, as also does the plant that fades and the animal that dies. However, man has a special significance in this cosmic process. Immortality for him has quite a different meaning. Indeed, immortality for man only has real meaning 'when he can "carry" his consciousness with him through the Gates of Death. Picture to yourselves an immortal human soul that was unconscious after death; such immortality would have absolutely no meaning at all.' [25]

It is, of course, true that for most people today consciousness extends only as far as death. This is, however, not the same as saying that we lack consciousness in the spiritual world — albeit a different form of consciousness from that of which we usually think. Steiner never tires of stressing that the 'life' of the human soul in the spiritual world is no inactive one. [26] As we have seen elsewhere in these pages man exists there in continuous activity. Among other things, he co-operates with the higher Hierarchies in the development of the Earth in the most important way. It is only for the modern consciousness of man a kind of sleep state; for another consciousness, however, it appears as a much more active, more real condition, than the one we know on earth.

Our consciousness has gone through, and will continue to go through, a process of evolution. [27] Our consciousness today is not that of, say, the ancient Hebrew people. Into the consciousness possessed by the Hebrew people — a consciousness limited to the period between birth and death — there shone the Divine Will — for example, in the Ten Commandments. But this Divine Will, this illumination, could not stimulate man's consciousness to such a degree that it could say to itself: I pass as a conscious being through the Gates of Death. As Steiner reminds us, Job, for instance, was not able to be certain of this.

To the Jews was given *Will*, through the Law. To the disciples of the Ancient Mysteries was given *Wisdom*. Here again we have the testimony from heathendom as to the uncertainty felt by man concerning his immortality: 'Better a beggar in the Upper World than a King in the Realm of Shades'.

In his search for certainty in regard to immortality, Man has to become increasingly aware of the fact that his own nature is inseparably bound up with love. 'Neither Will nor Wisdom can give to man what he needs during this search; only Love can give man what he needs'. [28] can give him certainty in regard to his immortality.

Love is nothing we appropriate to ourselves through the Will; Love is nothing that we appropriate to ourselves through Wisdom; Love dwells in the region of the feelings, and we know that we could not be the ideal human soul, if that soul could not be filled with love. When we penetrate into the nature of the soul, we realize that our human soul would no longer be a human soul if it could not love. [29]

'But now, let us suppose', suggests Steiner, 'that we were to pass through the Gates of Death in such a way that our human individuality were lost, and that we were to be united with some Universal Divinity. We should then be within this Divinity; we should belong to it. We could no longer love the Godhead; we should be within it. Love would have no meaning, if we were *within* the Godhead. If we could not carry our individuality' — and, therefore, consciousness — 'through death, we should in death have to lose love. One being can love another, only if that other being is separate from itself; if we carry our love of God through death, we must carry with us through death that which kindles love within us, our individuality' [30] — our individuality in Christ.

What came to pass through the Divine Deed of Love on Golgotha? Through this Deed the beginning was made, whereby the vision that man once had as a 'natural' gift, and through which his immortality was evident to him, was restored to him. 'In the overcoming of death on Golgotha the forces originated which could rekindle in the soul the powers which had been lost. And the path of man through earth evolution will henceforth be this: inasmuch as he takes the Christ more and more into himself he

will discover that within himself which can love beyond death —
that is to say, he can stand before his God as an immortal
individuality.' [31]

Will was given through the Ten Commandments, Wisdom
through the Mysteries. 'But Love was given when God became
man in Christ Jesus. And the certainty that we can love beyond
death', that we are immortal, that by means of the powers with
which our souls are endowed through the Mystery of Golgotha 'a
community of love can be founded between God and man and all
men among one another' [32] — this certainty proceeds from the
Mystery of Golgotha.

19.

SELF-LOVE

Progress in spiritual training is out of the question, unless progress is made at the same time in the ethical sphere. Lack of moral strength makes conquest of self-conceit impossible. [1]

19.

In 1918 Steiner published a book, *A Road to Self-Knowledge*, which he described as an amplification of *Knowledge of the Higher Worlds. How is it achieved?* — both of which were born of his spiritual vision, the nature of which was such that he could conduct his observations, at a very high level of consciousness, with full discriminatory power and 'scientific' exactitude. In *A Road to Self-Knowledge*, which he wrote in the form of eight meditations, Steiner is concerned to give an account of the experiences of the soul as it progresses along the path to the Spirit.

At a certain stage in our spiritual development we attain a special means of self-knowledge: we learn to contemplate ourselves from a standpoint outside ourselves. An example of this objective self-contemplation could be the painful realization that one has been in gross error in regard to an opinion of a fellow-man. Such a realization, together with the depressing feeling which arises in one's soul as a consequence of it, marks a clear step forward towards true self-knowledge, towards a recognition of the true nature of one's own soul. [2]

It is a common experience to feel such enlightenment in regard to oneself as painful. However, it is just through this experience of pain that, for example, we learn to see how strong is the desire to feel ourselves to be human beings of importance and special value — more important and of greater value to the community than our next door neighbour; an ugly fact, an ugliness of our self which we have to face without prejudice, a fact which, before embarking upon the path of spiritual self-development, we had not noticed — 'because we had never consciously taken ourselves in hand and penetrated deeply enough into our own being'. When we do this, sincerely and honestly, we cannot but perceive how dearly we love many traits within ourselves which, once recognized, must be felt as ugly. 'The power of self-love shows itself in all its enormity.' [3] Equally important, we also recognize how little inclination we normally have to discard this self-love.

Such a kind of self-knowledge manifests itself when experience 'outside' the physical body[4] begins, when supersensible experience begins, for then our self-knowledge becomes an objective, true one, and, as Steiner puts it, 'we are no longer troubled by any desire to find ourselves modelled in any particular fashion we may have set ourselves'. [5]

The need for absolute honesty — and courage — in ourselves, if we are truly to distinguish between self-love and love of others, is stressed by Steiner. In particular these qualities are called for in a very high degree if we are to undertake spiritual scientific research into reincarnation and karmic relationships.

Steiner indicates very clearly the things to which we should pay particular attention. [6]

Self-love is present in each one of us, even in those of us who imagine they are entirely free of it.

Steiner makes some cogent remarks concerning the nature of self-love in relation to our feelings of love for others. He prefaces the point he wishes to make by the statement that of all forms of knowledge, the knowledge of the human being himself, of self-knowledge, is decidedly the most difficult and most likely to be subject to illusion. 'It may be said that man is extraordinarily fond of himself and it is this self-love that causes him to transform self-knowledge into a source of illusion. For instance, a man prefers not to admit that in his thinking he is an anti-social being.' [7] But it is in particular in our feelings of love for others that we fall prey to illusion. 'However strange it may seem to ordinary, everyday consciousness, it is nevertheless true that the love manifesting itself between one person and another, if it is not spiritualized — and love is seldom spiritualized in ordinary life' is not really love as such, but an image the person 'loving' makes of love. 'It is generally nothing more than a terrible illusion, because the love one person believes he feels towards another is, for the most part, nothing but self-love ... *What he feels* as a state of rapture in his own soul in association with the other person, *what he experiences* within himself by reason of the fact that he is in the presence of the other person ... *this* is what he really loves.' [8] In general, we could, therefore, say that in his social relationships with the other person it is self-love that is enkindled. 'This', Steiner continues, 'is an important mystery in human life and is of enormous significance. This love that a person supposes is real, selfless love, is, in reality, masked Egoism. This self-love — masked as real love — is the source of the most widespread anti-social impulses. Through it a person becomes in preeminent degree an anti-social being.' [9]

'Love can actually become a strong force working in the direction of the anti-social life.' We can, in fact, assert that he who does not undertake self-discipline, does not undertake the difficult task of spiritualizing love, is invariably an anti-social being when he loves. 'Love, unless he who loves practises self-discipline, is pre-destined to be anti-social, for it is exclusive.' This statement is not to be understood as being condemnatory of all expressions of such love. 'In the very nature of things, a father will love his own son more than a strange child.' [10] However, viewed objectively, we must concede that such love is exclusive and, it follows, anti-social — such love does not embrace humanity.

In more general terms we may say, in regard to personal, social relationships, that the 'curing of the ills of our age depends largely upon whether people will cease to be so intensely fond of themselves'. [11]

There are very few of whom it could be said that they are entirely free of self-love, of self-esteem. [12] In such cases, says Steiner, a close investigation of karma would be called for to determine why such freedom exists. Now love of others may, of course, be absolutely genuine, but it is very seldom that it is not coloured by some element or other of self-love. We may love someone because he does us a kind service; because he shows us affection; because he is by our side, with sympathy, in a situation which would cause us extreme distress, if we had to face it alone. Many are the reasons which cause us to 'love' another. But if we look closely, objectively, at these reasons and at the feeling of love engendered in our souls, we recognize in most, if not all, cases, that an element of self-love is present to a greater or lesser degree.

'Nevertheless, there *is* such a thing as selfless love and it is within our reach.' [13] Once we are aware of the need for objective self-observation, we can learn, gradually, 'to expel from love every vestige of self-interest'. For some of us this may be relatively easy; for others extremely difficult. We then come to know what it really means to surrender ourselves to others in a true and complete sense. All vestiges of those aspects of our Ego attached to that which is personal, as distinct from universal, dissolve in the moment of complete self-surrender, of genuine selfless, spiritualized love.

Now the point Steiner makes in connection with incarnation

and karmic relationships is that it is in and from this self-giving, this selfless love, that we can kindle the feeling that has to be born in our soul, if we are to glimpse earlier earth-lives.

Steiner asks us to look at a concrete example. A man lived in, say, the eighth or ninth century. He is alive again now. The personality which was alive, in a physical body, some 1,000 years ago and the personality alive today are linked by the spiritual life 'stretching' between the death of the former and the birth of the latter. Now, before even so much as a glimmer can arise in the twentieth-century man of the personality who lived in the eighth or ninth century, 'he must first be capable of loving his own self in exactly the same way as if he were loving another human being ' — loving the other person selflessly. He must surrender his self in order to know himself. For, although the being who lived some 1,000 years ago is within him now, he is a 'stranger' exactly in the same way as another person may be a stranger to him now. 'He must be able to relate himself to his preceding incarnation in the same way as he relates himself now to some other human being — otherwise no inkling of the earlier incarnation is possible. Love that is truly selfless becomes a power of knowledge.' [14] When love of self becomes so objective that we can observe ourselves as we would, lovingly, observe other human beings, then this selfless love is the means by which earlier earth-lives reveal themselves to us.

*   *   *   *

In an open letter written to the members of the Anthroposophical Society a few weeks before he died, [15] Steiner draws our attention very forcibly to the distinction between 'spirit-love' and self-love, and brings the two into relation with the cosmic powers of the Christ and the Archangel Michael, the conqueror of the Dragon, of Ahriman.

When we seek freedom selflessly, with no element of Egoism in our striving; when freedom really is to us pure love for the action we seek to perform; then, says Steiner, it is possible for us to draw near to the archangelic power of Michael. [16] If, however, we seek freedom in order to create a platform for our Egoism; if freedom is to us 'the *pride* of feeling that in an action we give expression to *ourselves* — then we are in danger of falling under the dominion of Ahriman'. [17]

The deed performed out of love for others is a Michaelic Deed; the deed performed out of self-love is Ahrimanic.

Michael is our guide to the Christ. He goes through the cosmic world in clear spirit-love. He who follows Michael cherishes love for the earth-world; and love must unfold itself to this world — else it turns to self-love. The 'love for the other', if cherished in the Michael-heart and -mind, is reflected back into the self, and the self will then love, without self-love. In the light of such selfless love, the soul of man finds Christ. He who follows Michael cherishes love to the outer world and thereby finds that relation to the inner world of his own soul which brings him together with Christ. [18]

We grow ever more into our true humanity, as we grow to be an expression of the World. We find ourselves, not by seeking our selves, but by uniting ourselves to the World with will in love. 'In making himself an expression of his own separate self, man becomes ever less and less the expression of his innermost being. In *seeking* himself, he loses himself . . . ' [19] Man realizes his true self only when he loves the world. Human self-knowledge is world-knowledge. When friends asked for an autograph, Steiner often wrote down for them the following lines:

If thou would'st know thy Self
Look out into the Cosmic Spaces.
If thou would'st fathom the Cosmic Spaces,
Look inwards, into thine own Self.

Willst Du Dein Selbst erkennen,
Schaue hinaus in die Weltenweiten.
Willst Du die Weltenweiten durchschauen,
Blicke hinein in das eigene Selbst. [20]

We can attain no living conception of the world if we do not seek it by a spiritual perception of Man. For the ancient truth that Man is a microcosm — a true world in miniature — is as valid today as it ever was. Steiner goes so far as to say: 'Man has all the secrets and the riddles of the great world, the macrocosm, concealed in his own nature'. [21]

If we understand this in the right sense, then every time we look into our inner being, our attention will be directed to the world around us. Self-knowledge will become the door to world-knowledge. But if we take it in the wrong sense, our 'study of ourselves will become an imprisonment, and we shall lose our feeling for the world. World-knowledge is the door to self-know-ledge'. [22]

If we strive to know ourselves, what we gain in self-knowledge should quicken our vision to perceive how all that which is there within ourselves is there too in our fellow-men. We can feel what another man is undergoing, if we have experienced something similar within ourselves. So long as we are lacking in experience ourselves, we pass over the experience of another without really perceiving it. On the other hand, we have also to be inwardly alert to the fact that our feelings may become so fettered by our own experiences that we cannot enter with understanding into the experience of our fellow-man. [23]

If we remain alert to these 'dangers' then we can 'prevent self-knowledge degenerating into self-love'. Self-knowledge should always lead over to love and sympathy for our fellow-men. Once we have achieved genuine, selfless interest in our fellow-men, we shall certainly not be lacking in interest in the world, in world events, in general.

All too familiar is the refrain: my busy life leaves me no time and peace to study and assimilate spiritual science. Such a person feels himself overburdened with 'external' work, not realizing that it is just in the 'external' world that spiritual scientific work, spiritual development, must be pursued. What is equally import-ant to realize is that the reverse situation should not come about. 'Love of spiritual science must not prevent our joyous devotion to the needs of life. If it does, then any spiritual scientific work will never have the true warmth it must have, but will degenerate into cold selfishness', [24] into arid self-love. 'The study of spiritual science ought not to lead to a depreciation of external life.' [25]

*   *   *   *

Nothing is really so difficult in life for us as the attainment of real self-knowledge. We can experience many remarkable things in this respect not only in other people, but, of course, also in ourselves. For instance, we may convince others — and ourselves — that we are doing this or that from completely unselfish motives, that we want nothing at all for ourselves, and so on. Yet if we look a little deeper into ourselves, we often find that, though we imagine that we are selfless, in our subconsciousness we are thorough Egoists and only want what suits our Ego. As we have already noted, there is nothing in which we can be so easily deceived as about ourselves, if we do not always take care to exercise a genuine, honest self-knowledge. [26]

As already emphasized, true self-knowledge is absolutely necessary in making the ascent into higher worlds — indeed, without such knowledge the ascent is impossible. When we really know ourselves, then we cease to indulge in self-love. During the course of our spiritual development we will reach a stage when we have to say to ourselves: 'As I am *now*, I must eliminate myself'. [27]

Before making this stern statement, Steiner had indicated the necessity for self-surrender, which he describes as a preparatory step to the elimination of self-love, of egoistic love. Steiner is clearly not suggesting here that we should cease to love that which expresses itself, in no matter how small a measure, as the Higher Self, as the Christ Essence in us. It may serve to clarify what he does mean in this particular instance by referring to what he says regarding the necessity and meaning of self-surrender.

Surrender in the sense that Steiner means here can be described as 'a state of mind that does not seek to investigate truth (for instance) from out of itself (the mind), but which looks for truth to come from the revelation that flows towards it out of the things, and can wait until it is mature enough to receive the revelation. An inclination to judge, or form opinions, wants to be continually arriving at truth; surrender, on the other hand, does not seek to force an entrance, as it were, into this or that truth.' In such a state of mind we seek rather 'to educate ourselves and then quietly wait until we attain that stage of maturity where the truth flows to us from the things of the world, coming to us in revelation. To work with patience, knowing that patience will bring us further and further in wise self-education — that is the mood of surrender'. [28]

In this self-surrender we have gone a long way to overcoming self-love in the sense indicated above.

In such surrender lies the foundation for the unfolding and development of the love impulse in life. He who has never known what it is to 'surrender' his own self, to 'withdraw' from his own self, is quite unable to cultivate that devotion to another person which reveals itself in love. 'In such a person the apprehension of the spiritual can easily harden into lovelessness.' [29] He becomes a prey to the forces of Ahriman. A loveless, intellectual apprehension of the spiritual often brings with it a disdain for what is revealed in the outer, material world, and vice versa.

True spiritual science, says Steiner, does not seek the spirit because it finds nature devoid of spirit, and therefore worthy of contempt — on the contrary, it desires to seek the spirit in nature. [30]

> The sphere of the Spirit is the soul's true home,
> And Man will surely reach it
> By walking in the path of honest Thought;
> By choosing as his guide the fount of Love
> Implanted in his heart;
> By opening the eye of his soul
> To Nature's script
> Spread out before him through all the Universe,
> Telling the story of the Spirit
> In all that lives and thrives,
> And in the silent spaciousness of lifeless things,
> And in the stream of Time — the process of becoming. [31]

If we do not shut out completely all those things in us that we quite like to feel in us — errors, trivialities, prejudices, sympathies, antipathies — if we do not eliminate these, then our ascent into higher worlds cannot be made aright . . . for if we have anything left of self-love, or of desires that cling to the personal in us, or if we are still capable of making any judgement on purely personal grounds, then all such things can harm our health — both of our physical body and of our etheric body — when we follow the path of development into higher worlds. [32]

Steiner also considers self-surrender in a wider context. It should always be a matter for reflection, he points out, that during life on earth the human spirit is embodied in the material world. It has surrendered itself to an existence in matter. 'Life in the material world is, for man, that stage of existence in which he can perceive the spiritual *in a picture* separate from, but reflecting its reality; and a being who is unable to experience the spirit even in a picture-form cannot come to desire the spirit *freely*, out of his own inner nature.' [33]

*   *   *   *

At the beginning of this chapter the distinction between true love and self-love was drawn. What a man supposes to be true love for another person, as was said then, often turns out to be only self-love.

In this connection Rudolf Steiner says that when love appears

in the physical world and works within human life as the
foundation of moral life in the human order of the world it is
protected from every Luciferic attack. Lucifer cannot harm the
kind of love we have for another person that is cultivated for that
other person's sake. 'This love wherein the cause does not lie in
the one who loves, but in the one who is loved, this kind of love in
the physical world is immune to any form of Luciferic impulse.' [34]

We need not characterize egoistic and self-love again, but just
remind ourselves that a salient element in it is that a person loves
because he himself has certain propensities which thereby feel
satisfied. In other words, such a person loves for his own sake —
not for another's; he loves because his natural disposition finds its
satisfaction in loving another.

Now, with regard to egoistic love, though in general it needs to
be eliminated, nevertheless there is one all-significant exception.
When we turn our thinking, feeling and willing towards the
spiritual world it is justified. For all that love can cause to live in us
as a longing for and as impulse upwards to the spiritual world
must exist. [35] All that lives in us as an impulse to 'grasp' the beings
of the spiritual world, to recognize the spiritual world, springs
from an 'egoistic love' for the spiritual world. We are beings who
have our 'roots' in the spiritual world and we long to 're-root'
ourselves in that world of our origin. 'It is our duty', says Steiner,
'to make ourselves as perfect as possible', to spiritualize ourselves
as much as possible — not merely for our own sakes, but for that
of the whole of humanity, the Angels and Lucifer.

For this reason we must love the spiritual world, so that we may
draw as many forces as possible out of it into our being. In short,
in love of the spiritual this personal, individual element, this
'egoistic' element of love, is fully justified, for it leads us into the
spiritual world, it leads us to a fulfilment of the duty of perfecting
ourselves.

Lucifer, says Steiner, has the tendency to mingle these two
worlds, the physical and the spiritual, one with the other.
Wherever we love, in the physical world, with an admixture of
egoism, i.e. for our own sake, there Lucifer is active in his
endeavour to make physical love similar to spiritual love —
egoistic. All love in the physical world that does not exist for the
sake of the beloved but for that of the one who loves is exposed to
the impulses of Lucifer. Lucifer cannot touch selfless love, but
selfish love, directed towards the physical world, nourishes him.
'In our modern materialistic civilization there is every reason to

draw attention to the Luciferic allurements with regard to love —
for a great part of our present day outlook . . . is permeated with
this egoistic, Luciferic conception of love on earth.' [36]

In a lecture [37] given about the same time as he published the
basic work *The Threshold of the Spiritual World*, [38] Steiner imparts
to us knowledge he attained, through exact clairvoyance, of the
experiences of those souls who, in the spiritual world, look back
upon a life on earth in which lovelessness and a lack of feeling for
others held sway.

He introduces this theme by pointing out that those who learn
clairvoyantly to experience the higher worlds know that ordinary
sense-consciousness is, in reality and in comparison with what a
man feels and experiences in the spiritual worlds, a kind of sleep.
They also know that on entering into the spiritual worlds a
process of awakening begins, an awakening with a strengthened
feeling of the true self. Having stated this, Steiner then goes on to
say that there is, however, a force which does awaken man on the
physical plane, does awaken him out of spiritual sleep, and this
force is love. [39] He means here the kind of love that exists for the
sake of the beloved. Such love brings about an awakening of the
true self. Such love, as we have already seen, is protected from the
Luciferic forces — and, he says in this lecture, also from the
influence of Ahriman. The lack of such selfless love in the
physical world shows itself to clairvoyant consciousness. What we
develop in the way of egoism, lovelessness and selfishness, in the
physical world manifests itself clearly when it is 'brought up' into
the spiritual world. Steiner tells us that nothing is so disturbing,
no experience is so embittering, as that which we carry up as the
result of the lack of feeling 'for the other' in the physical world.
When we cross the Threshold, either through clairvoyance or
after death, everything manifests itself — not only the 'open but
also the hidden egoism that rages in the depths of our souls'. [40]

Lovelessness and lack of true sympathy, taken into the spiritual
worlds, transform themselves into hideous and frequently terrifying forms.

This experience confronts us all to a greater or lesser degree
when we cross the Threshold and it needs to be undergone with
courage and honesty. [41] Confronted with these disagreeable
aspects of ourselves — both here on earth when we have reached
a certain stage in our inner development and after death — we
need to say to ourselves: 'Well now, you are harbouring so much
egoism, you had better face it freely and honestly.' This would be

the healthy and positive approach. [42] But, as we all know, the soul has the tendency to take the easy way out and to turn a 'blind eye' to all that is disagreeable and terrifying within itself. Such a lack of conscious acceptance of, say, egoism, plays straight into the arms of Lucifer and Ahriman. Their purpose is to tempt the human soul away from the Christ, away from the 'true' spiritual worlds, and to lead it into their own 'kingdoms', 'where they can place before it all sorts of spiritual worlds, which the human soul then looks upon as the true spiritual world grounded in the cosmic order. We may say that the development of true, real love, earnest and honest sympathy, is a good preparation for the soul which aspires to rise with clear vision into the spiritual worlds', [43] into the world of the Cosmic Christ.

20.

EGOISM AND ALTRUISM

In purest outpoured Light
Shimmers the Godhead of the world.
In purest Love toward all that lives
Outpours the god-hood of my soul.
I rest within the Godhead of the world;
There shall I find myself,
Within the Godhead of the world. [1]

20.

Contrasting the soul qualities of egoism and altruism, Steiner makes the following interesting observation. There are instances in ordinary human life in which egoism may be said to expand beyond the personality and where, to a certain extent, we need to regard this 'expansion' of egoism as a necessary element in life. An example of this is mother-love. It is characteristic of much mother-love, particularly perhaps among the so-called less developed peoples, that there is what we might call a lioness-like way in which mothers protect their children. The mother's self is 'extended' to her child; an attack upon her child is felt by her to be an attack upon her self. What she feels in herself she carries over to her child 'and it is a fortunate provision of nature that egoism can be transferred in this way from one person to another'. We can see that egoism ceases to have a 'dark' side when a human being thus expands himself; when he transfers his feelings and thinking to someone, something beyond himself. Such an extended egoism may be said to be selfless in that the person who harbours it protects, cherishes and takes care of beings, objects, other than himself. On the other hand, under certain circumstances, what we call altruism may be very self-seeking. [2]

We can make beautiful systems with such ideas as egoism and altruism, says Steiner, but the facts of life often tear such systems apart. For, as just mentioned, when egoism so extends its interests that it feels itself responsible for what is around it, then it becomes selflessness to a large extent. On the other hand, when altruism takes on the form that one wishes to make the whole world happy and joyful only according to one's *own* ideas, when one wishes to impress one's *own* thoughts and feelings on the world, then altruism may become self-seeking. [3]

Selfish egoism and selfish altruism — from what has just been said, the meanings of both terms are apparent — can both be overcome when our interests include the whole of the earth and humanity. The interests of humanity must become our interests. To overcome these two qualities of soul our interests must cease to be solely connected with the merely personal. We need to reach the point of feeling, of knowing, everything connected with the development of the earth and of humanity as being an 'extension' of ourselves — not only what belongs to our family by blood, by inheritance, and so on, but the whole of mankind. Then we begin to experience true love and universal brotherhood.

It can be observed, says Steiner, that while, in many so-called occult societies selflessness, universal love, is preached as a moral principle and repeated again and again, yet egoism flourishes. Caution is called for, Steiner warns, when it is found that in such a society universal human love is made into a much-talked of axiom or, differently phrased, is always being spoken of as distinct from becoming a life-principle — for under certain conditions of soul-life a person speaks most frequently of what he least possesses. 'We can often observe that fundamental truths are most often emphazied by those who are most in want of them.'⁴

Universal human love should become something in the development of humanity which completely 'rules' the human soul, something which lives in the soul as self-evident. About the self-evident one needs hardly to speak. It exists. It is. Steiner states that just as the commandment says: 'Thou shalt not take the Name of God in vain', so might one say to a true and noble humanity: 'Thou shalt not utter so often in vain the requirement of Universal Human Love'. 'For if silence is in many cases a better means of developing a quality than speech, it is particularly the case in this matter!'⁵ To cultivate it quietly in the heart is a far better and more fruitful way of developing universal brotherly love than to be continually talking about it. Often such talk is counter-productive, it is coloured by both arrogance and egoism disguised as altruism.

Love is not only something which links men together; it is also needed by each of us as individuals. 'When a man is incapable of developing the quality of love, he becomes dried-up and withered in his inner being.'⁶

People who are incapable of love, who find it difficult to love, are a distressing sight as, devoid of the warmth that love alone can generate, they go about their daily tasks in a lifeless way. 'For love is a living force that stimulates something deep in our being, keeping it awake and alive.' In reality we are 'cradled in a body of love' or, in the terms of spiritual science, in an etheric body, in a body of life-giving, formative forces.⁷ The principal forces working in us and emanating from the etheric body are those creative forces that express themselves in a man's capacity for loving. If a man were able to empty his being of the force of love he would die. 'But that indeed is impossible for even the greatest egoist, for even in egoistical striving, there is still some element of love.' [8] Steiner gives the example of the man who, though unable to love anything else, is sufficiently avaricious to love wealth. He substitutes a love arising from greed, from egoism, for charitable love. But it cannot be said that he is completely devoid of the force of love. Were there to be no trace of love at all in a man, then the etheric body, 'that should be sustained by love-forces, would shrivel, and the man, empty of love, would actually perish; he would really meet with physical death'. The shrivelling of the forces of love is likewise a shrivelling of the forces belonging to the etheric body, the body of love. [9]

Here we see the lack of love, of the force of love, as being destructive of life. Steiner also speaks of the effect of deeds and thoughts of love in relation to our fellow-men and to the spiritual world in the following concise manner. In relation to the former we can recognize that 'deeds born of our compassion or of sympathy with the sorrows or joys of our fellow-men do not live on only within us but also in the other human being, indeed in our whole environment'. He for whom we have performed an act of compassion and love 'carries the influence and effect of our action on with him through life'. [10] Such an action works on as a constructive force. The obverse is also true, as Steiner points out when speaking of the effects of selfishness, egoism, and selfless love on the spiritual life of the world. 'The forces of selfish thoughts become forces of disturbance, even of destruction — they pass into the spiritual world actually as destructive forces. On the other hand, all forces of selfless thoughts enter into the spiritual life of Earth evolution, not as destructive but as upbuilding, constructive forces.' [11]

If during our earthly life we have filled our etheric body with devout and loving feelings and it then dissolves, shortly after death, into the Universal All, we 'hand over' to the Universe an etheric body filled with such feelings. It is then of benefit to the whole world for it is filled with constructive and creative force. If, on the other hand, we have not given loving devotion to the Christ and the spiritual world but have been both materialistic and egoistic in our attitude toward life and our fellow-men, then the etheric body which we lay aside after death, being more or less devoid of the creative forces of love and therefore 'sterile', will have a destructive effect when it dissolves in the universal ether.

'In the same measure in which we gain wisdom, we help not only ourselves, but indirectly the world also. And in the same measure in which we unfold loving, devout feelings, we help the world in a direct way, for love and devoutness act as creative forces in the universe.' [12]

It is incumbent upon those who are striving spiritually 'to have eyes for the quality of love and compassion', [13] for their constructive powers will be increasingly needed in all spheres of present and future human toil.

'The whole history of man is filled with egoism and endless harm has been wrought by it in ordinary life; but all the trouble that is due to egoism in ordinary life is a mere trifle in comparison with the harm it causes if it is able to work with occult knowledge' [14] — sobering words that anyone entering upon the path of spiritual scientific development cannot take too seriously.

The reader is reminded here of Steiner's insistence, in *Knowledge of the Higher Worlds*, that egoism is a hindrance on the path of spiritual development — egoism in the sense that we centre our attention upon our own 'I', that we value our Ego too highly. Steiner explains what he means by holding our 'I' in too high esteem in the following words:

We have, to begin with, our physical body that has been gradually formed and completed with such wonderful artistic power in four majestic phases of development. [15] Then we have the etheric body that has undergone three stages of development. And we have also the astral body that has undergone only two. The 'I', however, is no more than a baby. And if we are able to see *through* what shows on the surface, then, when we look at someone who is sailing through life on the sea of his own egoism, we have before us the Imagination of a fond fostermother or nurse, whose heart is filled with rapturous devotion to the baby in her arms. In *her* case the rapture is justified, for the child in her arms is other than herself; but we have a spectacle merely of egoism when we behold man fondling so tenderly the baby in him. And you can indeed see people going about like that today. Man of our times carries his 'I', his Ego, in his arms, fondling it and caressing it tenderly. [16]

However, there is a vital difference between holding our Ego in too high esteem in the sense in which Steiner is speaking here and recognising egoism, quite objectively, as an essential and irreplaceable 'ingredient' in our striving towards the creation of a

Cosmos of Love. As Steiner repeatedly stresses, man has to have egoism implanted into him during Earth evolution. 'Without egoism he could not fulfil his task on Earth, for his task consists in evolving from egoism to love; through love he has to ennoble and spiritualize egoism', transform it into love. 'At the end of Earth evolution man will be permeated through and through with love, but he could never evolve up to this *love in freedom*, had not egoism been implanted into his nature.' [17]

21.

LOVE AND THE MORAL LIFE

To be moral also means to acknowledge that one has a relationship to all men. That is why love of all humanity is self-evident to all moral people. [1]

Christ is the true moral impulse which permeates humanity with moral power. [2]

21.

There is no human soul, with the exception of black magicians (Steiner is adamant on this point), in which there is not the foundation of what is morally good — even in the most hardened of criminals; if we delve deep enough, we shall find moral impulses.

'If a person is wicked, it is because that which has originated in the course of time as spiritual errors overlies moral goodness.' Human nature, Steiner states categorically, is not bad; originally it was good. Human nature, in its essence, is good. 'It was through spiritual errors that man deviated from the moral path.'[3] The foundation for the improvement of a human being, morally, always consists in taking away his spiritual error. And what is necessary to accomplish this? Steiner's unequivocal answer is: Faith, Love, Hope.

The fundamental attitude we need to have towards our fellow-man is that we believe in the original goodness of man. This attitude is the first thing we must cultivate in ourselves, if we are to speak of true morality. We must have faith that something immeasurably good lies at the foundation of man, that divine spiritual forces underlie each human being, even him who has sinned.

This attitude of faith makes it possible for the power of love to manifest itself in our soul — the power that gives and helps morally, and even heals. No one, says Steiner, if he really develops the belief, the faith, in the original goodness of man, can do other than attain boundless love for human nature as such. 'It is primarily these two impulses that form the foundation of a truly moral life: the belief in the divine in man, no matter what appearances may otherwise suggest, and measureless love of man that springs from this faith.'[4]

The third element that man needs to develop in his soul, if he is to develop the right, morally fruitful attitude towards his fellow-men, is the hope that every single soul, even though it may have fallen far from the height of spiritual life, can find its way back to the divine-spiritual. Faith and Hope, either singly or together, do not work; one must, of course, have them, 'but only Love is effective'. [5]

Steiner reminds us of Plato's views on morals, on the virtues of man. According to Plato there are three main virtues: Wisdom, Valour, and Moderation or Temperance — all of which curb the sensual impulses active in man and, in his view, the harmonious balance of these three is brought about by a fourth virtue: Justice. In terms of Christian morality, however, we cannot describe, as Plato did, the only virtues as being wisdom, temperance, valour and justice, for, as Steiner points out, we would receive the reply: 'If you had all these and yet you had not love, you would never enter the Kingdom of Heaven'. [6]

Freedom in life, Steiner again reminds us, consists in man being able to err in one direction or another, to succumb to either the Luciferic or the Ahrimanic influence. Thereby the possibility of evil arises. 'Goodness consists in avoiding both these extremes.' [7]

The mean, the balance, must be found 'if man is really to be virtuous, if moral power is to pulsate through the world'.

We could now ask: Why should morals exist at all? What happens when evil is done, when there is no morality? Something is destroyed! 'Every evil or immoral act is a process of destruction, and the moment man realizes that, when he has done wrong, he cannot do otherwise than destroy something, deprive the world of something, in that moment an impulse for good awakens within him.' [8] A moral deed is constructive, is of a healing quality; an immoral deed is destructive, is of a disease-creating quality.

A powerful quality that can help develop moral impulses is what Steiner terms 'interest'. He places the role 'interest' plays in the following way before us. There is a soul element in man (called by Steiner the 'sentient-soul') which enables him to perceive the sense-perceptible world and to form relationships with the multiplicity of objects it contains. These relationships are mediated by 'interest'. It is much more important, says Steiner, that man should be conscious of the moral significance of 'interest' than that he should indulge in beautiful moral axioms 'which may be only paltry and hypocritical'. [9] Our moral impulses are never better guided than when we take a proper healthy interest in the human beings and world of nature around us.

The more we extend our genuine interests, our genuine inner participation in events around us, the more our mental horizons are widened, the 'closer we grow towards the creation of the universal brotherhood of mankind. Progress in this direction is not achieved by the mere preaching of universal love, but by the continuing extension of our interests, of our participation, so that, eventually, we are able to *transpose* ourselves with loving understanding into other human beings, into other human beings with widely different, often contrasting characters, racial and national characteristics, religious and philosophical views', [10] and so on. Loving interest and understanding call forth the right moral action from the human soul.

A person who is striving to become mature enough for spiritual development must widen the circle of his interest beyond his everyday life. In our time there are many who have a concerned interest for the whole of mankind. More often than not they are to be found among those who lead quite simple lives — not so much among the intellectuals. There are many today who have a humble place in life who have a live interest in and concern for the whole of mankind. Without such interest, such selfless concern, no progress can be made in spiritual development. [11]

In relation to the cultivation of interest we find ourselves having to hold a balance between two extremes: apathy and uncontrolled passion. An apathetic person lives more or less exclusively within himself — insisting, for instance, on the rightness of his own standpoint. In a moral sense, such insistence is always bad. The essential thing is to have an open mind. Apathy cuts us off from the world and nurtures egoism. 'The world loses us through our apathy and we thus become immoral.' [12] The other extreme — uncontrolled passion — is avoided by distinguishing between true and false interests. To throw oneself indiscriminately into the arms of each person we encounter is 'to lose oneself'. That is not true interest. In this way 'we lose ourselves to the world' and we become immoral. To hold the golden mean between these two extremes is to be moral. Through healthy, devoted interest we stand morally firm in the centre, in a state of conscious balance between apathy and uncontrolled passion. Here we are reminded of Steiner's statement: 'It is of the essence of real love that it is . . . an equilibrium of polarities'. [13]

In ancient times, and also at the time of Plato and Aristotle, the power to hold this balance between extremes was known as Wisdom. But this Wisdom in, say, the age of Ancient Egypt, was a gift from the gods. It was in other words instinctive wisdom. Thus it was a gift that enabled men to find the happy mean in action between apathy and sensuous, passionate devotion. This balance was maintained through 'external' institutions, we might say. For example, through the existence of blood kinship in the tribe, an obstacle was placed in the way of unbridled passion.

But inherent in the progressive development of mankind is, as has been stressed several times in these pages, the necessity for man to become independent of the divine spiritual powers for a period during this development, in order to achieve consciously reunion with them. Hence we see that since the Graeco-Roman age, since the time of Plato and Aristotle, it was considered that Wisdom must be *gained*. It was felt that this Wisdom was *no longer a gift* of the gods. With Plato we recognize that not to strive after the attainment of Wisdom is immoral. [14]

We, in our present age, have just begun to tread the path, by means of spiritual science, towards the raising into consciousness of what the gods once *gave* as Wisdom to the unconscious human soul. We are consciously beginning to fill our souls with enthusiasm and love for moral ideals. [15] We are, in a sense, in a kind of spiritual no-man's land and are therefore specially liable to err in both the directions just indicated. The dangers involved need to be counteracted by a spiritual conception of the world and a clear realization of our 'place' in the scheme of evolution, 'so that what we once possessed as instinctive wisdom may now become conscious wisdom'. [16]

If we transplanted ourselves back into the age when the gods gave us Wisdom, when we 'possessed' instinctive wisdom and we conducted our moral lives in accordance with the Law, we should find, as we discussed elsewhere, that we were not independent, free individuals, but should feel ourselves as integral parts of a group-soul. We should not, as individuals, be able to experience inner love to its fullest extent; our love and our moral conduct would be embedded in blood relationships and all the taboos and restrictions governing such a relationship. As we shall see in our discussion of the 'old and new bonds of love', men must free themselves more and more from this group-soul love and instinctive, group-soul sense of moral duty and proffer these inner qualities as free gifts of the independent Ego.

At the end of earth evolution, Steiner states, a time will come when the Ego, now become free of all Luciferic and Ahrimanic influence,

will receive into its inner being, in full self-surrender, the impulse to do the right and the good. When Love becomes spiritualized to such a degree that no one will wish to follow any other impulse than this, then that will be fulfilled which Christ Jesus wished to bring into the world. For one of the mysteries of Christianity is that it teaches the seeker to behold the Christ, to fill himself with the power of His Image, to seek to become like Him, and to follow after Him. Then will his liberated Ego need no other law; it will then, as a being free in its inner depths, do the good and the true. Thus Christ is the bringer of the impulse of freedom from the Law, that good may be done, not because of the compulsion of any law, but as an indwelling Impulse of love with the human soul.

This Impulse, Steiner continues, will need the remainder of the Earth period for its full development, and it is 'the Christ Figure Who will always be the Power that will educate humanity to its fulfilment'. [17]

The Christ Impulse raises us out of the world of nature, out of natural law and necessity. We must regard it as a kind of ideal for the moral life within us to be able to have moral principles which are not forced upon us from without. The moment we become truly conscious of our human dignity and feel we cannot be like beings driven by necessity, we rise to a world quite different from the world of Nature. [18]

There is a clear distinction between the laws of nature and those of morality. In any explanation of natural phenomena and processes we do not make use of moral ideas. For instance, confronted with a poisonous mushroom we endeavour to explain its poisonous qualities according to natural law and we do not condemn it for being poisonous. With regard to the animal kingdom there can, at the most, be a question of something resembling morality. A moral judgement regarding the actions of an animal is not applicable. However, in the human realm moral judgements begin to be of importance and are of relevance. In this realm, too, no one would consider the laws of nature as being identical with, or even similar to, moral law. [19]

However, says Steiner, as soon as we 'enter' the spiritual world other conditions prevail. 'The more spiritual the worlds which we enter, the more do moral law and what may be termed natural law in these worlds coincide. In the physical world we know that we are using figurative speech when we say that an evil deed burns heat are quite different from this experience of an evil deed. In the spiritual world, however, we find something quite different.

For instance, Steiner tells us, 'hate and envy are forces acting in such a way that we may term their effects the *natural laws* of that world. Hate and envy in the spiritual world have the effect that the being who is hated or envied reacts against him who hates or envies in a consuming, *extinguishing* manner, so that processes of destruction are established which are hurtful to the spiritual being emanating hate and envy.' In contrast, 'love acts in such a way in the spiritual world that its effect is an irradiation of warmth that is productive and helpful'. [20] This effect, incidentally, can also be observed in the etheric body of man living in a physical body. [21]

The spiritually-moral has become little more than an abstract idea for man today, representing to a very large extent something purely conventional. The original, instinctive feeling of a spiritually-moral element in man has 'withdrawn' increasingly into the background. This, as described above, is a necessary part of man's striving towards freedom. We are, as also mentioned earlier, in a kind of spiritual no-man's land at present. Nevertheless, it is still true to say that in general the education of modern civilized man inclines him to ask: What is the established convention? What is the law? Such education lays little stress 'on what emerges as impulse and is situated in that part of man he describes, vaguely, as his conscience. What is both moral and spiritual has become something that exists more or less only in conventions and traditions'. Steiner emphasizes that he does not in any way wish to detract from the value of tradition in morals, but 'think for a moment how very old the Ten Commandments are. They are taught as commands recorded from very ancient times. Can it be said that today something might be expected to arise from the original elemental nature of man at all resembling the Decalogue?' [22] It is not surprising that all around us traditions, customs and conventions are being ignored and that a state of chaos is entering into the moral sphere. In order to create a morality based on freedom and love we have to become quite clear as to how moral and spiritual qualities arise that link men together socially in a mutual respect for the dignity of each other.

'The real source of what is moral and spiritual in man is what we may call *human understanding*; mutual human understanding, and the *human love* that is built on it.' Human understanding and human love, 'these are the driving forces of all that is social, moral and spiritual in man', understanding and love imbued with the Christ Impulse. It is only through the development of such understanding and love that a new morality, in keeping with the consciously striving individual, can arise. 'Fundamentally, we can only live among our fellow-men as moral-spiritual beings through the development of human understanding and human love.' [23]

Earlier on we discussed the destructive power of evil. We can now say that through what is immoral, through lack of loving interest and understanding, we destroy something of the Christ Impulse. But if we give to the world what can be given to it through love, that is creative, we build, we are constructive. We build, in short, through loving, and wisdom-filled self-surrender. It is not without reason, Steiner reminds us, that it has often been said that Christ was crucified on Golgotha, but that He is crucified again and again through the immoral deeds of men, through this unkindness and lack of understanding and loving interest. [24]

'When we act out of love, in all cases where we use love, we strengthen the Christ Impulse, we help to bring it to life.' 'Inasmuch as ye have done it unto one of the least of those My brethren, ye have done it unto Me' (Matthew 25: 40). This, says Steiner, is one of the most significant statements of love, and it constitutes the most profound moral impulse, if it is once rightly understood. It becomes a tenet of our everyday lives, when with loving understanding we confront our fellow-men and offer them something in our actions, our virtue, our conduct towards them that is born of our understanding of their nature. 'Our attitude towards our fellow-men is our attitude to the Christ Impulse.'

'It is a powerful moral impulse, something which is a real foundation for a true moral life, when we feel whatever you do to men you do to Christ.'

We may now say: 'Whereas the gods of pre-Christian times gave instinctive wisdom to man, so now love streams down from the Cross — the love that is based upon the mutual interest of man in man.' [25]

*   *   *   *

In a most fascinating and far-reaching lecture given on 15 December 1922, Steiner speaks of the power of love we are able to unfold here on earth in relation to our existence in the spiritual world. If, he states, between death and a new birth we, as spiritual beings, are unable to work together, to commune with the Beings of the Higher Hierarchies (see Chapter 6), then in a subsequent earth-life we are not able to unfold the power of love. That we are able to unfold human love, a sympathetic understanding for another human being, is due to the fact that between death and a new birth we are able to live in communion with the Beings of the Higher Hierarchies. Those who, in a previous earth-life, cultivated few if any genuine inclinations towards a religious, spiritual life, acquired little aptitude for living together with the Higher Beings of the Hierarchies during a subsequent period between death and a new birth. Such people, Steiner says, are incapable of unfolding a love here on earth in which there is 'real strength'. They are unable to unfold the all-embracing love that comes to expression in the power to understand selflessly one's fellow-men. 'We may truly say: it is among the Gods, in pre-earthly existence, that we acquire the gift for observing our fellow-men, to perceive how they think, how they feel, to understand them with inner sympathy.' If, we learn from Steiner, man were deprived of this communion with the Higher Hierarchies, then we would be incapable of developing here on earth that insight into other human beings that alone makes earthly life a reality.

We see then, with Steiner, that, issuing from man's communion in the spiritual world with the Higher Hierarchies, the seed is sown in his soul to unfold true communion with his fellow-men on earth. 'Love and the outcome of love, morality, are a consequence of what man has experienced spiritually in pre-earthly existence.' [26]

22.

OLD AND NEW BONDS OF LOVE

Gazing down from the Cross upon Golgotha,
Christ beheld the mother, beheld the son;
and in that moment He founded that community
that up to then had existed only through the
blood.

Up to that time no mother had had a son, no
son a mother, without the tie being that of
blood relationship. However, blood ties
were not to be eliminated by Christianity,
but to them were to be added spiritual ties,
diffusing with their spiritual light those
ties created by the blood.

It was to this end that Christ Jesus on the
Cross spoke the words: 'Woman behold thy
son!', and to the beloved disciple: 'Behold
thy mother!' [1]

22.

In the peoples of ancient times — including ancient Greece — there existed what we might call a form of collective consciousness. Although a man felt himself, to a greater or lesser degree, to be an individuality, although he felt his personal ego within his skin, so to speak, he felt himself even more strongly to be a member of a tribe, or of a city community. Just as the individual soul can be felt to be the focal factor in our organism as a whole — uniting the various elements of his organism — so did man in ancient times feel himself to be a member of a group-soul. [2]

In these ancient times it was among blood relatives that closest affinity was experienced. [3] But the power of blood-relationship has diminished through the ages and it is now through the cultivation of the spiritual life that such affinity can be recognized. [4] Whereas, for instance, in ancient times marriages were always contracted within the tribe, we find consanguineous marriages becoming increasingly rare in the days of Roman supremacy, the days in which the Christ Event took place. The ties of blood were necessarily sundered to an increasing extent in the course of human evolution, because, as is repeatedly emphasized in these pages, man was destined to establish himself as an independent, free Ego-being. [5]

Christ's message: 'He who forsaketh not father, and mother, and brethren, and sisters for my name's sake, cannot be my disciple' (Luke 14: 26; Matthew 19: 39, also 19: 29) should not, however, be understood to mean that we should abandon our parents, brothers and sisters. What Christ is saying here is: he who makes love *conditional* upon the *natural* foundation of blood-ties, of blood-relationships, is not a Christian. [6]

In the ancient folk community it was said: he who is born within the folk, within the tribe, he is my brother. In the Christian Brotherhood of Man, embracing the whole human race, we should say: because you are a man, you are my brother. This is the very deepest principle of true Christianity.

We could now ask ourselves: if the community based on the

blood-tie has broken down and we are now to 'create' communities consisting of free human beings, how can these human beings who have now become free individuals, who are no longer held by the customs of the tribe, be brought harmoniously together, and live in harmony together? How can dissension, so rife in the world today, be overcome? Steiner's answer to this is: whereas in ancient times the sway of external law was necessary in order that men might be held together, in Christian times those who know the Spirit of Truth, the Christ, will of themselves feel drawn to one another. There can be no conflict or dissension, if natural love once tied to the blood-relationship is transformed into spiritual love, for there are no different 'standpoints' if the Spirit alone unites us. [7]

'Thus at the beginning of human evolution stands the Law; at the end, peace, harmonious cooperation. This is called Grace in esoteric Christianity, in contrast to Law. [8] It is nothing other than the capacity to share, in complete harmony, in the feelings of other men. This is one of the most profound concepts of Christianity.' [9]

In a lecture given in Paris in 1906, one of a series of eighteen in which he formulated a basic view of Esoteric Christianity, Steiner develops the theme of the true essence of Christianity in a way that sheds further light on what has been discussed so far. [10]

The brotherhood of man and the acceptance of the One God, of the Three in One, are fundamental elements, but 'they only represent the external, social aspect, not the inner, spiritual reality'. The new, mysterious and transcendental element in Christianity is that 'it creates divine love, the power that transforms man from within, the leaven by which the whole world is raised'. As we have already seen, the words contained in the Gospels of St Luke and St Matthew do not imply the cessation of natural links. They propound the deep esoteric truth that Love extends beyond the bounds of family, beyond the blood-tie, to all human beings throughout the world, and is a vivifying, creative, transmuting power. 'It is destined to change the very essence of all religions, of all cults, of all science.' The progress of humanity, Steiner continues, is from atavistic clairvoyance, from unconscious spirituality (pre-Christian), through intellectualism (the present age), to conscious spirituality imbued with the power of Love, divine and human. [11]

Christianity can, therefore, be recognized as being not only a universal religion but also the source of the highest development of individual freedom. 'The tyranny of dogma, of the Law, is replaced by the radiance of divine Wisdom, embracing intelligence, love and action. The science that arises from this cannot be measured by its power of abstract reasoning but by its power to bring souls to flower and fruition.' [12]

On many occasions Steiner speaks of the blood as being the external expression of the Ego. [13] 'In the course of evolution too strong a measure of egoism made·its appearance, which means that the egohood "impressed" the blood too powerfully. This "surplus of egoism"' in the stream of human evolution 'had to be expelled again if spirituality was to be restored to mankind. On Golgotha the impulse was given for this expulsion of egoism.' [14] When the blood flowed from the wounds of the Redeemer, Christ united himself mystically with the earth. [15] The Blood of Christ flowed out in the material world, while the superfluity of egoism passed over into and was transmuted in the spiritual world. In place of the process of increasing egoism, which would have dominated humanity irrevocably, universal human love entered into the spiritual evolution of mankind and is there as a real possibility for men to recognize and develop consciously.

Egoism is a hallmark of the materialistic age in which we live; a 'spiritual age will denote the overcoming of this egoism. Therefore Christianity and indeed all movements imbued with genuine religious life have worked consciously towards breaking through all the old blood-ties'. [16] Christianity has made a radical statement in this regard, not only in the words of Christ quoted earlier on, [17] but also, in one of the first proclamations of universal love, in His statement as given to us through St Mark: 'Then his mother and his brothers arrived, and remaining outside the house sent in a message asking him to come out to them. A crowd was sitting round and word was brought to him: "Your mother and your brothers are outside asking for you". He replied: "Who is my mother? Who are my brothers?" And looking round at those who were sitting in the circle about him he said, "Here are my mother and my brothers. Whosoever does the will of God is my brother, my sister, my mother" (Mark 4: 31-35). Here again is indicated nothing less than that in place of the ancient blood-ties there must enter the spiritual bond between soul and soul. This proclamation of universal love resounded once again from the lips of Christ, in His last words, to which reference has already been made. [18]

Steiner makes a pertinent remark which, although similar

thoughts have been expressed more than once in these pages, is included here, as its importance cannot be overemphasized. It is this:

> What are the ways and means by which humanity may attain spirituality, that is, may overcome materialism, and at the same time reach what may be called the bond of brotherhood, the expression of universal human love? One might imagine that universal human love need only be stressed strongly enough, and that then it must come about. Spiritual science is never of this opinion. On the contrary! The more a man speaks of universal brotherly love and humanity, becoming in a sense intoxicated by the phrases, the more egoistic he becomes. [19] For precisely as there is a lust of the senses, so is there a lust of the soul; and it is in fact a refined voluptuousness to say: 'I will become morally higher and higher'. This, to be sure, is not a thought which creates the ordinary, conventional egoism, but it does lead to a subtle form of egoism. [20]

Repeated talk about pity, sympathy, love, will not generate these qualities. We will be led to the bond of brotherhood through something quite different, namely, spiritual knowledge itself. 'There is no other means of bringing about a universal human brotherhood than the spreading of spiritual scientific knowledge through the world.' [21] Through such dissemination of spiritual knowledge mankind will grow increasingly free of physical blood-ties, and increasingly able to form groups, communities, founded in the recognition of the reality of the spirit. Moreover, states Steiner quite categorically, 'the concept of race will lose its meaning'. [22]

The more man becomes individual, a free individual, the more can he become a vehicle of love. [23] Where blood links men together, men love because they are guided to that which they shall love, but when the freedom of individuality is given to man, when he cherishes and brings to life within him the divine spark, the divine Christ-Essence, then the impulses of love, the waves of love, can stream forth from the free heart of man, from man to man. Imbued with this Christ Impulse, with the Essence of Divine Love, man can become the bearer of the essence of divine love, can become a true Christopherus. [24] Imbued with this Impulse man transforms the old bond of love, the bond bound to the blood. 'Love is gradually becoming transformed into that spiritual love which flows from individual soul to individual soul, and which will in due course embrace the whole of mankind in one common bond of brotherhood.' [25]

The power of spiritual love was brought into the souls of men for the first time by Christ when He appeared on the earth; and with the Blood that flowed on Golgotha from His wounds the overpowering influence exerted by the blood was surrendered. [26]

The Gospel of St John describes most succinctly what must be fulfilled by man in earth existence: 'the ordering of this existence in accordance with the Logos, the Sun Word'. Hence, for instance, John's gaze is directed to the ordering of life as proclaimed by Christ from the Cross. [27]

To reiterate: the principle of selfless love is what streamed into earth existence, into humanity, through Christ's Deed.

One day, in the future, when the Jew loves and understands the Christian, and the Christian the Jew, when the Pariah and the Brahmin love each other as men, and put themselves in each other's places, then we shall know how deeply it can be felt, in a Christian way, when we say: 'All men must feel themselves to be brothers, no matter what their blood and what their religious creed may be.' The Christ Impulse balances, harmonizes and unites all human differences. A Christopherus, a bearer of Christ, is one who knows that mere human distinctions are of little significance in comparison with the Impulse of Love streaming forth from the Cross, from the Mystery of Golgotha. [28]

When we understand what the Christ Impulse truly is, then, as already mentioned, we will establish communities and institutions based on the bond of love freely created between soul and soul. 'Just as in the blood of the Hebrew people and in the threads running through the generations, that which was *ordained* to be bound together was bound together and that which was *ordained* to be loosed was loosed according to the pattern of the Macrocosm', [29] so there is now to arise, through Christ in us, through the conscious Ego, in the form of ethical, moral and spiritual relationships, the inner force that either freely loosens the ties between human beings or freely binds them together in love. Human communities and institutions are now to be created, and harmonized, by the conscious Ego. This, Steiner points out, is the meaning of the words spoken by Christ to Peter: 'I will give unto thee the keys of the Kingdom of Heaven: whatsoever thou shalt bind on earth shall be bound in Heaven: and whatsoever thou shalt loose on earth shall be loosed in Heaven' (Matthew 16: 19). [30]

One of the deepest purposes of Christianity is to unloose everything that binds men within narrow egotistical, blood-tie limits. It is true, as we have seen, that it will 'split up' mankind into individuals, but they will be individuals imbued with love and, out of their own free will, they will unite, in love, again. In the Mystery of Golgotha this transformation, from the old ordained tie to the new freely formed union born of selfless love, is prepared. It begins to work, Steiner reminds us, at Whitsuntide, the first Whitsuntide, when the Holy Spirit is poured forth into men; that is, when the understanding of this new bond of Brotherhood is born. This birth is expressed in a beautiful symbol when we hear that the Apostles spoke to·men of all nations in their own tongues. 'That which had flowed through the Blood of Christ on Golgotha is in this Whitsuntide experience spread abroad by the Holy Spirit.' The narrow, egoistic blood-tie brotherhood has been transformed into universal brotherhood grounded in Spirit-Love. [31]

The pouring forth of the Spirit at Whitsuntide appears 'as the outpouring of the Spirit of Love, Concord and Harmony' upon all those who, assembled together from many different corners of the earth and who, although they had different mother-tongues, could all understand the language of the Logos, of the Sun-Spirit, of the Christ.

Steiner expresses this in very simple terms: 'Perhaps, in order to catch the exact purport of the Bible words [the second chapter of the Acts of the Apostles] we could express it thus: The message of the Whitsuntide revelation was so in tune with the human heart that each man could understand it, although he knew no other language than his own.' [32]

'Christ's suffering gave birth to the Spirit that was poured upon the Apostles on the day of Pentecost. Out of this suffering was born the all-prevailing Cosmic Love that, at the Baptism in the Jordan, had come down from the super-sensible world, from the heavenly spheres, into the sphere of the earth, had taken on the likeness of man, of a human body, and had endured that moment of utmost, divine powerlessness.' He underwent extreme suffering on the Cross in order to bring forth the Impulse of Divine Love and to permeate the evolutionary stream of earth and man with this Impulse. 'These are things of which we must be mindful if we would understand the real significance of the Christ Impulse. Men of the future will need such understanding if they are to make progress along their path of evolution and culture.' [33]

Steiner, 'entering the hearts' of the Apostles, gives a moving insight into what it was they experienced.

The Apostles felt as if something had descended upon them from the Cosmos which could only be called 'the Substance of the all-prevailing Love'. They felt as if they had been 'quickened from on high by the all-prevailing Love, and awakened from the condition of dream into which they had fallen. It seemed to them as if they had been wakened to life by the primal force of Love pervading and warming the Cosmos'.

> To others who could observe them it seemed as if these men had been transformed, as if their very souls had been made new; they seemed to have lost all narrowness, all selfishness in life, to have acquired largeness of heart, an all-embracing tolerance and a deep understanding for everything that is human on the earth. Moreover they were able to express themselves in such a way that everyone present could understand them. It was felt that they could look into every heart, could read the deepest, innermost secrets of the soul and so were able to bring consolation to every single individual, to say to him exactly what he needed to hear. [34]

The Apostles themselves, in whom this transformation took place, who had been awakened by the Spirit of Cosmic Love, by the Holy Spirit, now felt within them a new understanding of what had actually transpired on Golgotha.

For full understanding of the Golgotha Event the Whitsuntide experience, the 'quickening' by the Holy Spirit, the all-prevailing Cosmic Love, is necessary. [35]

The Apostles now knew that Jesus had died on the Cross, but that this dying was in reality a *birth*, was the birth of that Spirit outpoured as the all-prevailing Cosmic Love into their souls. Each one felt that he had been touched by 'a ray of the primordial, aeonic Love' that was born into the stream of evolution when Jesus Christ died on the Cross. Each one inwardly knew that it was only illusion that on the Cross a simple death had taken place. 'This death, preceded by infinite suffering', they felt, they knew, 'was the birth of the ray of Love now penetrating their souls'. [36]

Here Steiner explains that the all-prevailing Cosmic Love that had previously been present everywhere 'outside' and around the earth, beyond the reach of man, had, with the death of Christ, been born 'into' the earth. At the moment of Christ's death on the

Cross spiritualized love, previously only to be 'found' in the Cosmos, was born for the earth and the whole of humanity. 'The death of Jesus of Nazareth was the birth of Cosmic Love within the sphere of the Earth.' [37]

In the Acts of the Apostles we can read that many were baptised after Peter had spoken to the assembled crowd of the meaning of Golgotha and of the Cosmic Love that would also fill their souls if they took the Christ into their hearts. Freely and in love they 'held everything in common. They sold their property and possessions and made a general distribution as the need of each required'.

Emerging from this first Whitsuntide experience there grew a new bond of love, a new community, freely formed.

'The great goal of humanity consists in overcoming all differences and in founding the great love of humanity. This goal will not be gained in any other way than by people learning to penetrate more and more into the spiritual worlds. Humanity emerged from the unity with the Divine Being and developed the various egos. Ultimately this humanity will become completely individualized, but at the same time' — in freedom and in love — 'united in a brotherhood. It will form a Unity that will give birth to a new "star", to the star that in the Apocalypse is called The New Jerusalem.' [38]

23.

THE SOCIAL FUTURE

True health is only when
In the human soul is mirrored
The image of the whole community,
And in the community there lives
The virtue of each single soul. [1]

So long as thou dost feel the pain
Which I am spared,
The Christ unrecognized
Is working in the World.
For weak is still the Spirit
While each is only capable of suffering
Through his own body. [2a]

To be free means to realize oneself in actions which one loves.
Trust *is the one golden word which in future must rule*
social life. Love *for what we have to do is the other golden*
word. In future those actions will be socially good which
flow from a love for all men. This love has first to be
learned. [2b]

23.

In a series of lectures with the title *The Social Future* Steiner speaks in some detail of the urgent need to rethink and reformulate the nature of man's social future. In the final lecture he outlines the elements and qualities inherent in nationalism and internationalism. In particular he is concerned to show the true nature of egoism and love in relation to nationalism and internationalism.

It is a widespread view that the ethical law requires that egoism should be 'conquered' by love and that in the progress of human evolution pure love should supplant egoism. This is, as we have seen, the view of spiritual science too. This claim is put forward not only on the grounds of ethics, but also as a social need.

However, is the opposition implicit in egoism and love always sufficiently understood? asks Steiner. A closer look at the kind of opposition that actually exists between the forces of egoism and those of love shows that if we were to follow the dictum 'Love must conquer egoism' without discrimination and objective insight, we could well be 'throwing out the baby with the bath water'.

To say that egoism must be overcome by love certainly does not help us to understand the nature of egoism. The point to bear in mind is rather this: he who meets his fellow-men with a purely human interest and understanding certainly acts quite differently from one whose interests are narrow and self-centred, but the former need not necessarily be less egoistic in life than the latter, for his egoism may take the form of being of service to others; it may nurture in him a feeling of *inner* well-being, of *inner* self-satisfaction and bliss, even of ecstasy, to devote himself in a self-sacrificial way to the service of others. In other words, deeds that seem to issue from altruism may well proceed from egoism. Outwardly they appear altruistic and as being solely imbued with selfless love for others, but inwardly, in the life of feeling, they cannot be appraised otherwise than as egoistic.

We could pursue the question of the nature of egoism still further. For instance, it is clear that everything in the nature of creative imagination, of imaginative creation, arises out of the inner being. All creations in the sphere of art, to take one example, are of this nature. If we now, without bias, seek a right understanding of such things, we shall find that what instigates man's imaginative creation, of all that rises out of the depths of his being, has the same source, albeit at a higher level, as the physical bodily needs, i.e. egoism. 'The life of imagination which is developed in art, for instance, viewed *subjectively*, reposes on a feeling of *inward* satisfaction — more refined, nobler, to be sure, than the satisfaction of hunger, but not different in quality for the individual himself, even though that which is produced thereby may have a different significance for the rest of humanity.' [3]

All human egoism may be said to be directed by the fact that, as individuals, we have to live and work together with our fellow-man. Indeed, egoism itself requires that we should live and work with other men. Much of what we carry out together with others is founded on egoism and may yet be credited with the noblest human virtues. For example, if we contemplate maternal, paternal, or filial love, we recognize that it is founded on egoism — yet it manifests itself most nobly in the common life of humanity.

In the love of the achievements of one's country, in patriotism, egoism can clearly rise to a high level. It takes the form of an ideal and rightly so, but that ideal is nevertheless rooted in egoism. Cultural nationalism is an egoism that can be experienced by a whole nation; it is a form of egoism which is carried, we might say, into the spiritual region of life. This 'positive' form of egoism is aglow with the imagination and creative ability of the people in which it finds expression. Nationalism, patriotism, takes on the form of an ideal when it is an expression of cultural — also economic — achievement, in which the individual members can feel that they are doing something unique to themselves and also of value to their fellow-men throughout the world. 'This ideal, springing from human egoism, must be realized in order that the productivity and creativity of a people may be able to give something to humanity as a whole.'

The aspects of egoism just illustrated could be said to be of a positive nature rather than the reverse — the effects are beneficial to the community as a whole. [4]

Of a different kind is that characteristic of human nature which develops as internationalism. Nationalism could be described as 'a blossom on the growth of the individual human being, who is of the same blood as his tribe, or is bound by other ties to his people'. [5] Nationalism, the feeling of nationalism, arises out of our 'nature', we could say. Internationalism is not 'possessed' by us in the same way. Internationalism is somewhat comparable to the feeling we acquire when we contemplate nature or, let us say, a beautiful work of art. Here understanding, love and reverence are conjured up in us through the impression made upon us and the consequent dawning within us of a new reality and new value in life. We surrender ourselves to something that is not a 'natural' part of ourselves and allow ourselves, in this surrender, to be enriched and ennobled through the understanding, love and reverence that are born within us. Whereas, in other words, we *grow* 'directly' into our own people, because we are members of it, we *learn to know*, to understand, to love, other peoples. They work on us 'indirectly' through a relationship brought about by knowledge, by understanding and love. Whereas nationalism — which can, of course, degenerate into chauvinism, a less sympathetic aspect of 'egoism' — is an integral part of our nature, internationalism, a feeling and understanding for other peoples, has to be achieved. In proportion as our feeling for internationalism grows, in the same proportion do we learn to love and understand mankind in its different peoples.

There are then two distinct sources in human nature, egoism and love, loving understanding, from which arise respectively nationalism and internationalism. [6]

In the same lecture to which reference has just been made Steiner also makes a few salient remarks regarding the 'economic life'. Here again, the two impulses in the human soul, egoism and love, may be regarded as constituting the twofold foundation stone. Human needs and the desire to satisfy these needs, consumption and production, form the origin of the economic system. The satisfaction of human wants is really the whole task of economic life. And if we ask: what element, what impulse of human nature lies at the root of demand, of consumption, the answer is quite clear — egoism. Egoism is at the root of demand. If this is clearly understood, then no one will ask the misguided question, in regard to the economic life: How can we overcome egoism? Once it is recognized that egoism has a rightful place in the scheme of things, the more realistic question to be asked is: How can altruism, love, meet the *just* demands of egoism?

Let us now look at the polar element in the twofold foundation stone of the economic system, at production. The producer, whose task it is to satisfy demand, must not only have an understanding of the whole process of production, but also, ideally, of the life of his fellow-men, so that he can devote himself to the work of production in a manner corresponding to their needs. He must then devote himself — unselfishly and with understanding — to production.

We are clearly here dealing in basic terms with what we might call the fundamental elements of economic life. That this life has been distorted out of all recognition by the creation of artificial 'needs' and consequent over-production, etc., is all too obvious. But if the socio-economic life is to gain any kind of equilibrium — and, we could say, sincerity and true humanity — then the points made by Steiner are clearly valid, and constitute a goal toward which we should strive. We need to recognize that harmony and commonsense will reign in the economic sphere only when 'the *real* motive-power of production is self-sacrificing love towards humanity. The producer's selfless interest in his fellow-men and in life, his unselfish love for the different branches of production, must form the foundation of meeting the just demands arising in the consumer' — demands which arise out of his own 'natural' being, and not artificially inculcated by various means from 'outside'. [7]

Elsewhere Steiner speaks about the love the artisan had, in earlier times before the machine 'took over', for the product, for the result of his work. The machine in one form or another is here to stay, and what is required today is love of man and the brotherhood of man. This is not to suggest that the object should not be loved — though clearly the soul-attitude of the 'worker' to an object produced by his own manual skill is inevitably more of an intimate nature than that to an object 'produced' by a machine, and it is equally natural that in this mechanized, intellectual age an increasing number of people are finding their work, as work, uninteresting. To regain an interest, a living interest, will depend on our knowing as workers, how our every activity is an essential and integral element in the social organism of mankind. We will then know the reason for the duties we perform and learn to love them. [8]

Not only an understanding, a loving understanding, of the activity involved in production must gradually emerge, but also an understanding of 'universal' consumption. Just as it is true that members of one nation may 'develop to objective heights in which they find, as a spiritual perception, that which may also be found

by anyone of any other nation'[9] — meaning, in short, that
difference in nationality constitutes no barriers in spiritual
matters — so also is it true that difference in nationality does not
affect the needs of human consumers. Human wants are
international, as are spiritual perceptions also. But the internationality of human wants is the polar opposite in nature to
spiritual internationality, the internationality of the spirit. Once
this is fully understood the door is open to true internationality.
The internationality of the spirit must 'permeate with love the
understanding of other nationalities, and must be able to expand
that love to cosmopolitanism. Internationalism will only be able to
establish a connection with world-production when the latter
springs from a common spiritual understanding, from a common
spiritual conception of unity'. [10] Understanding of universal
consumption will never emerge from the egoism of the *separate*
nations. Only from a universal spiritual perception can that
develop which proceeds not from egoism, but from love, and
which therefore can govern production with understanding.

In a fascinating lecture dealing with the social basis for primary
and secondary education, [11] Steiner makes a comment in
connection with the need to bring about a synthesis between
characteristic trends prevailing, on the one hand, in the West
and, on the other, in the East, a comment which throws light on
the matter under immediate consideration from a different angle.

In the Anglo-American world everyone thinks so politically
that this political thinking is extended into economics. But in this
there is a peculiar feature. [12] Now Steiner, in his conception of
the threefold commonwealth [13] insists that in the economic
sphere *fraternity* should be the hallmark, and the 'peculiar
feature' to which he is referring is that fraternity has been 'driven
out' of the imperialist-political economic life of the West. The
consequence of the elimination of fraternity is a strongly
emphasized egoistic capitalism.

Characteristic of the East, however, is a strongly developed
sense of fraternity. Out of the Eastern peoples, who, since ancient
times, have had a highly developed spiritual life with an emphasis
on the life of soul and spirit, springs a true sense of brotherhood.
Whereas the characteristic of the West is an emphasis on the
economic life destitute of brotherliness — and tending,
therefore, towards capitalism — in the East there is an emphasis
on brotherliness without a realistic sense of economy. [14] We, in
Central Europe, says Steiner, 'have the task of synthesizing the

brotherliness of the East with the non-brotherly, but economic, way of thinking characteristic of the West. Were we to achieve this, we would be socialists in a world-embracing sense.' [15] We would achieve fraternity in the sphere of economics.

It is a great error in modern thought, remarks Steiner, to imagine that one common social programme could be issued for the whole of humanity and that individual nations should simply adjust themselves to it. Human beings are 'individualized', specialized, we might say, in the different regions of the earth, [16] and those who would learn to know the true, the inner, being of man must be able to develop love not merely for an abstract, universal humanity — for that would be nothing more than an 'idea' of humanity, 'a dead, empty idea' — but must 'develop love for the individual forms and expressions of human nature in the different regions of the Earth'. [17]

It is not an *intellectual* understanding, but a heart-warmed, living and loving understanding that must be developed. We need to cultivate a love for what is expressed in individual forms by the different peoples of the earth. Side by side with this selfless love we must also develop the awareness of the particular qualities that make one nation, one people, great, and that are not possessed by others, not possessed by one's own nation, for instance. We can understand these qualities — and gain knowledge from others that would otherwise elude us — only when we are able to love other peoples and appreciate to the full the value of their particular gifts. An attitude of love, essential to the harmonious working together of individuals, is equally essential to living cooperation between nations.

> Man in his *whole nature* is not expressed in the members of any one people or race. Full manhood is as yet only an urge within us, but this urge must grow into a love for all humanity, for those qualities we do not ourselves possess by nature, but which we can acquire if we sincerely seek for knowledge of the nature of other peoples of the Earth. [18]

Love for all humanity — love based on understanding — will create a living form of internationalism. The form of internationalism Steiner envisages as being necessary for the future development of mankind differs markedly from those 'preached' by politicians today. 'In its present form, internationalism is not a living pulse in the world; it is *preached* in the form of, say,

Marxism' — and Marxism is rooted solely in human intellectual thought. [19] Marxism visualizes human history as a natural process rooted in man's natural needs. This is the underlying idea of historical materialism. No heed is taken whatsoever to the spiritual essence of man. At the risk of overgeneralizing, we could say that all forms of internationalism today show the same shortcoming as Marxism. In it there can be no inkling of the differentiation of full and complete humanity over the earth. 'An abstraction is set up and is supposed to represent humanity, to represent man. The kind of internationalism which appears in Marxism and all that has developed from it is the result of remaining stationary within a one-sided and wholly unpractical system of thought, that is moreover merely applied to the world of sense-perception and has not penetrated to the true racial qualities.' [20] In contrast to this an internationalism, as envisaged by spiritual science, springs from a love which radiates out to all peoples and races, in order that the light received from them may be kindled in the deeds, conceptions and creations of one's own people. 'Each individual nation must so find its place in the great chorus of the peoples of the earth that it contributes to the full understanding which can alone unite them all in real and mutual knowledge.' [21] By 'real' knowledge Steiner clearly does not mean knowledge rooted in one-sided materialistic thought, but a living knowledge based on a spiritual-scientific comprehension of the totality of man, of man as a being of both worlds, of the world of matter and the world of the spirit, of man as a being who activates his thinking by the forces of the heart, by love.

Steiner then speaks of the need for indifference, antipathy and hatred to be replaced by international love. Human love alone, he says, has the power to heal the wounds wrought by antipathy, indifference and hatred. 'If mankind has no wish for this love, chaos will remain.' We must wake up out of a state of lethargy, of spiritual sleep, warns Steiner, otherwise 'the healing waves of love will not be able to flow over the waves of hatred' and transmute them.

Those who realize this need will acquire the kind of knowledge that flows from a spiritual conception of the relationships between peoples. They will take this knowledge into their feelings — 'love for humanity will be born'. They will also take it into their will — 'deeds for humanity', deeds born of love, will be accomplished. To counteract and overcome the destructive elements we need to gather together all that can unite mankind in love. 'This quest for loving unification, for unifying love, is not merely a vague feeling' [22] — it is a solemn duty men of love must carry out.

In the nineteenth century two impulses took stronger effect than ever before. The first was that of nationalism, chauvinistic nationalism. A re-emergence of the old blood principle took hold of men; the Christian impulse towards universal humanity, towards universal love, was over-shadowed by this principle of nationalism. [23] The old Luciferic principle of the blood came to life again in narrow nation consciousness. 'We see a revolt against Christianity in the nationalism of the ninteenth century. The one and only reality befitting the present age would be to overcome bellicose nationalism and for men to be stirred by the impulse of universal humanity.' [24]

The second impulse is that men sought, and still seek, in greater measure than before to draw their knowledge of the world, of the human being himself, not from 'awakened powers of soul, but from the material images of these powers'. Vision of the soul has faded, and in his physical being man is no more than an image of the spiritual. 'This image can bring forth intellectualism, but not knowledge of the spirit'. Steiner never tired from emphasizing that man can only recognize and know the spiritual by lifting himself to the spirit. [25] Strange as this may sound — and only mention of this can be made here — our thinking must be completely transformed and grow 'free' from the physical brain if it is to 'perceive' the spiritual. Intellectualism is a 'dead' form of thinking, is materialistic thinking. All thinking that is a 'product' of the physical brain is materialistic. [26] One manifestation of such thinking is Bolshevism, declares Steiner. Bolshevism owes its negative destructive power to the fact that, being a 'product' of the material brain, pure and simple, it is alien to the spirit, to the spiritual core of man. Steiner often described how the material brain really represents a process of decay, how materialistic thinking unfolds on the basis of processes of destruction, death processes, taking place in the physical brain. [27] 'If this kind of thinking', which by its very nature is 'cold' and abstract ('abstracted' from the reality of the spiritual world), 'if this kind of thinking is applied to the social life of man, as it is in, for example, Leninism and Trotskyism, a destructive process is inevitably set in motion, for such ideas about the social order issue from what is itself the foundation of destruction, namely the Ahrimanic impulse.' [28]

These two impulses, the Luciferic form of anti-Christianity, chauvinistic nationalism, and the Ahrimanic form of anti-Christianity, culminating in the tenets of Lenin and Trotsky, 'have insinuated themselves into what ought to have been the Christian impulse of the nineteenth and twentieth centuries. They are the spades with which the grave of Christianity is being dug today. Wherever these principles, these impulses, even in a mild form, become a cult, there the grave of Christianity is being prepared.'

Those who have insight can discern here a mood that is, in the real sense, the mood of Easter Saturday. Christianity lies in the grave and men place a stone over it. In truth, two stones have been laid over the grave of Christianity — the stones of chauvinistic nationalism and of external forms of Bolshevism. It now behoves humanity to inaugurate the epoch of Easter Sunday, when the stone or stones are rolled away. [29]

Taking up once more the question of the nature of intellectual thinking, a remark made by Steiner in a lecture in which he speaks on spiritual science and sociology is instructive. The intellect, he states here, separates man from man. It is only through what he calls 'vital thinking', which reapproaches *consciously* 'certain instinctive conceptions of the cosmos', that we can reestablish our position in the social life as healthily and wholly as the man of instinct did in earlier times. The development of a revitalized and enlightened thinking, grounded in heart-warmed brotherliness, will make it possible for social organisms — living social organisms, not abstract social programmes — to emerge. Social organisms which would be in keeping with the dignity of man as a threefold being of body, soul and spirit. [30]

The following statement by Steiner is as relevant today as it was when he made it nearly sixty years ago. Who, he asks, will be the reformer; who will have the power and the love to establish peace and harmony amid social strife and disharmony? Steiner's answer to this question is, quite simply, Christ. The Christ — He and He alone will be the Reformer and the Bringer of Peace and Harmony.

When men lead a social life hallowed by acts of consecration, when they do not say 'I', but rather: When two or three, or many are gathered together in the name of Christ, then He is in the midst of us.

Activity in the sphere of social life then becomes a hallowing, a continuation of the sacred acts of cult and rite in olden times. Christ Himself will be the great social Reformer, for He works today, since the Mystery of Golgotha, as a *living entity* within the being of man. [31]

*   *   *   *

We cannot possibly do justice to Rudolf Steiner's far-reaching conception of a threefold commonwealth in these few pages and refer the interested reader to his fundamental books and lectures in this field. [32] We must confine ourselves to the theme of the significance of the power of love and trust that the following few remarks will stimulate the reader to a deeper study of what Steiner has to contribute towards the realization of a truly human economic, socio-political, and spiritual life.

Taken in isolation and out of context the following statement about the true nature of labour may appear far-fetched, perhaps, but it is included here because of its relevance to the paramount importance Steiner attaches to the power of love. In the statement in question he gives an indication of the true nature of man's labour. Steiner stresses that in the society of the future a proper understanding of labour will be vital. In his view, what is usually said about the *nature* of labour is invalid. For instance, labour is usually considered to be primarily concerned with the production of goods — Karl Marx calls commodities 'crystallized labour power'. This is not so, for what really takes place when a man works is that he 'uses himself up' in a certain sense. Self-consumption is the primary element; but this self-consumption can be brought about in countless ways, i.e. not merely in producing goods. For instance, you might exert yourself in sports and use your 'working power' in this way. You might, of course, chop wood or do some other chore. The work-power used — the power you expend — may be the same whether you clean someone's house, chop wood in your own backyard for your wife and family, or play a game of tennis. Indeed, you may well expend, consume yourself, more in the latter activity than in the former! In other words, the important thing is not how much work-power you exert, but for what purpose you use it in social life. Labour, as such, cannot be said to be the prerogative, as it were, of the activity of producing goods.

The next step to be taken in the direction of regarding labour in a different way from that which has overwhelmed humanity in the last century or so is this: instead of 'What can I get for my labour, for the power I expend?' we could say: 'What can I give to my fellow-men through my efforts?'. Once this attitude has been changed, then the idea put forward by Steiner does not seem far-fetched: 'That which must be the basis for a man's work must be the joy and love for work itself.' [33] A truly social structure for society will be achieved only when we find the way to *love* and *want* to work.

In future, men will never be warmed through by joy and love for work (as was the case in the past when things were more instinctive) if society is not permeated by such ideas and feelings which can enter the world of humanity through the inspired concepts imparted by spiritual science. In order that joy and love for work be reborn in us we need a spiritual science of man that can permeate the hearts and souls of us *all*. Such joy and love cannot be inspired in men on the basis of the hollow, spiritless concepts proclaimed in one-sided socio-political programmes, such as that put forward by Karl Marx, no matter how right they may be, theoretically, in some respects. Only concepts based on a loving understanding of the totality of the threefold social organism — of the economic, socio-political and spiritual spheres and their functions in the community and in the individual — only such concepts will give birth to love for work given and love for work acknowledged.

Love for the Divine in man — no matter what his function in society — can form the basis for a relationship to work which will be truly satisfying to man's aspirations in all three spheres of the social organism.

Steiner also speaks in very clear terms regarding the significance of inspired concepts of labour. The significance of such concepts imparted by spiritual science, producing joy and love for work, will be realized only if one person meets another as an equal, if real equality governs in the life of rights; that is, if every individual be permitted to contribute what of value lives in him. [34]

In all spheres of human activity, be it in education, economics, science, and so forth, we could say, with Steiner: whereas the egotistical point of view makes man more and more abstract, theoretical, inclines him towards one-sided 'head-thinking', the unegotistical point of view urges him to understand the world and his fellow-men with love, with warmth of soul, with 'heart-thinking'.

This unegotistical point of view can be transformed into a

selfless, loving and understanding attitude to life and to one's fellow-men when one undertakes to replace the analytical intellect by the faculty of imagination, by the creative, artistic, image-forming powers that dwell in human thinking. This faculty brings experiences that may be described as a form of spiritual vision, spiritual seeing. In a series of lectures Steiner gave in Dornach shortly after the end of the First World War, which in English bears the title *The Challenge of the Times*, [35] he repeatedly stressed the urgent need to transform our mode of thinking if there is to be any real hope of creating a society truly worthy of man. Among many statements as relevant today as they were over fifty years ago — and also pertinent to our theme — are those dealing with the necessity of the transformation just mentioned.

Steiner reminds us that the social, personal relationships into which men entered in ancient times had their origin in the 'unconscious spirit vibrating in the blood' and furthermore that, in accordance with Jehovah wisdom, whereas the heathen peoples had their myths in pictorial form, created through atavism in ancient cultural forms, the Jewish people were given the Law, were given abstractions, not myths in pictorial form. The basic Hebrew command 'Thou shalt make unto thyself no image' still holds sway over us today. We think primarily in terms of abstractions. But, to quote Steiner, 'Man must again attain the capacity of soul that can form images — and consciously this time'. It is only on the basis of man's faculty of imagination, of living, creative thinking, that the relationships between man and man, that the social life in all its aspects, economic, legal and spiritual, can be rightly established in the future. 'The future form of the social life will depend upon the capacity to exercise in a conscious way the same force that once existed atavistically, in unconsciousness or semi-conscious form, in man's myth building capacity.' Should we continue to disseminate mere abstractions, mere abstract formulae and laws, then we 'should be completely filled with anti-social instincts'. [36]

We must, then, says Steiner, cultivate the 'pictorial', consciously cultivate our faculty of imagination. If we do this, then we shall no longer pass one another by as one spectre passes another, so that we form no living, creative picture of each other, but merely define each other with abstract concepts. 'The truth is that we do nothing more at present. One spectre forms the conception, "That is a nice fellow", and the other, "That is not such a nice fellow" ... "He is a bad man" ... "He is a good

man" — all sorts of such abstract concepts abound. In the
relationships between man and man we have nothing but a
bundle of abstract concepts. This is the essential thing that has
entered into humanity out of the Old Testament form of life:
"Make unto thyself no image". It must inevitably lead to an
anti-social life if we should continue in the same way.' [37]

However, the capacity to be stimulated in such a way that,
when we confront another person, a picture of his real being
arises within us, 'will come to realization. It will enter as a special
social impulse into human life' — if we undertake a self-education that leads to spiritual 'seeing', to the development of innate
seeds that can grow into the creative, artistic, image-forming
powers that dwell in our thinking.

In answer to the obvious question, how we should set about
gradually attaining the capacity to cause the living picture of
another person to emerge before our inner vision, Steiner gives
us an exercise that can help us develop this faculty. By way of
introducing us to this exercise he states that it is most important
that the impulse be implanted in us to look back through our lives
in a special way. For the most part what usually develops as
memories of earlier experiences of our lives is markedly selfish in
character. We have to look back in a far more unselfish way to
what we have experienced in childhood, in our youth, and so on.
'You have to look back into your life and pay less attention to what
interests you in your respectable person, and much more to those
people who have come into contact with you — educating you,
befriending you, assisting you, perhaps even injuring you, often
hurting you in a helpful way. One thing will then soon become
evident: how little reason you really have to ascribe to yourself
what you have become.' [38] In a comprehensive sense, an unselfish
survey of our lives comprises all manner of situations and events
that do not give us cause to immerse ourselves selfishly in
ourselves, 'to brood egotistically over ourselves', [39] but induce us
to widen and fill our view of ourselves to embrace those who have
come into contact with us, who have given of themselves to us.
'Let us immerse ourselves with real love in what has come into
our life.' [40] Such an exercise, frequently undertaken, gives rise to
the self-observation: 'How little cause do I have to occupy myself
with myself! How rich my life has become due to all those who
have entered my life in one way or another.' In this way, Steiner
continues, 'We free ourselves from ourselves, when we carry out
such an unselfish, loving survey. We free ourselves from that evil

of our times — brooding over ourselves. Anyone who has once felt the power of such self-observation as just described will find himself far too uninteresting to spend much time brooding over his own life.' [41]

Through such a cultivation of selfless recollection, through the development of our creative faculty of picturing, imaging, imbued with gratitude and love for those who have 'met' us in our lives, we gradually acquire the imaginative forces necessary to confront our contemporaries in such a way that it is no longer our self-centred sympathies or antipathies which form abstract judgements and opinions — allowing us only to see the spectre of the other human being, but the essence of the other speaks to us.

To reiterate: through the developed power of love and the faculty of imagination we can acquire powers of knowledge that enable us to 'perceive' the eternal in human nature. 'And through this we acquire a new feeling, worthy of the human being, as to what man really is'. In consequence, for instance, 'in meeting our neighbours we notice in them what is born out of the spiritual world, and see in them a part of this spiritual world. The ethical aspect of human life is then ennobled, social life is ennobled by the spirit.' We also gain the ability to know that what we do in our actions has meaning not only for us and our fellow-men here and now, not only for the earth, but for the whole world. When we develop social ideas which are born of love, we are developing something which has meaning for the whole of humanity, for the present and the future, for the cosmos. [42]

Our creative, image-forming powers, nurtured in selfless and loving recollection of others, grow into a living and ever present faculty, which brings about a transformation of our everyday consciousness, our analytical intellect, into a creative, imaginative, artistic consciousness, into what Steiner terms, in short, Imagination — an exact, fantasy-free form of spiritual vision. Once we have experienced this ourselves we recognize the validity of Steiner's statement that the intellect, which by its very nature is analytical, can only deal with and understand the non-living, i.e. the world of matter, whereas forms of consciousness such as Imagination are needed to be able to enter into a real relationship with life, with the soul-spiritual in man and nature. Fundamental to this ability is the power of love.

We may now say, with Steiner: 'The cultivation of the social life, which in earlier times had its source in the bonds of blood, does not, for our present age and in the future, depend so much upon any sort of socialistic programmes, but upon man's becoming a spiritual-social being.' We could say: upon his *becoming aware* of the fact that he is such a being. He will become so aware 'he will become such a being by awakening within himself the deeper forces that can bring to birth within him the capacity for conceiving, in imaginative consciousness, the other human being'. Otherwise, to reiterate and emphasize the point already made, 'we shall always remain anti-social beings, capable of approaching others only according to our sympathies and antipathies'. [43] If we can conceive 'pictorially' our fellow-men, then we become aware of the following two inner occurrences: the invisible, the essential in the other human being becomes inwardly visible to us, and we enrich our own soul, or, as Steiner puts it: 'We bestow a treasure upon our own inner soul life with each human acquaintanceship. Then we no longer live so that A lives "there", B "here", C "there", but A, B and C live in D; A, B and D live in C, and so on. We gain the capacity to have other human beings live in us.' [44] We become one with our fellow-men. And the foundation for this is our own loving, selfless understanding and recognition of the other through the newly won capacity of liberating oneself from oneself. [45]

'But this', says Steiner, 'must be acquired.'

It is not born in us. If we should continue simply to cultivate those characteristics that are born in us, we should continue within the limits of a mere blood culture, not the culture to which could be ascribed in the true sense of the word human brotherhood. Only when we carry the other human being within us can we really speak of human brotherhood. When we form a picture, an imagination of the other person which is implanted as a treasure in our own souls, then we carry within the realm of our soul-life something essential of him, just as in the case of a brother or sister we carry around something within us through the fact that there is common blood. *This elective affinity as the basis of social life must take the place in this concrete way of the mere blood affinity*. [46]

There is a further important element that must be borne in mind in our endeavour to overcome the present 'spectre' mentality outlined above, in our efforts to see in another person standing before us a particular human being, not human beings in general — 'the generalized human being, the abstract man, does not exist'. [47] This element, fundamental to Steiner's conception of a threefold social order, may be described as follows. All enslavement of thought, all moulding and manipulating of the thinking of one man by another, that has come from earlier ages in which it was justified — be it the Mosaic law, religious dogma, political propaganda, and so forth — all such restrictive practices must be eliminated from the world of man if true socialization is to come into being. Or, in other words, freedom of spiritual life, freedom of thought, is essential to the realization of a process of socialization that is true to man's soul-spiritual essence.

Human beings have hitherto been separated — this process of separation has come to a head in the last few centuries particularly through the one-sided stress on man's intellect. As Steiner shows on countless occasions, this process was fully 'justified', but we have now reached the stage in human evolution when this onesidedness needs to be overcome. Instead of the analytical, 'separating' intellect dealing with matters for which it is entirely inept (with, for instance, the creation of a dynamic social organism) we need to cultivate the kind of living thinking to which reference is made throughout these pages.

Human beings, then, have gone through and are still going through the experience of separateness from each other. We have discussed briefly one important issue involved in the process of creating a true brotherhood, namely, the nurturing of an imaginative consciousness in order to bring into being the inner experience of being at one with another human being. Now, Steiner points out, it is equally important that this experience does not lead to the annihilation of the individuality; that, to express it rather extremely perhaps, humanity does not end up dimly experiencing itself as an amorphous mass.

It has previously been stated that to expound Steiner's conception of a threefold social [48] order is beyond the bounds of the present thesis, but the following two paragraphs, quoted here in full, not only give a fair summary of this conception, but are also relevant to the points made in this chapter.

The threefold social order aims at establishing an independent self-grounded life of the spirit, and therewith a free field where a man may learn in life's fullness to understand what this human society is, for which he is called on to work, a free field where he may learn to see what each single piece of work means for the combined fabric of the social order, and see it in such a light that he will learn to love the single piece of work because of its value for the whole. This social order aims to create, in this free life of the spirit, the deeper principles which can replace the motive forces arising from desire of personal gain. Only in a free life of spirit can some such love spring up from the human social order, the love which an artist has for the work growing before his eyes, under his hands. If one is not prepared to consider a free life of spirit in which to cultivate this kind of love, then one may as well renounce all attempts to construct a new order of society. Those who doubt that men are capable of being educated to this kind of love must give up all hope of eliminating personal gain from economic life. Anyone who fails to believe that a free spiritual life in man begets this kind of love is unaware that it is just the dependence of spiritual life upon state and economics which creates the desire for personal gain, and that this desire of gain is not a primary outcome of human nature.

Whilst the free life of the spirit will create the motives for developing individual ability, the democratically ordered life of the 'rights'-sphere will give the needful impulses for the will to work. Real relations will grow up between the people united in a common social body, when every adult person has a voice and rules his own rights with every other person. Real relations will grow up that can fire the will to work for the community. One must reflect that a truly communal feeling can only grow up from such 'man-to-man' relations and, from this feeling, the will also to work. [49]

Earlier in this chapter mention was made of a characteristic feature of the East — a strongly developed sense of fraternity — and of a characteristic feature of the West, particularly of America — an economic life destitute of brotherliness; and it was indicated that we, in Europe, have the task of synthesizing these two contrasting trends. Our concern was the economic aspect of a true brotherhood of man.

Side by side with this aspect we can also place another vital task to be undertaken: the creation of a philo-sophia of life that will bring about a harmonizing union and subsequent step forwards towards universal love, a philosophy of life that will 'inject' new life into the spiritual conceptions of both East and West.

Let us consider East and West in the light of their 'philosophical' conceptions of life.

We, in the West, are accustomed to sharply delineated concepts, concepts closely linked to external observation. In contrast, the notions of the Orient — 'shifting, fluctuating, less closely and less sharply linked to externals' — appear dreamlike to our Western minds. We realize, perhaps, that from this dreamlike spiritual life, embodied in the most splendid poems, the Vedas, there did of course develop the clear-cut concepts of a comprehensive philosophy — for example, Vedanta. But these concepts were not gained by examining external data, that is, analytically, but emerged from an inwardly experienced and apprehended spiritual life. [50]

At the time when the Oriental was developing the finest part of his philosophy of life (which has since come down to his descendants in a partially decadent condition), the East created everything with devoted love. 'Love lives in each of its ideas, concepts and images. In them all we perceive love. This love seeks to flow out into the sense-world. And it flows out and conjures up before our soul the symbols that the Oriental established, with an inner understanding of much that functions supersensibly, in seeking to establish what he perceived as the spiritual element in the world of nature.' [51]

Against this configuration of spirit we may set the outlook that has developed, with no less justification, in the West. Here, we find, it is regarded as an ideal to stand back from what the senses observe directly and to test what nature offers in regard to position, motion, dimensions and weight. What presents itself directly to the eye is dissected and placed under a microscope. Notions of the world then emerge that are entirely dependent on the use of such instruments. In the laboratory we grow increasingly rich in concepts remote from direct observation and experience. For instance, by means of intricate instruments we examine light flooding through the universe and our investigation gives rise to all manner of abstract concepts. We certainly need such concepts in order to deepen our understanding of the nature of light, but how remote are the observations recorded from what we encounter as light and colour in nature itself! What we formulate in our sharply delineated concepts — with the help of various instruments — may bring us nearer to a solution of this or that riddle, but it does not bring us to direct observation of nature. One often hears the view: direct your attention to sensory observation and then try to derive your philosophy of life from it. But this is too simplistic a view, for the scientific view of life we establish in the Western world is, in fact, far removed from what the senses observe. Steiner suggests that what we need to do in order to reach the essence of nature again is this: if we establish a corpus of knowledge based on the use of equipment of technological knowledge 'with which we have harvested perhaps the finest fruits of present day natural science', then we need to 're-tune our soul' before we can approach nature, the essence of nature, again. If, for example, as botanists, we have used the microscope extensively — and, thereby, gained much valuable knowledge regarding cell-life, and so forth — and, as a result of our observations formulated concepts in the atomistic manner characteristic of the modern scientific approach, 'then we shall have to re-tune our soul before we can recapture a love of the immediate world of plants as it grows and flowers'. [52] Again, if we have formed a scientific concept of the structure of animal and man, then we shall have to 're-tune' if we want to move to direct observation of the animal's shape and actions, if we want to enjoy the way it plays in the meadow or turns its gaze upon us.

The Oriental had no re-tuning to do in this sense. Since what he called science — until the influence of the West had ousted it to a large extent — was shot through with love, and he was led by it to immediate observation of nature. 'And this was a direct echo of what he experienced in his soul.' [53]

The ancient Oriental sensed that the spiritual world is a reality with which he felt closely linked, and he sensed that nature, including the natural element within himself, is a 'replica of the spiritual — that it provides an external garment for the revelation of what is spiritual'. Something of this ancient attitude of soul can still be sensed in the East today in a diluted form. From everything that he faithfully observed and lovingly honoured as a 'replica', something of the spirit shone. 'Nature shone spirit upon him, revealed spirit to him. And this spirit was his reality.' [54] What lay before him as sense world, as physical nature, was Maya.

However, Steiner reminds us, we can sense how, already in Buddhism, from the sixth century B.C. onwards, the experience of the great non-being Maya gradually became predominant and the sense of inhabiting a spiritual world paled. He no longer saw the world of nature as a 'replica' of the spiritual and he turned away from it, regarding it as mere illusion.

If we wish to regain something of the spirit of the ancient Oriental conception of nature, if we strive to imbue our philosophy of life with spirit, we must do so 'with complete self-possession and lucid consciousness' — not in the instinctive way of the Orient — and, most certainly, 'the impairment of human activity relative to the demands of the physical, external world must not occur a second time in the world's development.

Man must never again *escape* into spiritual activity and so prevent himself from devoting his strength and love to earthly tasks.' [55]

If we now consider Western civilization we see that there has developed an outlook diametrically opposed to what had long prevailed in the Orient and still survives in a diluted form. The most extreme form of the Western outlook is, as we have previously discussed, to be found in economic materialism. The scientific method, with its increasing emphasis on matter, has given rise to the view that historical reality consists simply of economic struggles, economic patterns, class struggles; in short, of the immediate material elements, externally sensuous and physical, in human life and history. Economic forces are considered to be the true reality. Moreover, what the soul experiences is not reality. True reality is only what exists externally in the form of tangible, visible elements and facts.

In the East: true reality is what is experienced within, in the soul and spirit, and physical actuality is illusion, is Maya. In the West: Maya is what is experienced in the soul and spirit, and reality is what is tangibly displayed, visibly perceptible in the world.

These are polar extremes, it is true, and there are a multiplicity of modifications in both outlooks. But the point to bear in mind is that the one could only have arisen in the East and the other only in the West.

Before us, then, are two pictures: spiritual world as reality and world of the senses as Maya, on the one hand, and world of the senses as reality and spiritual world as Maya, on the other.

Now, we need a philosophy of life, says Steiner, that is capable of injecting the spiritual world, regarded by the Western world in general as ideology, as Maya, with 'spiritual imagination, inspiration and intuition, so that what today appears unutterably empty may be filled once more with spiritual meaning and content'. [56] At the same time this philosophy of life must be able to perceive that what the Orient regards as illusion and Maya is a reality in the sense that it is a true and faithful 'replica', a manifestation of the spiritual world, and that it is in this 'replica' that man can develop spiritual freedom. What Steiner means by statements of this kind is this: when a man *feels* closely linked to the spiritual world — as he did, instinctively, in the East — he feels at the same time 'inwardly determined and dependent on it'. Therefore, in order to be able to act, morally, out of freedom and love, man, during the course of evolution, had to turn, with his consciousness, from the spiritual world to the world of mere fact. Confronted with this external actuality, the life of man's soul becomes an image of it. The spirit informing this life turns into abstract concepts and gradually becomes a mere image. Now, says Steiner, 'by having images within us, we can be free. Mirror-images do not determine our actions. If we wish to conform to mirror-images, the impulse to do so must come from us. The same is true of abstract concepts.' Abstract thinking must evolve to pure thinking. 'In making its appearance in pure thinking the moral and religious element', rooted in love, 'becomes for us an impulse of freedom.' [57]

We can see development, therefore, in the following way: from instinctively felt spirit-reality in the ancient Orient to the spirit as abstraction in Western ideology, dialectic materialism. And we are now called upon to create out of our own spiritual essence — in freedom — living concepts, and to infuse into this 'ideology' a spiritually perceived and experienced world. A new and spiritually real form of the higher worlds must infuse with love the initially unreal concepts of dialectic materialism.

The one philosophy, that of the East, is, in some respects, 'senile'. Yet it contains things of such great value that we should approach it with reverence and love. What we encounter in the West, on the other hand, has the 'character of youthfulness, of a first step'. The 'ideology' of the West is young — and it must develop youthful power in itself so that it may attain real spiritual meaning in its own way. [58]

We should honour the Orient for its spirituality, says Steiner, but we in the West, particularly in Europe, must build up our own spirituality. If, 'for all our respect, love and admiration' for its spirituality, we learn what we need from the East, not with passive receptivity, but with a busy activity rooted in what, today, is still perhaps unspiritual in the West yet contains the germ of spirituality; if we add youthful strength to respect, love and admiration, then 'we shall do the right thing for the future of human development', [59] we shall lay a sound foundation for a realistic brotherhood of man.

The liberated spirit will bring us to real vision of the spiritual world. The spirit will also help us find the way to the equality of man. For human equality can never exist in the external economic order only. As soon as man understands the supersensible nature of his own ensouled spirit being, however, he will be able to find the law that makes him an equal among equals. He will also deepen science; for with spiritual vision . . . medicine, law, and the art of education will find their real source. Science will then lead neither to the mechanization of the spirit as it has hitherto, nor to the inequality of man, for complete freedom of the spirit will come to man when the spirit seeks it on spirit paths; human equality will come to human souls when the spirit seeks it on paths of the soul; and finally, when the human being who knows himself to be a supersensible spirit being approaches another person lovingly, then — because human beings will be associating with one another as conscious spirit beings in a loving way — in addition to having a liberated spirit and a soul that is equal with its neighbours, man will have, both in his human nature and in social life, a true, spiritualized, ensouled, thoroughly human brotherliness! [60]

24.

LOVE, CHRIST AND OUR IDEALS

The weaving essence of the Light rays forth
From Man to Man
To fill the world with Truth.
Love's blessing warmeth Soul by Soul,
To call forth bounty of all worlds,
And Angel-beings, they unite
Man's deeds of blessing with World-aims Divine.
And when Man, welding both, beholds
Himself in Spirit-Man,
Then Light of Spirit
Rays through Warmth of Soul. [1]

24.

He who accepts the truth of spiritual science 'lives for others, even if at first he is impelled by an egoistic longing for the spiritual worlds. If the path is right then it is of itself the destroyer of selfseeking and is the best educator of selflessness'. [2]

Spiritual science is necessary for humanity for its further progress. What is to take place for the transforming of mankind must be brought about through men themselves. [3]

Occult development is now needed by mankind and must be implanted into it. An earnest, selfless striving for truth, step by step, this alone leads to genuine brotherliness, this is the magician which can best bring about the uniting of humanity. This will serve as the means to bring about humanity's great goal, unity; and we shall reach this goal when we develop the means to it in ourselves, when we seek to acquire these means in the noblest, purest way, for it is a matter of hallowing humanity . . . . [4]

If Spiritual Science has been understood, not merely abstractly, but so that feelings have been evoked through knowledge of facts, then it can work directly into life. When this knowledge flows into our whole organism, from head to heart and thence into the hand, into all that we are and create, then we have grasped the foundations of true spiritual science. [5]

True social love, the right feeling of love which ought to exist between human beings, will come into the world as the fruit of true spiritual science. [6]

It will be apparent from Steiner's statements just quoted and from the foregoing pages that it is not enough merely to know about supersensible things. We must know with feeling, and feel with knowledge. Our knowledge must be acompanied by feeling, and our feeling by knowledge. [7]

Steiner warns repeatedly that those who undertake to develop themselves spiritually should not neglect Nature.

If, in our striving for spiritual knowledge, we tend to 'lead the soul away from love of Nature, confusion alone ensues. The true starting-point of spiritual-scientific thoughts cannot be found in the belittling of what Nature reveals to us.' To despise Nature, to disregard the truth which flows to us from the phenomena of life and the world of nature, to turn our backs on the beauty that pervades these phenomena and not to recognize the tasks they set us to perform — this attitude of mind and soul 'can at most produce a caricature of spiritual truth'. Such a 'caricature', continues Steiner, will always "be tinged with the personal element", and, moreover, experienced in a dreamlike way. [8] Spiritual science, rightly experienced, unites man with man, in full consciousness. In a dreamlike state man separates himself from his fellow-men. He who lives in his own dreams, cuts himself off from Nature and he distances himself from the world of men. In waking life we find each other, in dreaming life we isolate ourselves from each other.

Now it is true that in everyday waking life we have a sense of community, but we also sense that this community is circumscribed and confined within narrow limits. We sense, in our hearts, that the true community of human life embraces far more than what everyday life offers us, and, just as we look upwards, outwardly, to the heavens, to the sun, to find the source of light that irradiates the life of common day, so, too, do we inwardly direct our attention, not to the world of Nature, to the world of sense-perception, but to the reality of the Spirit in order to find the true source of humanity where the soul can experience the fullness of community it seeks and needs. [9]

This inner direction of our attention to the spiritual source is clearly what spiritual striving is all about, but, and this is the point Steiner makes, in so doing we should be wary of despising the world of Nature. We may all too easily turn our backs on life, instead of entering more fully and lovingly into it. We may all too easily fall into that isolation of the soul of which 'dreaming' is a good example.

Let us rather educate our minds by contact with the light of truth which streams into the soul of man from Nature. Then we shall best develop the sense for the truths of Man, which are at the same time the truths of the Cosmos. The truths of Nature, experienced with free and open mind, lead us already towards the truths of the Spirit. When we fill ourselves with the beauty, greatness and majesty of

Nature, it grows in us to a fountain of true feeling for the Spirit. And when we open our hearts to the silent gesture of Nature revealing her eternal innocence beyond all good and evil, our eyes are opened presently to the spiritual World, from whence — into the silent gesture — the living Word rings forth, revealing good and evil.

Spiritual dreaming, elaborated in contradiction to true knowledge of Nature, can but impoverish the human heart. Spirit perception, brought up in the loving perception of Nature, brings to life the true riches of the soul. [10]

'The greatest contribution to the development of spiritual life and culture will be accomplished when human beings meet in such a way that each presupposes and then senses the sacred mystery in the other. Then will the right relationship be established from man to man, and love will permeate the soul in a truly human way.' It is only in a relationship founded on the recognition of the sacred essence in each other that the right feelings of love can be cultivated. That 'we should be able to understand and love every human soul really means that we should be able to sense the sacred mystery of the other, for then love permeates the soul in a truly human way'. [11]

True love, Steiner stresses, must be guided by another virtue — by the interest in and understanding of the person to whom we give our love. Warmth of heart, love, can cause harm 'when it is passionately manifested; when it appears merely as a quality of human nature without being guided by wisdom and truth'. [12]

Interest and understanding, which connect us with the world in the right way, must lead and guide us when, with our love, we turn to the world. [13] Love is 'flanked' by what man has developed as truth — manifesting itself, in due course, as the belief in supersensible knowledge, for instance, on the one side; and by life-wisdom, originating in ourselves, on the other, and manifesting itself in such a way that we sense it to be a 'divine spiritual regulator that, like conscience, leads securely along the true middle path'. [14]

In ancient times man had not yet descended so deeply into the physical plane as he finds himself today, but was still closely connected, *instinctively*, with divine impulses, a condition that, in the future, he will *consciously* strive to reattain 'when he is imbued more by truth, love and life-wisdom in regard to the physical plane, and when, in regard to spiritual knowledge, he is actuated by faith in the divine, supersensible world'. It is not necessarily so, Steiner says, that faith will directly lead into that world, but it will, in due course, be transformed into supersensible knowledge.

'Faith, Love, Conscience [15] — these three forces will become the three stars of the moral forces that shall enter into human souls.' [16]

* * * *

In a lecture given just a few weeks before the outbreak of the First World War Steiner speaks at some length on the significance and attainment of ideals. [17]

He begins by mentioning that in addition to the pleasure, satisfaction and benefit we derive from the sunlight we also enjoy the sure knowledge that the setting sun will rise anew for us on the following morning. 'This is a part of the confidence that lives in our soul — confidence in the lasting reality of the physical world order.' [18] We could, of course, find many examples of such confidence in our everyday experience of life.

But, Steiner says, there is something of special significance for our inner soul life. This 'something' comprises our ideals. When we feel and think 'in a higher sense', our ideals belong to those things that are of greater importance to us than external reality. 'It is our ideals that set our souls inwardly aflame and make life valuable and precious to us. But when we look at external life and at what assures for us the reality of this life, we are often troubled by the thought: does this external reality contain something that assures to us just that which is most precious to us — the realization of our ideals?' [19]

Innumerable inner conflicts arise in our souls because we doubt, to a greater or lesser degree, the realization of our ideals. Certainly it is true that, on the basis of our experience of physical reality, we cannot conclude that our ideals will prove to be the seed of a future reality in the same way as, for instance, plant seeds will bear fruit during the course of their growth. We may cherish the belief that our ideals will have some real significance for life, but certainty in the sense just described in regard to the sunrise, or next year's harvest, we cannot have. 'We should like our ideals to be the seeds for a future, but we look in vain for that which can give them assured reality.' [20] Moreover, we can so easily feel in regard to our ideals that they not only have no inherent guarantee of reality in the general, everyday life of men, but that they actually tend to alienate us from our fellow-men. [21]

But, declares Steiner, this need not be. When we permeate with Christ's Divine Love 'all that we attain spiritually, when we feel the Christ in us, knowing that what we receive' — in the way of a spiritual impulse towards the realization of an ideal — 'is also received by the Christ in us — "Not I, but Christ in me" — then we do not look upon our ideals as though they tended to alienate us from the world, from our fellow-men.' True, through this realization, our ideals have not as yet 'that guarantee of their own reality, their own actuality, which inheres in the plant seed for the coming year, but when they are committed to the Christ within us, then they are real seed'. Our ideals are then real germs of future reality. 'Christ-enfilled idealism is permeated with the seed of reality. Christ bears our ideals on into the future — just as the God of Nature bears the plant-seeds of this year into the coming year. This gives reality, certainty to idealism.' [22]

But something else can also become a reality in a matter of immense human significance. If we can experience this 'Not I, but Christ in me' in such a way that it is inner truth, then, and only then, may we say and mean the words: 'Yes, I love Him above all, even above myself.' When the 'Not I, but the Christ in me' forms the foundation and content of my thoughts, deeds and feelings, then I have fulfilled the exhortation, 'Love thy neighbour as thyself' — for what I have attained for myself will, given reality by Christ's Love, become the common possession of all humanity and bear fruit for the whole of mankind. [23]

APPENDIX

AHRIMAN AND LUCIFER

Steiner sees evil as being embodied in two forces, which are not only opposed to man's spiritual development but also, in a certain sense, to one another. To the leaders of these forces he gave the time-honoured names of Lucifer (Isaiah 14: 12) and Ahriman (from the old Persian 'Aingra Mainyu', the spirit of darkness and evil).

Whereas the generally accepted view is that good and evil are polarities, Steiner emphasizes a threefold nature: two opposing forces of evil with the good 'standing' in the middle. The good strives to balance, redeem and heal, not merely to fight the forces of evil. [1]

Let us consider a few examples to show how two opposing 'evil' and undesirable traits, predispositions, which enter the human soul, are balanced, raised and transformed by the 'good':

pedantry	*orderliness*	disorderliness (chaos)
cowardice	*bravery*	recklessness (foolhardiness)
apathy	*concern*	over-sensitivity
indifference	*compassion*	effusiveness
sluggishness	*steadfastness*	excitability
miserliness	*thrift*	wastefulness
rigidity	*equanimity*	vacillation
love of ease	*controlled creative activity*	thoughtless over-activity

From these examples, which could be added to *ad infinitum*, we can readily see that the 'positive', the 'good' in each case, situated between two extremes, does indeed bring about a process of balance and transformation. For instance, 'bravery' is born in man's soul as a result of an effort of will to conquer two opposing tendencies — cowardice and recklessness. [2] If the effort of will were not made, then either one or the other extreme would assume the upper hand; or, if they were of equal power, they would annul each other and a situation of stalemate, even of regression, would ensue. We see here the truth of the contention that 'evil' is necessary in order that 'good' should manifest itself. [3]

In general terms we may say that the manifestations induced by Ahriman (on the left-hand side of the table of examples) are indicative of ossifying, hardening processes, of paralysis and inner stagnation, whereas those encouraged by Lucifer (on the right-hand side of the table) are expressive of processes of dissolution, self-intoxication, illusion and formlessness.

If we consider these two forces in a broader context we could say that both endeavour to distort man's powers of inner freedom, of spiritual activity.

Lucifer, the master of delusion, tempts man to believe that he is 'like unto a god', more powerful and beautiful than in reality he is; he appeals to man's pride and instils in him the thought that he has no limitations (the story of Icarus illustrates this point well). We can also recognize that what lives in the human soul as surging emotion and passion is brought into being by the influence of Lucifer. Indulgence in excessive expressions of feeling is fruitless in regard to real, everyday life and so easily leads man into illusory fantasies about the spiritual world that have no basis in real life. Hazy occultism and mysticism, characteristic preoccupations of such souls, nourish the creation of a spectral and hallucinatory world.

In contrast to this is the petrifying power of Ahriman. He would have man develop a one-sided, coldly analytical intellect capable of comprehending the world of matter and its underlying laws, but closed to the influence of the spiritual world. Working predominantly with lifeless formulae — Ahriman is the master of formulae and clear-cut, once-and-for-ever definitions — the human soul is subject to processes of dessication and under peril of being reduced to a barren wasteland.

There are, then, two main possibilities, two main directions of error: we can either fall prey to an over-estimation of and craving for the material world; or we can fail to find a healthy relationship with the requirements of earth existence and, as a consequence, 'float' in some fantasy world of our own making. Ahriman would reduce the human being to little more than an automaton who finds contentment in the satisfaction of his material needs; Lucifer would render man conceited in self-deification and arrogantly neglectful of the physical world. [4] To illustrate a certain aspect of the point just made we could say that cowardice is a manifestation of the over-estimation of one's material body and physical safety, whereas recklessness could be seen as a tendency towards a thoughtless disregard of one's physical life.

Much else could be mentioned in regard to the soul and its conflicts with Lucifer and Ahriman, but enough has been indicated to enable the interested reader to pursue further self-exploration in the direction outlined.

Now, man is a threefold being. He is a being of body, soul and spirit. These three 'components' are clearly so intimately interconnected that it is not difficult to realize that an influence on or damage to the one inevitably affects the other two sooner or later. We may, therefore, justifiably speak of the activities, the manifestations of detrimental forces of 'evil' not only in man's soul but in his spiritual being and physical body too. However, to go into such detail is beyond the scope of this appendical note. [5]

*   *   *   *

The emphasis so far has been on the 'negative', 'evil' aspects of the Luciferic and Ahrimanic forces. To omit some mention of the 'positive' and helpful aspects of these two mighty spiritual forces would be a disservice to those unfamiliar with Steiner's work, since it would leave an untruthful picture of these forces and the contributions which they, in spite of themselves, make towards man's spiritual development.

Both forces play an essential role in the liberation of the individual. [6] Without them man would and could not attain to love- and wisdom-filled freedom of spiritual activity. We could say that their very 'negative', 'evil' qualities act as a spur in our souls towards such an attainment.

Lucifer acts as the midwife at the birth of the human soul and its liberation from the paradisal state. The separation from the Divine World had to take place in order that man should eventually achieve selfless love in full consciousness. [7] It is just through the activity of this Spirit Being (beginning with the temptation of man in the Garden of Eden) that a seed was sown that can grow and blossom into man's attainment of spiritual freedom.

Ahriman, the spirit of soul-less material abundance and ease, also places us in a situation where we have freedom of choice. For instance, through his activity we are given the possibility of either succumbing to a robot-existence, or of availing ourselves of the technological and scientific achievements he has inspired in us in order to lead a life more free from the limits of natural law and necessity than it otherwise could be. It is to Ahriman that we owe our technological ingenuity. Technology is a positive fruit of his activity.

Steiner gives many examples of Ahriman's 'legitimate' tasks in the spiritual world and in the affairs of man. One example of the latter is to be seen where Ahriman creates a disharmony between physical facts and our ideas about and memories of such facts. If Ahriman were not to do this, 'there would be no lying in the world'. [9] 'Suppose,' continues Steiner, 'Ahriman were not active at all. If he were not there we should be like innocent lambs, for the impulse would continually be *never* to form concepts which did not tally with the facts. We should only express what we actually observed as fact but we should do this of *necessity*. It would be impossible for us to do anything else and there would be no question of free spiritual activity. In order to be able to speak the truth as *free* beings, the possibility to lie must also be in us. In other words, we must acquire the power to conquer Ahriman within us at every moment.' [10]

It is to the Luciferic forces that we owe our artistic gifts. Art is a positive fruit of their activity. Rightly approached these forces can free us from Ahriman, who would direct our full attention solely to the prosaic, factual circumstances of the physical world. Through this liberation we can gain the faculty of creative, imaginative thinking, by means of which the first steps towards a conscious experience of the reality of the spiritual world are taken and the barriers to supersensible knowledge, erected by our sense-bound intellect, broken through. [11]

Similarly, approached rightly, the Ahrimanic forces can help us lead responsible lives in the world into which we have incarnated. They can assist us to remain consciously aware of every step we take in our spiritual striving and prevent us creating a Luciferic fanciful world permeated by illusion.

Held in balance by the Christ-imbued heart, both Lucifer and Ahriman are the servants man needs to fulfil his mission on earth as the one and only being who, in full consciousness and freedom, can assist the Michaelic forces to redeem, spiritualize the earth and bring into being The New Jerusalem. [12]

In short, with Rudolf Steiner, we may say: 'The task of evil is to promote the ascent of man'. [13]

ABBREVIATIONS USED IN THE NOTES

AEC	*An Esoteric Cosmology* (1978)
AI	*Anthroposophy: an Introduction* (1961) [1982]
ALT	*Anthroposophical Leading Thoughts* (1973). See also MM.
AQ	*Anthroposophical Quarterly*, 1956-1978
ASJ	*Apocalypse of St John, The* (1958) [1977]
AC	*Awakening to Community* (1974)
BDR	*Between Death and Rebirth* (1975)
BSMG	*Building Stones for an Understanding of the Mystery of Golgotha* (1945) [1972]
CT	*Challenge of the Times, The* (1979)
CHS	*Christ and the Human Soul* (1956) [1972]
CRR	*Christianity began as a Religion but is greater than all Religions* (1959)
CM	*Cosmic Memory. Atlantis and Lemuria* (1976)
DSHH	*Deeper Secrets of Human History* (1957)
DFSP	*Driving Force of Spiritual Powers, The* (1972)
ECM	*Earthly and Cosmic Man* (1948)
EDCL	*Earthly Death and Cosmic Life* (1964)
EMSL	*Education and Modern Spiritual Life* (1954). Published 1972 and 1981 with the title *A Modern Art of Education*.
ESD	*Effects of Spiritual Development, The* (1978)
EC	*Evolution of Consciousness, The* (1966) [1979]
FS	*Festivals of the Seasons* (1928)
FDLD	*Forming of Destiny and Life after Death, The* (1927)
FBC	*From Buddha to Christ* (1978)
GSJ(C)	*Gospel of St John in relation to the other Gospels, particularly to that of St. Luke, The* (Cassel, 1948) [1982]
GSJ(H)	*Gospel of St John, The* (Hamburg, 1973)
GSL	*Gospel of St Luke, The* (1975)
GSM	*Gospel of St Matthew, The* (1965)
GET	*Guidance in Esoteric Training* (1972) [1977]
HVE	*Human Values in Education* (1971)

ISBM   *Influence of Spiritual Beings upon Man, The* (1961)
         [1982]
KR   *Karmic Relationships. Esoteric Studies. Eight volumes.*
         For dates see notes.
KHW   *Knowledge of the Higher Worlds. How is it achieved?*
         1969 [1976]
LDR   *Life between Death and Rebirth. The active connection*
         between the living and the dead (1975)
LNCA   *Life, Nature and Cultivation of Anthroposophy, The*
         (1976)
MWS   *Man and the World of Stars. The Spiritual Communion*
         of Mankind (1963) [1982]
MLO   *Man in the Light of Occultism, Theosophy and*
         Philosophy (1964)
MK   *Manifestations of Karma* (1976)
MBWE   *Man's being, His Destiny and World Evolution* (1966)
MS   *Metamorphoses of the Soul* (1st edition, n.d.)
MM   *Michael Mystery, The* (1956). See also ALT.
MG   *Mystery of Golgotha, The* (1940)
ODCC   *Occult Development & Christ in the Twentieth Century*
         (1947). Published together with *The Pre-Earthly*
         Deeds of Christ. Republished [1978] separately with
         the title *Occult Science and Occult Development and*
         Christ at the Time of the Mystery of Golgotha and Christ
         in the Twentieth Century.
OS   *Occult Science. An Outline* (1979)
OSOE   *Origin of Suffering, The; The Origin of Evil; Illness* and
         Death (1980)
PKHW   *Paths to Knowledge of Higher Worlds* (1980)
PF   *Philosophy of Freedom, The.* The Basis for a Modern
         World Conception. Some Results of Introspective
         Observation following the Methods of Natural
         Science (1979). English translations of this work
         from 1922 to 1963 were published with the title *The*
         Philosophy of Spiritual Activity.
RSK   *Road to Self Knowledge, A* (1975). Published together
         with *The Threshold of the Spiritual World.*
RE   *Rosicrucian Esotericism* (1978)
ST   *Secrets of the Threshold, The* (1928)
SFM   *Spiritual Foundation of Morality, The. Francis of Assisi*
         and the Mission of Love (1979). Previously published
         with the title *Anthroposophical Ethics.*

SGE	*Spiritual Ground of Education* (1947)
SGM	*Spiritual Guidance of Mankind, The* (3rd Edition, n.d.). Published [1970] with the title *Spiritual Guidance of Man and Humanity.*
SHK	*Stages of Higher Knowledge, The* (1974)
TEW	*Tension between East and West, The* (1963)
TR	*Theosophy of the Rosicrucian* (1966) [1981]
TSW	*Threshold of the Spiritual World, The* (1975). Published together with *A Road to Self Knowledge.*
UEM	*Universe, Earth and Man. In their relationship to Egyptian Myths and Modern Civilization* (1955)
VM	*Verses and Meditations* (1961) [1972]

NOTES

In a number of instances, after consulting the original German text, the author has taken the liberty of slightly changing an authorized English translation. In other cases, where there are two or more translations, a similar liberty has been taken in that words or phrases in one translation — because they seem to the author to be more felicitous — have been substituted for those in the rendering to which reference is made.

Dates in round brackets refer to the edition from which a quotation has been made. In most cases the latest edition has been consulted.Where this has not been feasible the date of the most recent edition has been shown in square brackets.

It should be mentioned that correct academic procedure has frequently not been observed. For example, no indication is given in those instances where words, phrases, or longer passages, have been omitted in a number of the more lengthy quotations. Nor have slight adaptations — which in no way alter the sense of the original passage — been indicated, and so on.

References are to works readily available to the reader who wishes to study this or that aspect of Steiner's work in greater depth. The author hopes that the reader will find it rewarding to read the whole lecture or chapter — in some cases the whole lecture cycle or book — to place a quoted passage in its proper context. Often lectures in their entirety are relevant to the theme of the power of love.

With very few exceptions references are to books, essays and lectures by Steiner that have been translated into English. All works are by him unless otherwise stated.

Works currently in print are obtainable from the Rudolf Steiner Bookshop, 38 Museum St, London, WC1, and from The Bookshop, Rudolf Steiner House, 35 Park Road, London, NW1 6XT.

All works mentioned may be borrowed from the Lending Library at Rudolf Steiner House.

Details regarding the works of Steiner published in English can be found in the two Bibliographical Reference Lists published by Rudolf Steiner Press, Vol. I (1977), Vol. II (1979). Details of more recent publications can be obtained from the two bookshops mentioned above.

INTRODUCTION

1   VM p. 119 Cf. also OSOE pp. 19-20.

2   MS p. 55.

3   Ibid. p. 76.

4   VM p. 43.

5   *Jeshu ben Pandira* (1942), p. 2.

5a   'Anthroposophy is a path of knowledge to guide the Spiritual in the human being to the Spiritual in the universe. It arises in man as a need of the heart, of the life of feeling; and it can be justified only inasmuch as it can satisfy this inner need.'

These words, which are the best descriptive 'definition' of the meaning of the term 'Anthroposophy', were written by Rudolf Steiner in February 1924. ALT p. 13.

The terms 'Anthroposophy' and 'spiritual science' were used interchangeably by Steiner himself. With few exceptions the latter has been used in the present work.

6   *Theosophy. An Introduction to the Supersensible Knowledge of the World and the Destination of Man* (1973), p. 13.

Re Steiner's use of the term 'Theosophy' see ibid. p. 5.

Cf. also

a)   *First Steps in Supersensible Perception* (1949), pp. 53-54

b)   ESD p. 17.

c)   MLO p. 59.

d)   LNCA pp. 15-16.

e)   ODCC p. 42.

7   KHW p. 70. Cf. also PKHW pp. 27, 30.

8   KHW p. 50. Cf. also

a)   ASJ p. 30.

b)   *The Education of the Child* (1947), p. 40 [1979].

c)   *Anthroposophy and the Human Gemüt* (1946). Republished with the title *Michaelmas and the soul-forces of Man* (1982).

The untranslatable word 'Gemüt' means something like this: The mind warmed by a loving heart and stimulated by the soul's imaginative power.

Steiner's opening words to the series of four lectures are: 'One of the many misstatements made about spiritual science

(Anthroposophy) is that it is intellectualistic, that it appeals predominantly to the scientific mind, and that it does not sufficiently consider the needs of the human *Gemüt'*. (p. 1).

In the second lecture Steiner makes the following statement which is particularly relevant to our main theme: 'Our thinking appears to us cold, dry, colourless — as though spiritually emaciating us — when our thoughts take an abstract form, when we are unable to imbue them with the warmth and enthusiasm of feeling. We can call a man *gemütvoll* only when something of the inner warmth of his *Gemüt* streams forth to us when he utters his thoughts. And we can really make close contact with a man only if his behaviour towards us and the world is not merely correct and in line with duty, but if his actions manifest enthusiasm, a warm heart, a love of nature, love for every being. This human *Gemüt*, then, dwells in the very centre of man's soul life.' Ibid. p. 20.

9   MS pp. 85-87. Cf. also:
    a)   Ibid. pp. 92-98.
    b)   PKHW p. 35.
10 MS pp. 88-89.
11 Ibid. p. 89.
12 Ibid. pp. 89-90.
13 Ibid. p. 90.
14 Ibid. p. 92.
15 Cf.
    a)   AC Lecture III.
    b)   *Mystery Knowledge and Mystery Centres* (1973), pp. 11-12.
    c)   PKHW pp. 4-5, 11, 19, 54.
    d)   PF.
    e)   *The Redemption of Thinking* (1956), pp. 105-110.
    f)   Numerous passages in CL.
    g)   Otto Palmer: *Rudolf Steiner on his book The Philosophy of Freedom* (1975).
    h)   Canon A.P.Shepherd: *A Scientist of the Invisible* (1983).
16 Op. cit. (1968), p. 202.
17 *Macrocosm and Microcosm* (1968), p. 203.
18 Ibid. p. 204. Cf. also ibid. Lecture IX and the first part of Lecture XI.
19 Cf. *The Gospel of St Mark* (1947), p. 91.
    In MS Steiner comments:
    'Dissociation from the truth leads to humanly degrading egoism. Nothing but the love of truth ensures the ego's self-emancipation. To ignore truth in favour of something else signifies a corresponding lapse into selfishness. The moment a man prefers himself and

his own opinions to truth he manifestly exerts an anti-social influence and tends to alienate himself from the human community.

'Consider those who make no effort to love truth for truth's own sake, but "install" a number of their own opinions as "truth". Such people love nothing but the possession of their own soul and they are the most intolerant. The lovers of truth for the sake of their own views and opinions will not suffer others to seek truth along quite different paths. They cast a stone in the way of all who, relying on different abilities, reach different opinions from their own. Hence the many conflicts in life.

An honest striving for truth leads to human understanding in general, whereas the love of truth for the sake of one's own personality tends to intolerance and the destruction of others' freedom.' pp. 57-58.

Cf. also BSMG pp. 124-125.

1. THE MISSION AND ESSENCE OF SPIRITUAL SCIENCE

1   *The Soul's Probation* (1925), p. 160.
    Steiner wrote four Mystery Plays: *Portal of Initiation; The Soul's Probation; The Guardian of the Threshold; The Soul's Awakening.* A more recent translation of all four plays, by Ruth and Hans Pusch, was published in 1973.

2   EDCL p. 27.

3   BDR p. 168.

4   Ibid. p. 88. Cf. also *The Threefold Order of the Body Social.* Study Series II (1st edition, n.d.), p. 6.

5   *The Mission of Spiritual Science* (1917), pp. 54-55.

6   *Supersensible Knowledge as a Demand of the Age. Anthroposophy and the ethical-religious Conduct of Life* (1943), pp. 52-53.

7   AC p. 6.

8   *The Four Temperaments* (1949), p. 46 [1980].

9   CT p. 170.

10 *The Four Temperaments*, p. 46. Cf. also *Reincarnation and Immortality* (1977), p. 171.

11 *The Four Temperaments*, pp. 45-46.

12 'The Fundamental Impulses of the Old and New Mysteries'. AQ XXI, No. 2, 1976, p. 35. Cf. also *Reincarnation and Karma* (1960), p. 71.

13 ST p. 101.

14 *The Four Sacrifices of Christ* (1944), pp. 1-2 [1981].
    Cf. also:

a) 'Karmic Effects of Traits of Character'. AQ VII, No. 1, 1962.
b) LNCA pp. 36-37.

2. LOVE AND ITS MEANING IN THE WORLD

1 *The Guardian of the Threshold* (1925), p. 56.
2 *Love and its Meaning in the World* (1960) [1972].
3 Ibid. p. 9.
4 Ibid. p. 11.
5 Ibid.
6 Ibid.
7 Ibid. p. 12.
8 Ibid.
9 Cf. *Christmas. The Festivals and their Meaning.* Vol. I, (1955), p. 96.
10 *Love and its Meaning in the World*, p. 14.
11 Ibid. pp. 18-19. Cf. also *The Inner Nature of Man — and the Life between Death and a new Birth* (1959) re the threefold Rosicrucian saying: Ex Deo Nascimur — In Christo Morimur — Per Spiritum Sanctum Reviviscimus.

3. KNOWLEDGE OF THE HIGHER WORLDS

1 *The Portal of Initiation* (1925), p. 64.
2 Ibid. p. 80.
3 KHW pp. 24-25.
4 Cf. PF pp. 134-142.
5 KHW p. 111.
6 KR Vol. VII (1973), p. 99.
7 Ibid.
8 Ibid. pp. 96-97.
9 Ibid. p. 97.
10 Ibid.
11 Ibid. p. 100.
12 Ibid.
13 KHW pp. 113-114.
14 Ibid. cf. pp. 129-132.
15 LNCA p. 27.
16 KHW cf. pp. 147-149.
17 Ibid. p. 149.

What has just been stated may suggest that the 'personal' has no role at all to play in esoteric development. This is not what Steiner meant, however. The following observation may serve to clarify this point:

As certainly as Inspirations, * rooted in healthy feeling and will, may be a revelation from a higher world, so certainly do mistakes, delusions and errors concerning a higher world, spring from disorderly feeling and will.

Esoteric training therefore sets itself the task of indicating how man may make his feelings and his will-impulses productive in a healthy way for Inspiration. As in all matters of such training, the need here is for an intimate regulating and 'moulding' of the life of the soul. First of all certain feelings must be developed which are known only to a slight degree in ordinary life. One of the most important of these feelings is that of a heightened sensitiveness to 'truth' and 'falsehood', to 'right' and 'wrong'. True, everyone has such feelings, but they must be cultivated by the esoteric student to a very much higher degree. For example, let us suppose that a logical error has been made by someone. Somebody else sees this mistake and puts the matter right. Now, what we need to bear in mind is that usually a very large part is played by the faculty of judgement and the intellect in such a correction, whereas the feeling of 'pleasure' for what is true or that of 'repugnance' for what is false is generally slight. This is not to suggest that such feelings are non-existent, but the degree to which they are present in ordinary life must be vastly enhanced and intensified in esoteric training. A logical error should cause the esoteric student pain — in no way less excruciating than acute physical pain. And, conversely, what is 'right' should give him real joy and delight.

Whereas then we usually only avail ourselves of our power of judgement and our intellect, we must, as estoeric students, 'learn to live through the whole gamut of emotions, from grief to enthusiasm, from afflictive tension to transports of delight in the possession of truth. In fact, we must learn to feel something like hatred towards what the *normal* man experiences only in a cold and sober way as *incorrect*. We must enkindle in ourselves a *love of truth* that bears a personal character — as personal, as warm, as the lover feels for the beloved.' SHK pp. 36-37.

18 GET pp. 15-16.
19 Ibid. p. 24.
20 Ibid. p. 37.
21 Ibid. p. 85.
22 Ibid. p. 74.

*For the meaning of the term 'Inspiration' in the sense in which Steiner uses it, see SHK p. 8.

23 Speaking on one occasion about the Chakras, the inner sense organs of the soul and spirit, Steiner points out that their structure is extemely delicate and that, in order to 'come into bloom', they must be cared for and guarded. 'He who fails to do so will never enjoy true spiritual perception.'

Among the many facets of this caring and guarding Steiner stresses the importance of love, of empathy for one's fellow-men — 'for both saint and criminal'. For instance, it is absolutely necessary to acquire a positive manner of judging others. Loving understanding most replace negative criticism. Advance in self-development is suppressed if, as soon as we hear someone express a viewpoint, we immediately allow our disagreement or criticism to give rise to a counter viewpoint. We must first hear the other out and refrain from hasty criticism and judgement. 'Listening is an extraordinarily effective means of developing the inner sense organs of the soul and spirit.' *The Inner Development of Man* (1974), pp. 18-19.

Further re the development of the Chakras, see KHW pp. 117-159. Also:

a) ODDC p. 37.

b) OS Chapter V.

c) ST pp. 42-44.

24 GET p. 74.

25 Ibid. p. 72.

26 Ibid.

27 Cf. *Truth and Knowledge.* Published in one volume with *The Philosophy of Spiritual Activity* (1963). More recent editions of the latter bear the title *The Philosophy of Freedom.*

28 (1978).

29 TEW p. 84. Cf. also CT pp. 122-126; 141-142.

30 TEW p. 84.

31 Ibid. p. 85.

32 A better understanding of what Steiner meant by 'vital thinking' can be gained by a careful study of TEW. In particular pp. 28-30; 42-44; 58-59; 92-93; 104-105; 108-109; 130-131.

See also note 15 to the Introduction.

Re the meaning of the term 'empty consciousness' see TEW pp. 43-45 for a concise description.

See also EC Lectures I and II, and *What can the Art of Healing gain through Spiritual Science?* (1st edition, n.d.) pp. 4-8.

33 TEW pp. 87-88.

34 Ibid. p. 88.

35 The third lecture in LDR.

36 Ibid. p. 60.
37 Ibid. p. 62.
38 Ibid.

4. LOVE — THE BRIDGE BETWEEN TWO WORLDS

1   VM p. 213
2   Ibid. p. 215. See also *Truth-Wrought-Words* (1979), p. 93.
3   *First Steps in Supersensible Perception* (1949), pp. 27-28.
4   Published together with RSK (1975).
5   1975.
6   *Occult Reading and Occult Hearing* (1975), p. 53.
7   Ibid. Cf. also TSW. Section X.
8   *Occult Reading and Occult Hearing*, p. 53.
9   Ibid. pp. 54-57 re exercises aimed at cultivating a loving interest.

5. LINKS BETWEEN THE LIVING AND THE DEAD

1   *The Dead are with Us* (1952), p. 15 [1973].
2   (1927).
3   Op. cit. p. 42.
4   Ibid. p. 44, re memorial festivals and days of remembrance Cf. *Man as a Being of Sense and Perception* (1958), lecture III, re memory and love.
5   VM, pp. 212-213.
6   FDLD p. 43.
7   KR Vol. I (1972), p. 109 [1981].
8   AEC, p. 28. Cf. also OSOE p. 19.
9   FDLD p. 43.
10 LDR p. 25.
11 *Links between the Living and the Dead* (1973), p. 13.
12 Steiner points out that it is not a violation of karma when the dead feel eased through the love streaming to them from the earth, or when they encounter hindrances in their good endeavours. Ibid. pp. 13-14.
13 Ibid. p. 19.
14 Cf. *Supersensible Man* (1961), pp. 56-57. Also *Human Questions and Cosmic Answers* (1960) re Venus-forces and love.
15 *Links Between the Living and the Dead* (1973), p. 10.
16 Ibid. p. 11. Steiner develops the theme of the role of spiritual science in some detail in this lecture.
17 EDCL (1964), p. 121.
18 Cf. CT pp. 129-130.
19 EDCL p. 123.

20 Cf. Ibid Lecture VI.
21 Ibid. pp. 129-130.
22 *At the Gates of Spiritual Science* (1970), p. 144.
23 Given at Nuremberg, 10.11.1918.
24 Steiner said on more than one occasion that it is not the task of spiritual science to offer those who mourn shallow consolation for their pain, or to try to talk them out of their sorrow. Sorrow is justified — one should grow stronger to bear it, not let oneself be talked out of it.
25 *The Dead are with Us*, p. 19.
26 Cf. ibid. re Services for the Dead, pp. 19-20.
27 Cf. LDR pp. 70-71. Also *The Easter Festival in relation to the Mysteries* (1968), p. 3.
28 LDR p. 83.
29 Cf. ibid. p. 109.
30 Cf. ibid. pp. 6, 130-131. Also BDR pp. 26, 31 and 55.
31 TEW p. 49.
32 BDR (1930), p. 114. Also 1975 edition, p. 164.
33 Ibid.
34 Ibid. (1975), p. 165. Cf. also *The Mission of Christian Rosenkreutz* (1950), p. 75.
35 LDR p. 212. Cf. also ODCC pp. 23-24.
36 LDR p. 243.
37 TR p. 49.
38 Cf. RE 47-48.
39 Ibid. p. 48.
40 Cf. also *On the Meaning of Life* (1946), pp. 14-15.
41 RE p. 49.
42 *Results of Spiritual Investigation* (1971), pp. 64-65.
43 Cf. *Man as a Being of Sense and Perception* (1958), p. 49.
44 TR p. 50.
45 Ibid.
46 Ibid. p. 51.
47 Ibid.
48 *How the Spiritual World interpenetrates the Physical* (1927), pp. 18-19.
49 VM p. 205.
50 Ibid. p. 217.

6. MAN AND HIS ANGEL

1 VM p. 165.
2 *Cosmic Forces in Man* (1948), pp. 30-36.

3 (1959).
4 (1975).
5 Cf. Rudolf Steiner's Mystery Play *The Soul's Awakening*, Scene IX. Also MBWE re consequences of materialistic speech and thinking p. 52.
6 See notes 3 and 4.
7 *Cosmic Forces in Man*, p. 35.

7. ST LUKE'S GOSPEL OF LOVE — BUDDHA AND CHRIST

1 *The Foundation Stone* (1957), p. 19 [1979].
2 Cf. GSL p. 201. Also FBC, p. 24.
3 Cf. *The Course of My Life* (1951), p. 276.
4 Cf. *Background to the Gospel of St Mark* (1968), p. 143.
5 GSL p. 75.
6 Cf. ibid. p. 57.
7 Cf. KHW in which a path, suitable for our times, is described.
8 Cf. GSL p. 173.
9 Cf. ibid. p. 167. Also GSJ(H) pp. 76-77.
10 Cf. GSL p. 175.
11 Cf. ibid.
12 Cf.
   a) *The Occult Significance of Blood* (1978).
   b) RE p. 111.
13 See Ch. 8, note 5.
14 Cf. GSL p. 176.
15 Ibid. p. 179.
16 Cf. BSMG p. 35.
17 Cf. FBC, pp. 32-40. Also
   a) *Easter. The Festivals and their Meaning*. Vol. II, (1956), pp. 114-117.
   b) FS pp. 27-28.
   c) RE pp. 113-114.
18 Cf. FS pp. 72-73.
19 Cf. ibid. pp. 77-79. Also *Love and its Meaning in the World* (1960), pp. 13-14 [1972].
20 Cf. FS pp. 80-81.
21 Cf. MM p. 97. Also ALT p. 138.
22 Cf. *Newborn Might* and *Strength Everlasting* (1977), pp. 1-2.
23 Cf. ibid. p.11.
24 GSM, p. 22.
25 DSHH pp. 20-21.
26 Ibid. p. 12.

27 GSM, p. 20.
28 Ibid. p. 21.
29 DSHH, p. 12.
30 Ibid. pp. 12-13.
31 Ibid. pp. 13-14.
32 Cf. ibid. pp. 15-17.

8. THE MYSTERY OF GOLGOTHA

1 VM p. 133.
2 (1975), pp. 196-199.
3 BSMG pp. 39, 56-57.
4 GSL p. 198. Cf. also
   a) CRR.
   b) *The Etherization of the Blood. The Entry of the Etheric Christ into Earthly Evolution* (1971).
   c) *Macrocosm and Microcosm* (1968). Lectures V, VI and VIII.
   d) *Rosicrucianism and Modern Initiation* (1965).
5 Re blood as an expression of the ego see:
   a) *The Occult Significance of Blood* (1978).
   b) OSOE p. 25.
   c) RE p. 111.
   d) *The Ten Commandments and the Sermon on the Mount* (1978), p. 32.
   e) V. Bott: *Anthroposophical Medicine: An extension of the Art of Healing* (1978).
6 GSL p. 198. Cf. also:
   a) FS pp. 16-17.
   b) UEM p. 155.
7 *Christmas. The Festivals and their Meaning.* Vol. 1, (1955), p. 96.
8 *Jesus and Christ* (1976), pp. 16-17.
9 Ibid. p. 18.
10 Ibid. p. 19; cf. also pp. 10-13.
11 Ibid. p. 21.
12 'A Christmas Lecture' in FS.
13 Ibid. p. 86. Cf. also MG, p. 14.
14 FS p. 86.
15 Ibid. p. 87.
16 GSJ(C) p. 113. Steiner qualifies this statement later in the same lecture: 'John had aroused this feeling in his disciples, but, of course, only in a few. Most of them were not mature enough for such an experience during immersion. Nevertheless a few there were who recognized that He was approaching — the Spirit Who

was afterwards called Christ.'
17 Ibid. pp. 116-117.
18 'Faith, Love, Hope'. In *The Golden Blade* (1964), p. 23.
19 See Chapter 12 'Duty and Love'.

9. LUCIFER AND AHRIMAN*AND THE LOVE OF CHRIST

1 *The Guardian of the Threshold* (1925), p. 55.
2 Ibid. pp. 126-128.
3 MM pp. 106-107. Cf. revised translation in ALT, pp. 146-147.
4 Ibid. p. 108 and p. 148 respectively. Further re Ahriman and Lucifer in relation to love: cf. ibid. pp. 124, 168 and pp. 163, 204, respectively. Also MWS Lecture III.
5 MK p. 255.
6 Cf. *The Sun-Mystery in the Course of Human History* (1955), pp. 13-14.
7 MK p. 256. Cf. *The Spiritual Hierarchies* (1931), p. 14 re the nature of light; also *Curative Education* (1972), pp. 55-56.
8 MK p. 256. Cf. also OSOE p. 20.
9 MK p. 257.
10 *The Spiritual Hierarchies*, p. 113.
11 CHS, p. 31 [1972].
12 GSJ(C), p. 94.
13 TSW p. 144.
14 GSJ(C), p. 96.
15 TSW p. 145.
16 *Influences of Lucifer and Ahriman. Man's Responsibility for the Earth* (1954), pp. 41-42 [1976].
17 TSW p. 144.
18 'Inasmuch as he brings about head-activity he is a benefactor of mankind. But the counterweight must be there: *Love* must be there.' *The Occult Movement in the Nineteenth Century* (1973), p. 94.
19 FBC, p. 13.
20 CHS, pp. 32-33.
21 Ibid. p. 33.
22 Ibid. Cf. also:
    a) AEC, p. 32.
    b) *The Sun Mystery in the Course of Human History* (1955), p. 11 [1978].
23 LDR p. 172.
24 Ibid. p. 173.
25 Ibid. pp. 173-174. Cf. also:
    a) Ibid. p. 192.

b)   *The Driving Force of Spiritual Power in World History* (1972), p. 60.

c)   *The Mysteries of the East and of Christianity* (1972), pp. 30-31.

d)   *Results of Spiritual Investigation* (1971), p. 89.

26   Cf. CM. Essays VI and VII.

27   Ibid. pp. 95-105 re sensual love.

28   Cf. *Gospel of St Matthew* (1965), p. 195: 'Christ uses the word "Satan" for Ahriman, whereas elsewhere in the Bible the word "Devil" applies to everything of a Luciferic nature.' See also Alfred Schütze: *The Enigma of Evil* (1978).

29   CM pp. 94-96.

30   Ibid. p. 96.

31   Cf. OS pp. 123-132.

32   CM p. 96.

33   Cf. OS pp. 193-194.

34   CM p. 97.

35   OS p. 184.

36   *From Jesus to Christ* (1956), p. 139 [1973].

37   Ibid. p. 140.

38   'Men *should* not be able to lay hold of the thought of freedom without the thought of Redemption through Christ: only then is the thought of freedom justified. If we *will* to be free, we must bring the offering of thanks to Christ for our freedom. Then only can we perceive it.' Ibid.

39   Cf.

a)   *A Sound Outlook for Today and a Genuine Hope for the Future* (1954, Available as typescript). Lecture II.

b)   Cf. notes to Appendix: 'Ahriman and Lucifer'.

40   Ibid. a)   p. 40.

41   Cf. *World History in the Light of Anthroposophy* (1950), pp. 129-130 [1977].

10. LOVE AND FREEDOM: THE ESSENTIAL NATURE OF THINKING

1   *Philosophy, Cosmology and Religion* (1984), cf. pp. 7-8.

2   Third lecture in *The Bridge between Universal Spirituality and the Physical Constitution of Man. Freedom and Love* (1958).

3   Ibid. p. 50.

4   Ibid. p. 54.

5   Ibid.

6   'Between the will-permeated life of thought and the thought-imbued life of will lies the balancing factor that unites the two;

unites the will that rays towards the head with the thoughts which, as they flow into deeds wrought with love, are, so to say, felt with the heart. This means of union is the life of feeling which is able to direct itself towards the will as well as towards the thoughts.' Ibid. p. 57.

7 Ibid. p. 59.

8 References throughout these pages are to the 7th English edition, 2nd impression (1970) translated by Michael Wilson. A paperback edition — with identical pagination — was published in 1979.

9 AC p. 45.

10 Cf. Michael Wilson's Introduction to his translation — pp. XVII — XVIII.

11 PF pp. 11-12. In 1895 Steiner wrote in a guest book a few lines that express the same motif:

> 'The lover's eyes are blind to the beloved's weaknesses',
> Runs the old saying.
> It never seemed to me the right statement of it,
> For I would say that only loving eyes see truly,
> Since only they perceive the loved one's virtues.

Quoted in Otto Palmer's book, *Rudolf Steiner on his book The Philosophy of Freedom* (1975), p. 52. See also p. 53.

12 *Methods of Spiritual Research* (1971), pp. 79-80.

13 PF p. 70.

14 *Mystery Knowledge and Mystery Centres* (1973), p. 12.

15 Ibid. pp. 11-12.

16 PF pp. 119-120. Re Steiner's use of the term 'intuition' here see Michael Wilson's Introduction, pp. XVIII-XIX.

17 Cf. ibid. Chapter V and Steiner's addition to Chapter VIII.

18 Cf. ibid. Chapter XII.

19 'Anthroposophy's Contribution to the Most Urgent Needs of our Time'. AQ XXII, No. 1, 1977, p. 8. See also Chapter 12 'Duty and Love'.

20 *Spiritual Hierarchies* (1931), pp. 115-116.

21 *Foundations of Anthroposophy* (1947), pp. 62-63.

22 *Theosophy* (1973), pp. 142-143. Re Steiner's use of the term 'Theosophy' see ibid. p. 5.

23 Ibid. p. 143.

24 Ibid. p. 144.

25 Ibid. p. 88.

26 Ibid. p. 144.

27 Ibid. p. 145.

28 *Methods of Spiritual Research*, p. 80.
29 Ibid. p. 88.

11. LOVE AS A COGNITIVE POWER

1 *Methods of Spiritual Research*, p. 79. Cf. also *True and False Paths in Spiritual Investigation* (1972), p. 59.
2 *Reincarnation and Immortality* (1977), p. 101.
3 Ibid. p. 115.
4 *Supersensible Knowledge (Anthroposophy) as a Demand of the Age* (1943), p. 21 Cf. also EC pp. 34-37.
5 *Supersensible Knowledge* etc., p. 22.
6 Because the terms 'Imagination', 'Inspiration' and 'Intuition' in these pages have a specialized meaning the initial letter has been capitalized. The meaning and description of each term can be found in four articles by Steiner published with the title, *The Stages of Higher Knowledge* (1974). Cf. also:
    a) EC pp. 9-56.
    b) GSL pp. 20-25.
    c) OS pp. 235-297.
    d) *Knowledge and Initiation* (1936).
7 *Supersensible Knowledge*, etc., p. 23.
8 Ibid. See also Chapter 18 'Clairvoyance, our Ego and Love'.
9 RSK pp. 45-46.
10 Ibid. pp. 48-49.
11 EC pp. 52-53. Cf. also
    a) *Curative Education* (1972), pp. 55-56.
    b) *Spiritual Hierarchies* (1931), p. 14.
12 TR p. 45.
13 EC p. 54.
14 Ibid. p. 53.
15 In a lecture given in 1904 — published under the title, *The Inner Development of Man* (1974), Steiner speaks about some of the processes involved in the practice of meditation and the preparation of soul leading up to meditation. One of the elements of this preparation is that the would-be meditator should 'surrender' himself to 'eternal thoughts, concepts and sentiments' — the content of which 'must be true not only for today, yesterday, a century or tomorrow, but forever'. Sentences containing such thoughts are to be found in, for instance, the Bible and the Bhagavad Gita. Such thoughts do not belong to one man, they are universal and timeless. They awaken the slumbering soul faculties. However, it is not sufficient to assume that one comprehends,

intellectually, the meaning of such sentences — they must be allowed to quicken and come to life in one's inner self. One must allow the whole significance of such sentences to radiate in one's inner being. 'One must learn to *love* such sentences ... The intellectual comprehension is not important; the *love* for such a spiritual truth is.' The more the love for the truths contained in such sentences streams through us, the more the power of inner sight grows in us. Op. cit. p. 13. Cf. also VM p. 232.

16 See Chapter X, note 17. Cf. also:
    a)   AI pp. 76-89.
    b)   EC pp. 24-25, 29-36.

17 AI p. 78.

18 Steiner points out that, for future man, there are yet higher stages of cognition. Cf. SKH, p. 3.

19 Ibid. pp. 3-20.

20 EC pp. 35-36.

21 Ibid. p. 36.

22 Ibid. p. 37.

23 Ibid. p. 35.

24 Ibid.

12. DUTY AND LOVE

1 This rendering is taken from the 1st edition (1930) of BDR pp. 11-112. For the 2nd edition translation (1975) see ibid. p. 161.

2 (1970), pp. 134-144.

3 Steiner deals with the obvious objection to this in PF pp. 136-138.

4 For a characterization of what Steiner means by the 'ideal part of my individual being' see ibid. p. 137.

5 The ethical individualist has the capacity to experience for himself the particular moral principle for each single situation. In this sense we can say that the only true morality is purely individual, born in each case of spiritual devotion, love, for the action chosen. Cf. PF pp. 130-134.

6 *Critique of Pratical Reason*, Ch. III.

7 *The Younger Generation. Educational and Spiritual Impulses for Life in the Twentieth Century* (1976).

8 Ibid. p. 75.

9 Ibid. p. 74.

10 Ibid. p. 75.

11 Ibid. p. 77.

12 Ibid.

13 Ibid. pp. 77-78.

14 Ibid. p. 78. Re education in relation to the development of moral love, see Ch. 17, 'Love — the Root of Education'.

15 (1977).

16 *The Balance in the World and Man. Lucifer and Ahriman* (1977), p. 42.

17 Ibid.

18 Ibid.

19 Ibid. pp. 42-43.

20 Ibid. p. 43.

21 Ibid.

22 See Ch. 9, 'Lucifer and Ahriman and the Love of Christ'. Also Appendix.

23 *The Balance in the World and Man*, p. 43.

24 Ibid. pp. 43-44.

25 Ibid. p. 44.

26 Ibid.

13. LIGHT — LOVE — ILLNESS AND HEALTH

1 *The Portal of Initiation* (1925), p. 66.

2 MLO p. 78.

3 MK.

4 Ibid. p. 211.

5 In TR Steiner says: 'When, as seers, we seek for the Dead, we can find them within the Light — if we perceive the Light not merely in a material way. The Light that surrounds us forms the "bodies" of the Dead; they have bodies woven out of Light. The Light that enfolds the earth is "substance" for the Beings who are living in the spiritual world.' p. 45.

6 MK p. 222.

7 Ibid. pp. 223-224.

8 See OS, pp. 182-185, re Luciferic Beings and the Cosmos of Wisdom.

9 Many illnesses are more directly due to an Ahrimanic influence. Further re this see notes to Appendix.

10 It is clearly beyond the scope and purpose of the present work to discuss 'the right remedies'. See notes to Appendix.

11 MK p. 90.

12 Steiner gives the following example: Pneumonia in this life *may be* 'a karmic effect which follows when during his life in kamaloca the person in question looks back to a character which had within it the tendency towards sexual excess and a desire to live a sensual life'. Ibid. p. 93.

13 Ibid. p. 91 See also:
    a) Appendix
    b) CT p. 169.
    c) GSL pp. 158-163.
    d) MG where Steiner speaks of Christ's special mission as Healer.
14 Re this threefoldness see, for instance, OS, Ch. II, and *Theosophy*.
15 MK p. 92.
16 Ibid. pp. 224-225.
17 Ibid. pp. 225-226.
18 Ibid. p. 226.
19 Ibid.
20 Ibid. p. 228.
21 Ibid.
22 Ibid. p. 229.
23 Ibid. pp. 230-231.
24 Ibid. p. 233.
25 LDR p. 233.
26 SFM (1979) Previously published with the title *Anthroposophical Ethics* (1955). Translation and pagination are identical.
27 Ibid. p. 25.
28 Ibid.
29 Ibid. pp. 27-28.
30 Ibid. p. 28.
31 Ibid. p. 52.
32 *How the Spiritual World interpenetrates the Physical* (1927), p. 4.

14. THE POWER OF LOVE IN THE EVOLUTION OF EARTH AND MAN

 1 *The Foundation Stone Meditation* (1979). Seventh and eighth verses. Re the circumstances surrounding the giving of this Meditation by Rudolf Steiner, see G. Adams' Introduction to his translation. Cf. also F.W. Zeylmans van Emmichoven, *The Foundation Stone* (1963).
 2 Through, for instance, Lao-tse, Confucius, Buddha, Zarathustra, Pythagoras.
 3 ECM p. 114.
 4 Ibid. pp. 107-113.
 5 Ibid. p. 115.
 6 See Ch. 9 'Lucifer and Ahriman and the Love of Christ'.
 7 ECM p. 115.
 8 Cf. OS.

9 *The Mission of the Individual Folk Souls* (1970), pp. 93-94.
10 Ibid. pp. 94-95, 98, re the relation of the Hierarchies to the development of Love.
11 GSJ(H), p. 46.
12 Ibid. p. 47.
13 OS p. 311. Cf. also:
   a) ASJ pp. 75-76, 79, 92, 127-128, 148-150.
   b) *Egyptian Myths and Mysteries* (1971), pp. 43-44.
   c) AEC, p. 33.
   d) GSJ(H) pp. 46-49.
   e) ISBM pp. 97-100.
   f) *The Mision of the Individual Folk Souls*, pp. 93-95, 98.
   g) OSOE pp. 18-20.
   h) UEM p. 114.
14 OS p. 311.
15 Cf.
   a) CM, pp. 95-105.
   b) GSJ(H), p. 47.
   c) ISBM p. 97.
   d) OSOE pp. 18-19.
   e) UEM p. 114.
16 GSJ(H) p. 49.
17 ISBM p. 100. Cf. also ibid. p. 101.
18 OS p. 218.
19 Ibid. pp. 311-312.
20 Ibid. p. 312.
21 Ibid.
22 GSJ(H) p. 48.
23 Ibid. p. 50.
24 Ibid. p. 51.
25 Ibid. pp. 51-52. Cf. also:
   a) UEM p. 89.
   b) MG, p. 11.
26 UEM p. 89. Cf. also ASJ pp. 128-130.
27 OS p. 309.
28 UEM p. 114.
29 Ibid. p. 115.
30 Cf. *How Anthroposophical Groups prepare for the Sixth Epoch. Community above us. Christ in us* (1957), pp. 16-17. Republished, 1976, with the title, *Preparing for the Sixth Epoch*. Cf. also *The Ego. The God within and the God of External Revelation* (n.d.). in particular Lecture I.

31 UEM p. 115.

32 Ibid. p. 115.

33 Ibid.

34 Ibid. p. 116.

35 Ibid.

36 Ibid. p. 127.

37 Ibid. p. 128.

38 Ibid. p. 142.

39 Ibid. pp. 155-156. A statement made by Steiner relative to the Second Coming of Christ is all-important and although not directly relevant to our main theme is of such significance that a short reference here seems justified:

> During the Graeco-Latin period Christ worked on earth in a physical body. Since the human being was then primarily able to receive the influences of the forces existing in the physical world, Christ had to appear on the physical plane . . . Whereas at *that* time men could not have perceived Him otherwise than in a physical body, there are actually awakening in *our* age the forces in us through which we shall see the Christ, not in His physical body, but as an etheric form. Even in our century, from the 1930s on, and ever increasingly . . . men will behold the Christ as an etheric form. This will constitute the great advance beyond the earlier epoch, when human beings were not yet mature enough to behold Him in such a form. This is what is meant by the saying that Christ will 'appear in the clouds' . . .

> But it must be emphasized that He can be seen in our time *only in the etheric body.* Anyone who would believe that Christ will appear again in a physical body loses sight of the progress made by man during the course of evolution. It is a blunder to suppose that such an event as the appearance of Christ can recur in the same manner as that in which it has already taken place. *Jeshu ben Pandira* (1942), pp. 8-10. Cf. also:

a) *Christ at the Time of the Mystery of Golgotha and Christ in the Twentieth Century* (1947), pp. 48-52.

b) MG, p. 15.

c) *The Right and the Wrong Use of Esoteric Knowledge* (1966), pp. 12-13, 21, 23, 25.

d) SGM pp. 75, 95.

e) *The Three Paths of the Soul to Christ* (1942), p. 44.

f) *The True Nature of the Second Coming* (1971).

g) *Wonders of the World* (1963), Lectures II and IV.

40 Cf. GSJ(H) p. 68: 'We have seen that in the course of human

evolution, the true Earth-mission is the evolution of love, but that love is only conceivable when it is given as a voluntary offering by self-conscious human beings.' Cf. also MBWE p. 88.

41 GSJ(H) pp. 54-55.
42 DSHH, p. 14.
43 See Ch. 22, 'Old and New Bonds of Love'. See GSJ(H) pp. 76-77 re the significance of the Miracle at Cana.
44 Cf.
    a) *The Foundation Stone* (1979).
    b) BSMG.
45 DSHH, p. 45.
46 Ibid. p. 46.
47 Ibid. Cf. also GSJ(H) pp. 76-77.
48 DSHH, p. 47.
49 Ibid.
50 Lecture XI in GSJ(C).
51 Ibid. pp. 137-138.
52 Ibid. pp. 138-139.
53 Ibid. p. 140.
54 Ibid.
55 ISBM pp. 107-108.

15. REINCARNATION AND KARMA

1 *The Soul's Probation* (1925), p. 264.
2 KR Vol. II (1974), p. 59.
3 *Theosophy* (1973).
4 See KR in eight volumes. Cf. also:
    a) *Facing Karma* (1975).
    b) 'Karma and Details of the Law of Karma'. AQ XXIII, No.1, 1978.
    c) *Karma of Human Vocation. In connection with Life of Goethe* (1944).
    d) 'Karmic Effects of Traits of Character'. AQ VII, No. 1. 1962.
    e) RE Lecture X: 'On Karma, Reincarnation and Initiation'.
    f) *Reincarnation and Immortality* (1977).
    g) *Reincarnation and Karma* (1977).
    h) *Reincarnation and Karma and How Karma works* (1962).
    i) MK.
    j) 'The Significance of Repeated Lives on Earth'. In *Anthroposophical News Sheet*, Nos, 17-18, 1936.
    k) 'The Soul's Progress through Repeated Earth Lives'. In *The Anthroposophical Review*. Vol. III, No. 1, 1981.

l) *The Wisdom of Man, of the Soul, and of the Spirit* (1971). Lecture IV in section 'Wisdom of the Spirit'.
This is not by any means a comprehensive list. Moreover, there are lengthy references in many lectures not specifically dealing with reincarnation and karma.

5 In RE Steiner makes the following statement: 'Reincarnation and Karma will in time cease to have significance. Man will then enter permanently into a spiritual world in which he will continue to be active. When, for example, man has developed the impulse of brotherliness in himself, the growth of races will cease, will be surpassed. Karma will then also be overcome.' p. 118.

6 We could also say that such an individual will come under the dominance of the ossifying Ahrimanic forces in a later life.

7 'Karma and Details of the Law of Karma', AQ XXIII, No. 1, 1978. Cf. also RE pp. 119-120.

8 From a lecture given in Cassel on 2 December 1910. Not yet translated into English.

9 In *From Jesus to Christ* (1956) [1973] Steiner makes the statement that in 'the Mysteries it was made very clear indeed to the pupil that when, for example, anyone tells a lie or falls into error, it is a real process which has not merely to do with himself ... Thoughts belong to the objective world; they are not merely experiences of the soul. The pupil of the Mystery saw: "When thou tellest a lie it signifies in the supersensible world a darkening of a certain light; and when thou doest perpetrate a loveless action, something in the spiritual world is, in consequence, burned up in the fire of lovelessness; with errors thou doest extinguish light in the Macrocosm".' p. 119. Cf. also *The Significance of Spiritual Science for Moral Action* (1978), pp. 5-7.

10 See note 8.

11 See note 8.

12 See note 8.

13 See note 8.

14 Lecture IV in *Reincarnation and Karma. Their significance in Modern Culture* (1960).

15 Ibid. p. 70. Such alternation is clearly not a hard and fast rule, but certainly such qualities are mutually fruitful and complementary. The same may be said of male or female incarnations; or of an incarnation with a more intellectual trend alternating with one more inclined towards faith, and so on.

16 Ibid. p. 71. Steiner goes on to say: 'We are living in a time when devoted willingness for sacrifice only too often goes to waste.

Although lack of love is in evidence everywhere, there is also an enormous waste of love and willingness for sacrifice. This must not be misunderstood, but it should be realized that love, if it is not accompanied by wisdom, by wise insight into the prevailing conditions, can be very misplaced and therefore harmful rather than beneficial.'

17 Published in eight volumes entitled *Karmic Relationships. Esoteric Studies.*

18 KR Vo. I (1972). Lecture IV.

19 Ibid. p. 64.

20 Ibid.

21 Ibid. p. 65.

22 Ibid. p. 67.

23 Ibid. Steiner makes the following interesting remark here: 'A man may harm his fellows out of a positively criminal sense of hatred. Or — to omit the intermediate stages — he may merely be a critic. To be a critic you must always hate a little — unless you are one who praises.' Ibid. pp. 67-68.

24 Ibid. p. 68.

25 Ibid. p. 69.

26 Ibid.

27 Ibid. p. 70.

28 Ibid.

29 Ibid. p. 72.

30 MK Lecture II.

31 Ibid. p. 53.

32 Stated thus baldly this is a startling statement and may meet with incredulity and scepticism. Unfortunately it would take us well beyond the scope of the present study to substantiate the claim and the interested reader is referred to MK Lecture II, and to Hermann Poppelbaum: *Man and Animal. Their Essential Difference* (1960). Cf. *The Inner Realities of Evolution* (1953) re the significance of sacrifice (renunciation) in respect of the evolution of our whole cosmic system.

33 MK p. 53.

34 Ibid. p. 54.

35 Ibid. p. 53.

36 Ibid. p. 55.

16. THE POWER OF LOVE IN THE PROCESS OF IN-CARNATION

1 RE p. 49.

2 Op. cit. 10 lectures held in Budapest, 3-12 June 1909.

3 RE p. 51.

4 Ibid.

5 Ibid. p. 54.

6 Ibid. p. 55.

7 *Planetary spheres and their influence on Man's Life on Earth and in the Spiritual Worlds* (1982), p. 33.

8 TR p. 74.

9 Hermann Poppelbaum: *New Light on Heredity and Evolution* (1977), pp. 55-56. Cf. also BMWE p. 64.

10 TR p. 75.

11 'Karmic Effects of Traits of Character'. AQ VII, No. I, pp. 7-8.

12 Ibid. p. 8.

13 Ibid.

17. LOVE — THE ROOT OF EDUCATION

1 EMSL p. 95.

2a The author is indebted to Benedict Wood for this rendering. Cf. *Prayers for Mothers and Children* (1943), p. 6 [1968].

2b *Education as a Social Problem* (1969), p. 49.

3 EMSL p. 105. Cf. also HVE p. 42.

4 EMSL p. 109. Re child learning to walk, talk and think, and the spiritual hierarchies:

    a)   MBWE pp. 47-51, 65-66.

    b)   MWS p. 9.

5 Re the parent's and teacher's religious attitude towards the child: SGE pp. 57-58.

6 EMSL p. 179.

7 Cf. *Essentials of Education* (1948), pp. 73-76, re duty and love in relation to moral life. In the 6th Lecture of the cycle HVE Steiner speaks of gratitude in relation to the moral sense: 'Gratitude is the basic virtue in the child between birth and the change of teeth. If he sees that everyone who stands in some kind of relationship to him in the outer world shows gratitude for what he receives from this world; if, in confronting the outer world and wanting to imitate it, the child sees the kind of gestures that express gratitude, then a great deal is done towards establishing in him the right moral human attitude'. pp. 125-126 [1982].

8 The first Waldorf (Rudolf Steiner) School was founded in 1919 by Rudolf Steiner in response to the wishes of the workers and the director, Emil Molt, of the Waldorf Astoria Factory in Stuttgart, W. Germany. Today (1989) there are over 500 such schools throughout the world — many of them providing a comprehensive

education from Kindergarten to University Entrance. In addition there are numerous Schools, Homes and Village Communities for children and adults in need of special care.

9 Not yet translated into English. Cf. also:
   a) *The Four Temperaments* (1949), pp. 37-38, 43 [1980].
   b) *The Roots of Education* (1968), pp. 66-67 [1982].
   c) SGE p. 127.
   d) *Spiritual Science and the Art of Education* (1921), p. 20.
10 EMSL p. 188.
11 *Lectures to Teachers* (1948), p. 92.
12 (1947) [1975]. First published, in German, in 1909.
13 Op. cit. p. 34.
14 Cf.
   a) *The Essentials of Education*, pp. 78-79.
   b) MWS p. 59.
   c) RE p. 59.
   d) *Spiritual Science and the Art of Education.*
   e) *Supersensible Knowledge (Anthroposophy) as a Demand of the Age* (1943), p. 51.
15 *The Education of the Child* (1947), p. 46 [1981].
16 *Supersensible Physiology and Balance in Teaching* (1945), p. 19, re the generation of veneration of love in the teaching of history.
17 *The Education of the Child*, p. 47.
18 Ibid. p. 48.
19 SGE p. 59.
20 Ibid.
21 HVE p. 126.
22 Ibid. Cf. SGE p. 114. See also Ch. 12, 'Duty and Love'.
23 Cf. CM. In particular the two chapters: 'The Division into Sexes' and 'Before the Division into Sexes'. In ECM Steiner puts forward the view that in our present age of materialism it is difficult to find a true perspective of the concept of love. It is often distorted in that this concept is associated so closely with that of sexuality — 'with which, *fundamentally*, it has nothing whatever to do . . . The fact that under certain circumstances sexuality may be associated with love between man and woman is no argument for bringing so closely together the all-embracing nature of love or compassion with the specific character of sexuality.' p. 115. Cf. also:
   a) John F. Gardner: *Love and the Illusion of Love* (1976).
   b) A. Howard: *Sex in the Light of Reincarnation and Freedom* (1980).
24 *Supplementary Course for Teachers. The Upper School* (1956), Lecture

VIII, pp. 10-11. Published 1980 with the title, *Waldorf Education for Adolescence.*

25   *Curative Education* (1972), p. 44.
26   Ibid. p. 213.
27   (1971).
28   HVE p. 17.
29   See Ch. 10, 'Love and Freedom: The Essential Nature of Thinking'.
30   HVE p. 18. See also Ch. 11, 'Love as a Cognitive Power'.
31   Cf. SGE p. 133.
32   HVE pp. 19-20.
33   Ibid. pp. 41-42.
34   Cf. TR pp. 144-145.
35   *Ancient Myths. Their Meaning and Connection with Evolution*, (1971), p. 83. Re 'head-knowledge' and 'heart-knowledge' see ibid. Lecture VI. Cf. also *Macrocosm and Microcosm* (1968). Lectures IX, X and first part of XI.
36   *Ancient Myths*, p. 84.
37   Ibid.
38   Cf. HVE pp. 15-17, 42-43. Also *How can Mankind find the Christ again?* (1947). In particular pp. 103-104.
39   HVE p. 20.
40   Ibid.
41   See note 8.
42   SGE p. 94.
43   Ibid. p. 95.
44   'Love only can beget artistic power/And make an artist's work bear fruit and live'. *The Soul's Probation* (1925), p. 172.
45   *Education as a Social Problem* (1969), p. 16.
46   *The Christ Impulse and the Development of Ego Consciousness* (1976), pp. 34-35.
47   *Education as a Social Problem*, p. 16.
48   Ibid. Here Steiner also makes the following comment: 'After puberty, between the fourteenth and twenty-first years, it is not only the life of sexual love that develops in man; this develops merely as a special manifestation of universal love [cf. note 23]. This power of universal human love should be specially fostered when children leave school and go to technical colleges or similar institutions. For the sphere of economics . . . will never be warmed through as it should be by brotherly love — that is, universal human love — if this is not developed during the years between fourteen and twenty-one.'
49   Ibid. p. 17. et al.

18. CLAIRVOYANCE, OUR EGO AND LOVE

1 *The Soul's Probation* (1925), pp. 175-176.

2 Cf. KHW.

3 TSW pp. 133-136.

4 Ibid. p. 136.

5 Ibid. p. 134.

6 Ibid. pp. 139-140.

7 Ibid. p. 135.

8 Ibid.

9 Ibid. p. 136.

10 *The Ten Commandments and the Sermon on the Mount* (1978), pp. 18-19.

11 Op. cit. pp. 38-39.

12 GSJ(H), pp. 48-49.

13 See Ch. 20, 'Egoism and Altruism' and Appendix 'Ahriman and Lucifer'. Cf. TR pp. 97, 141-143.

14 TR p. 142. See also Appendix 'Ahriman and Lucifer'.

15 Ibid. pp. 141-142.

16 ASJ p. 137.

17 To enumerate Steiner's many expositions and references dealing with the nature of the ego — 'lower' and 'higher' — would require several pages. Some idea of his insight into the nature and essence of the 'Ego', the 'I', may be gained from the following:

a) BDR pp. 106-107 et al.

b) *The Christ Impulse and the Development of Ego Consciousness* (1976).

c) CM. Essay XVIII, 'The Fourfold Being of Man' (1976).

d) ESD Lecture VIII. Re lower and higher Self. Cf. ibid. pp. 14-15 re the ego and alcohol in relation to the blood.

e) *The Ego. The God Within and the God of External Revelation* (n.d.).

f) FBC. Lecture III, 'Buddhism and Christianity'.

g) KHW = Basic.

h) MS Lecture V, 'The Nature of Egoism' ("higher Ego within the ego" p. 144).

i) OS = Basic. Past, present and future development of the 'I', the 'Ego'. See, for instance, pp. 73-88, 102-103, 109-114, 182-188, 215-216, 241-244 (re awakening of the Higher Ego), 278-282, 290-292, 318-319.

j) *Paths of Experience* (1934), pp. 191-200 re 'limited ego' and 'Divine Ego'.

k) RE Lecture III.

l)   RSK. The Sixth Meditation.

m)   SHK = Basic.

n)   *Theosophy* (1973) = Basic. See, for instance, pp. 35-45, 63-65.

o)   TSW. The Ninth and Fourteenth Meditations.

p)   *The Wisdom of Man, of the Soul, and of the Spirit* (1971).

18 Cf.

a)   *The Spiritual Beings in the Heavenly Bodies* (1951), p. 202 [1981].

b)   *Ascension and Pentecost. The Festivals and their Meaning.* Vol. III (1958), pp. 64-69.

19 ASJ pp. 137-138.

20 *Ascension and Pentecost,* pp. 68-69.

21 ASJ p. 138.

22 Ibid. p. 203.

23 Ibid. p. 204. Re the possibility for those in the Abyss to follow the 'good' in the future, cf. ibid. pp. 204-205.

24 Ibid. pp. 130-131. Cf. also *Ascension and Pentecost*, pp. 68-69.

25 CHS, p. 16.

26 Cf. TR p. 105.

27 Cf.

a)   *The Christ Impulse and the Development of Ego Consciousness.*

b)   ESD.

c)   EC.

d)   OS. In particular Ch. VII.

e)   SHK.

f)   *True and False Paths in Spiritual Investigations* (1969).

g)   *World History in the Light of Anthroposophy* (1977).

28 CHS, p. 17.

29 Ibid. pp. 16-17.

30 Ibid. p. 17.

31 Ibid. p. 18.

32 Ibid.

19. SELF-LOVE

1 OS p. 242.

2 RSK pp. 38-39 cf. also OSOE p. 20.

3 RSK p. 39.

4 One illustration of what is meant here by 'experience "outside" the physical body' is given by Steiner in AI p. 77. Cf. also:

a)   *Goethe's Secret Revelation* (1932), p. 120.

b)   MS p. 149.

c)   ODCC p. 34.

d)   *Results of Spiritual Investigation* (1971), pp. 83-85 et al.

e) RSK The Fourth Meditation.

f) *The Spiritual Beings in the Heavenly Bodies*, p. 71.

5 RSK p. 40.

6 See, for instance, KR Vol. VII (1973), pp. 89-90.

7 CT p. 121. See Ch. 23, 'The Social Future'.

8 Ibid. pp. 134-135.

9 Ibid. pp. 135-136.

10 Ibid. p. 136.

11 Ibid. p. 146.

12 Cf.

a) OS. p. 242.

b) KR Vol. VII, p. 89.

13 KR Vol. VII, p. 89.

14 Ibid. pp. 89-90.

15 a) ALT pp. 97-101.

b) MM pp. 53-57.

16 Cf. MWS p. 92: ' . . . with the deeds of man which spring from the impulse of love, Michael has his own particular close relationship'.

17 a) ALT p. 99.

b) MM p. 55 (this translation used).

18 a) Ibid. p. 100.

b) Ibid. p. 56-57.

19 a) Ibid. p. 100.

b) Ibid. p. 56 (this translation used).

20 KR Vol. VII, p. 35. Cf. also LNCA p. 41.

21 LNCA p. 40. Cf. also MBWE p. 25.

22 LNCA p. 40.

23 Ibid.

24 Ibid. p. 41.

25 Ibid. p. 49.

26 ST p. 100. Cf. also CT pp. 121, 126.

27 *The World of the Senses and the World of the Spirit* (1947), p. 32.

28 Ibid. p. 24.

29 LNCA p. 50.

30 Ibid. p. 51.

31 VM p. 139.

32 *The World of the Senses and the World of the Spirit*, p. 32. Cf. also KR Vol. VIII (1975), pp. 53-54, re self-surrender.

33 LNCA p. 50.

34 ST p. 24.

35 Ibid.

36 Ibid. pp. 24-25 Cf. also:

    a)   ibid. 26-27.

    b)   OSOE p. 20.

37   ST. Lecture VIII.

38   First published in German in 1913.

39   ST p. 101.

40   Ibid. p. 102. Steiner also makes the point here that a man who manifests an external egoism, frankly admitting that he wants this or that, may well be far less of an egoist than those who constantly proclaim selflessness, tolerance and love, on the basis of a spiritual scientific insight which, in reality, has remained mere theory and not become inner experience. Cf. ibid. pp. 97-99 and 102.

42   Cf.

    a)   KHW Chapter: 'The Guardian of the Threshold'.

    b)   TSW Lectures II and VIII.

42   ST. p. 102.

43   Ibid.

20. EGOISM AND ALTRUISM

1   ESD pp. 99-100.

2   Ibid.

3   Ibid. pp. 100-101.

4   Ibid. pp. 98-99.

5   Ibid. Translation 1945 edition, p. 115. Cf. also MS pp. 149-150.

6   'Faith, Love, Hope'. In *The Golden Blade* (1964), p. 9.

7   Ibid. p. 10.

8   Ibid.

9   Ibid.

10   ECM p. 147.

11   Ibid. p. 155.

12   'Anthroposophy in Daily Life'. AQ XXII, No. 4, 1978, p. 8. In *The Problems of our Time* (1943) Steiner says: 'At birth we bring with us creative forces from our existence in the supersensible world into the physical sense-world ... They work in all that we develop as spiritual life in this world ... There would be no possibility of developing any spiritual life at all (no poetry, philosophy, science, etc.), if we did not carry with us through birth those impulses which come from our pre-natal life. All that belongs to our spiritual life is of pre-natal origin. On the other hand, what we ourselves develop within the economic life, through our will-impulses, brotherliness, love for humanity, thought and work for others, rather than for ourselves ... all that provides the most important impulses for what we take within us, at death, into the spiritual world. Just as at

birth we bring with us from the spiritual world the forces which, above all, build our spiritual life here on earth, so we take the forces developed by human love and brotherliness back into the spiritual world at death. There they accompany us and are our most fruitful impulses.' p. 88.

13 ECM p. 118.

14 MLO p. 12.

15 Cf. OS.

16 *Curative Education* (1972), pp. 211-212.

17 MLO p. 12. Cf. also:
a)   *Anthroposophy and the Social Question* (1958), pp. 30-33.
b)   OSOE p. 20.
c)   'The Present Crisis in Man's Development'. AQ XIII, No. 3, 1968, pp. 50-52.
d)   'The Riddle of Faust'. In *Goethe's Secret Revelation* (1933). In particular pp. 124-128.
e)   *Study of Man* (1947), pp. 8-9.[1981]
f)   TR pp. 97, 141-143.

21. LOVE AND THE MORAL LIFE

1 LDR p. 288.

2 *Jeshu ben Pandira* (1942), p. 11.

3 SFM pp. 49-50.

4 Ibid. p. 51. Cf. also Lecture IV in *Reincarnation and Karma. Their significance in Modern Culture* (1960).

5 SFM p. 52.

6 Ibid. p. 54.

7 Ibid. p. 57. See also Appendix: 'Ahriman and Lucifer'.

8 SFM pp. 58-59. Cf. also *The Significance of Spiritual Science for Moral Action* (1978), p. 5.

9 SFM p. 60.

10 Ibid. p. 61.

11 *The Occult Significance of the Bhagavad Gita* (1968), pp. 18-20.

12 SFM p. 61.

13 *On the Meaning of Life* (1946), p. 31.

14 SFM p. 64. Re Plato's conception of Love, cf. *Christianity as Mystical Fact and the Mysteries of Antiquity* (1972), Ch. 'Plato as a Mystic'.

15 Cf. *The World of the Senses and the World of the Spirit* (1947), pp. 8-9.

16 SFM p. 65.

17 GSJ(H) p. 75. See Ch. XXII, 'Old and New Bonds of Love'.

18 Cf. AI p. 54. Also MG pp. 22-23.

19 RSK pp. 66-67. Cf. also BSMG pp. 55-57 and Lecture IV.
20 RSK p. 67.
21 Cf. 'Faith, Love, Hope'. In *The Golden Blade* (1964), p. 24.
22 *Man as Symphony of the Creative Word* (1945), p. 194 [1978].
23 Ibid. pp. 194-195.
24 SFM p. 72.
25 Ibid. 72-73.
26 MWS pp. 51-52.

22. OLD AND NEW BONDS OF LOVE

 1 FS p. 37. Cf. also GSJ(C) p. 146.
 2 *Occult History* (1957), p. 35. Cf. also TR p. 125.[1982]
 3 Cf.
     a) TR p. 131.
     b) AEC, p. 19.
 4 AC p. 99 et al.
 5 GSJ(C) pp. 137-138.
 6 *Christmas* (n.d.), p. 24. Cf. also:
     a) CRR pp. 13-14.
     b) RE pp. 111-112.
 7 CRR p. 17. Cf. also:
     a) *Jesus and Christ* (1976), pp. 10-23, where Steiner speaks succinctly of the nature of the Ancient Mysteries in contrast to that of the Mystery of Golgotha.
     b) TR Lecture XIV, 'The Nature of Initiation'.
 8 See *The Gospel according to St John*, I, 16-17: 'For the Law was given by Moses, but Grace and Truth came by Jesus Christ'.
 9 CRR pp. 17-18.
10 AEC Lecture I.
11 Ibid. pp. 19-20. Cf. also: *The Christ Impulse and the Development of the Ego-Consciousness* (1976), pp. 79-86.
12 AEC, p. 20. Steiner continues: 'That is the difference between "Logia" and "Sophia", between science and divine Wisdom, between Theology and Theosophy.

In this sense, Christ is the centre of the esoteric evolution of the West. Certain modern Theologians ... have tried to represent Christ as a simple, naive human being. This is a terrible error. The most sublime consciousness, the most profound Wisdom live in Him — as well as the most divine Love.' Ibid. pp. 20-21.
13 E.G.
     a) *Egyptian Myths and Mysteries* (1971), pp. 132-133.

b) OSOE p. 25.

c) RE p. 111.

Elsewhere Steiner comments: 'The external physical expression of the ego is the blood, and where it brings itself most clearly to expression is in the heart, as expression of the purified ego. Christ said, therefore, "Blessed are the pure in heart, for they shall see God". Thus we are shown how in the most intimate sense the heart is the expression of the ego, the divine in man.' *The Ten Commandments and the Sermon on the Mount* (1978), p. 32. Cf. also Ch. 8, note 5.

14 *Egyptian Myths and Mysteries*, p. 133. Cf. also:

a) GSJ(H) pp. 76-77.

b) UEM p. 155.

15 Cf. FBC, pp. 19-20.

16 TR p. 142.

17 I.e. 'He who forsaketh not father, and mother, and brethren, and sister for my name's sake, cannot be my disciple'.

18 *The Gospel according to St John*, XIX, 26-27. See note 1.

19 Cf. 'The present Crisis in Man's Development'. AQ XIII, No. 3, 1968, p. 56.

20 TR pp. 142-143. Cf. ibid. p. 14.

21 Ibid. p. 143. 'The aim of the sixth epoch [beginning, according to Steiner, about AD 3500] of humanity will be to popularize occult truth in the widest circle.' Ibid. p. 144. Cf. also OS p. 306.

22 TR p. 145.

23 Cf. ASJ 'Man will develop his "I" to the necessary height so that he will become independent and, in freedom, show *love* towards all other beings . . . '. p. 76.

24 FBC, p. 21.

25 *Spiritual Science, Christianity, and the Future of Mankind* (1921) p. 23.

This lecture was given by Steiner as an Introduction to the cycle on *The Apocalypse of St John*. See also the 1958 edition of this cycle, pp. 26-27.

'Christ died and rose as much for the Chinese, Japanese, Hindus, and so forth, as for the Christians . . . All men have been redeemed from the Riddle of Death by Christ.' MBWE p. 89.

26 RE p. 112. Cf. CT p. 167, where Steiner states that the culture of the future cannot base the social order upon mere blood connections, i.e. upon Jehovah-wisdom. Jehovah-wisdom must be superseded by Christ-love. See also CT pp. 170-171.

27 Cf. GSM, pp. 220-221.

28 SFM p. 73. Cf. also MLO 'Love of one's neighbour is connected in its impulse with the Christ.' p. 207.
29 GSM, p. 195.
30 Ibid. p. 196.
31 FS p. 9. Cf. also ibid. pp. 17, 19, 37. Re spiritual science and the Brotherhood of Man, cf. ibid. pp. 10-11.
32 Ibid. p. 142. Cf. ibid. p. 65.
33 *The Fifth Gospel* (1951), pp. 62-63.[1978]
34 Ibid. pp. 25-26.
35 Cf.
   a) ibid. pp. 27, 34-44.
   b) MBWE pp. 96-97.
36 *The Fifth Gospel*, p. 35.
37 Ibid. pp. 35-36. Cf. also ibid. pp. 38, 40, 48.
38 FS p. 21.

23. THE SOCIAL FUTURE

1 I am indebted to Benedict Wood for this rendering. Cf. VM p. 117.
2a VM p. 191. Cf. also:
   a) ibid. p. 232.
   b) ESD pp. 79-80.
   c) OSOE pp. 11-15.
2b *Threefolding. A Social Alternative* (1980), pp. 40-41. Cf. ibid. p. 39.
3 *The Social Future* (1935), p. 194 [1972].
4 Ibid. pp. 194-195.
5 Ibid. p. 195.
6 Cf. ibid. p. 196.
7 Cf. ibid. pp. 196-198.
8 Cf. TEW pp. 145-146.
9 *The Social Future*, p. 211.
10 Ibid.
11 *A Social Basis for Primary and Secondary Education* (1958). Lecture II.
12 Cf. ibid. p. 17.
13 Cf.
   a) *Anthroposophy and the Social Question* (1958).
   b) *The Inner Aspects of the Social Question* (1974).
   c) *The Social Future.*
   d) *The Threefold Order of the Body Social. Study Series I, II and III (n.d.).*
   e) *Threefolding. A Social Alternative* (1980).
   f) *Towards Social Renewal. Basic Issues of the Social Question* (1977).

g) *World Economy. The Formation of a Science of World Economy* (1977).

14 *A Social Basis for Primary and Secondary Education.* Lecture II, p. 17.

Steiner gave this lecture in 1919 when the situation in the East, in particular, was a different one in regard to the economic life than it is today. However, it should be borne in mind that although the element of brotherliness may be on the decline in the East and the Western form of economic thinking manifesting itself more predominantly there, this trend cannot be regarded as being in accord with the true, inner soul-spiritual quality of the East.

15 Ibid.

16 Cf. *The Mission of the Individual Folk Souls* (1970).

17 'The Peoples of the Earth in the Light of Anthroposophy'. In *The Golden Blade* (1980), p. 12.

18 Ibid. p. 22.

19 Ibid.

20 Ibid. pp. 22-23.

21 Ibid. p. 23.

22 Ibid. p. 24.

23 *Easter. The Festivals and their Meaning.* Vol. II, (1956), p. 32.

24 Ibid.

25 Ibid.

26 Ibid.

27 Cf.

a) *Curative Education* (1972).

b) ESD.

c) *Geographic Medicine* (n.d.), p. 11.

d) *The Invisible Man within us* (n.d.).

e) ODCC p. 33.

f) *The Right and the Wrong Use of Esoteric Knowledge* (1966), p. 54.

g) ST pp. 20-21.

h) *The Study of Man* (1981).

i) See also: V. Bott, *Anthroposophical Medicine* (1978).

28 *Easter. The Festivals and their Meaning.* Vol. II, (1956), p. 33.

29 Ibid.

30 TEW p. 109.

31 *First Steps in Supersensible Perception and the Relation of Anthroposophy to Christianity* (1949), p.53.

32 See note 13.

33 *Education as a Social Problem* (1969), p. 56.

34 Ibid. p. 57.

35 CT.

36   Ibid. p. 171. Cf. also pp. 141-142.
37   Ibid. p. 172.
38   Ibid. p. 174.
39   Ibid. p. 175. Cf:
     a)   ibid. p. 146.
     b)   MS pp. 146-148.
40   CT p. 175.
41   Ibid. pp. 175-176.
42   *Methods of Spiritual Research* (1971), p. 88.
43   CT p. 176.
44   Ibid. p. 177.
45   Cf. *Mystery Knowledge and Mystery Centres* (1973), pp. 13-14.
46   CT p. 177.
47   Ibid. p. 142.
48   See note 13.
49   *The Threefold Order of the Body Social.* Study Series III (n.d.), pp. 38-39.
50   TEW p. 67. It is, of course, clear that we are here discussing that which may be described as being characteristically Eastern — not the East influenced by Western thought.
51   Ibid. pp. 68-69.
52   Ibid. p. 69.
53   Ibid. p. 70.
54   Ibid. p. 74.
55   Ibid.
56   Ibid. p. 78.
57   Ibid. p. 77.
58   Cf. ibid. pp. 80-81.
59   Ibid. p. 81.
60   'The Supersensible Being of Man and the Evolution of Mankind'. In *The Anthroposophical Review*, Vol. II, No. 3, 1980, p. 25.

In Otto Palmer's book, *Rudolf Steiner on his Book The Philosophy of Freedom* (1975), we find an extract from a lecture, not yet translated into English in its entirety, which is highly relevant to Steiner's conception of the need for an entirely new approach to social and economic problems: 'What anthroposophical knowledge enkindles in us with its pursuit of the supersensible is *love of man*. It teaches us how precious a human being is and imbues us with a feeling for human dignity, a love-imbued will — these are life's fruits garnered as one learns to experience the findings of spiritual science . . . Anthroposophy (Spiritual Science) is able to show how *love of duty* goes on growing into *love of man* and thus becomes a real quickener of social life. We can gain insight into the huge, burning social problems that confront us today only if we take the trouble to realize the connection between freedom, love, man's being, spiritual and natural necessity.' pp. 63-64.

24. LOVE, CHRIST AND OUR IDEALS

1 VM p. 127.
2 TR p. 167.
3 Ibid. p. 166.
4 Ibid. p. 167.
5 Ibid. pp. 167-168.
6 Cf. BDR pp. 30-31.
7 Cf. ibid. p. 168.
8 LNCA p. 30.
9 Ibid. pp. 30-31.
10 Ibid. p. 31.
11 LDR p. 78.
12 SFM p. 70.
13 Ibid. 'Sympathy in grief and joy is the virtue that in the future must produce the most beautiful and glorious fruits in human social life. In those who rightly understand the Christ Impulse this sympathy and this love will arise quite naturally.' Ibid. p. 71.
14 Ibid. p. 82.
15 Cf. ibid. pp. 85-86.
16 Ibid. 83. Cf. 'Ancient Wisdom and the Heralding of the Christ Impulse'. AQ XVIII, No. 1. 1933, pp. 9-10. Here Steiner discusses the relation of the three soul-qualities 'wonder', 'compassion' and 'conscience', in relation to Christ.
17 CHS.
18 Ibid. p. 20.
19 Ibid.
20 Ibid. p. 21.
21 Ibid. Cf. ibid. pp. 26-27 re Lucifer and our Ideals.
22 Ibid. p. 27.
23 Ibid. p. 29.

APPENDIX. AHRIMAN AND LUCIFER

1 Cf.
   a) *Christ in Relation to Lucifer and Ahriman* (1978).
   b) *The Mysteries of Light, of Space and of the Earth* (1945), pp. 9-10, 26-28.

c) *Rudolf Steiner's Sculpture* (1975) by Fant, A., Klingborg, A., and Wilkes, A.J.

2 Cf. SFM pp. 55-57.

3 Cf. *From Symptom to Reality in Modern History* (1976), pp. 118-119.Also:

   a) CHS pp. 32-33.

   b) MWS pp. 71, 77.

4 Cf. *The Birth of Christianity. Christianity and the Mysteries of Antiquity* (1950), pp. 52-53.

5 A closer understanding of the significance and roles of Ahriman and Lucifer may be gained by a closer study of the following list of works (not, by any means, comprehensive):

   a) ALT.

   b) *The Balance in the World. Lucifer and Ahriman* (1977).

   c) *The Deed of Christ and the Opposing Spiritual Powers* (1976).

   d) ESD Lecture IX.

   e) FS pp. 142-146 et al.

   f) *Goethe's Standard of the Soul* (1925).

   g) *The Influences of Ahriman and Lucifer* (1976).

   h) *Luciferic and Ahrimanic in their Relation to Man* (1933).

   i) MWS. In particular Lecture III.

   j) *Planetary Spheres and their Influence on Man's Life on Earth and in the Spiritual Worlds* (1982). In particular Lecture V.

   k) *The Mission of the Archangel Michael* (1961). In particular Lecture V.

   l) ST.

   m) *Spiritual Science and Medicine* (1975).

   n) *Three Streams in the Evolution of Mankind* (1965).

   o) TSW. In particular pp. 111-118, 143-146

Also: i) V. Bott: *Anthroposophical Medicine. An extension of the art of healing* (1978).

ii) B.J. Lievegoed: *Towards the 21st Century: doing the good* (1972).

iii) Alfred Schütze: *The Enigma of Evil* (1978).

iv) Carl Stegmann: *The Other America. The Western World in the Light of Spiritual Science* (n.d.).

6 Cf. OS. Also:

   a) OSOE p. 20.

   b) ST. In particular Lecture II.

   c) *Spiritual Beings in the Heavenly Bodies* (1951). In particular Lecture X [1981].

   d) SGM pp. 45, 48-49, 58.

7 Cf. UEM pp. 87-88. See also note 5.

8 See note 6.
9 *Memory and Habit* (1948), p. 17.
10 Ibid. p. 19.
11 See Introduction.
12 Re the Archangel Michael see:
   a) ALT.
   b) ODCC pp. 41-53.
   c) *The Cycle of the Year* (1956).
   d) *The Four Seasons and the Archangels* (1968).
   e) MWS Lecture VI.
   f) *Michaelmas. The Festivals and their Meaning.* Vol. IV, 1957.
   g) *The Mission of the Archangel Michael* (1961).
   h) *Rosicrucianism and Modern Initiation* (1965). Lecture VI.
13 *At the Gates of Spiritual Science* (1970), p. 74. Cf. also:
   a) *From Symptom to Reality in Modern History* (1976). In particular Lecture V where Steiner speaks of the 'Mystery of Evil'.
   b) OSOE pp. 17 and 21.
   c) TSW p. 140.

SELECT BIBLIOGRAPHY

This list contains works by students of Rudolf Steiner's spiritual science which the author has found useful in the preparation of this book and which are not mentioned in the foregoing notes.

Adams, G. *The Mysteries of the Rose-Cross* (1955).
Adams, G. and Whicher, O. *The Plant between Sun and Earth and the Science of Physical and Ethereal Spaces* (1980).
Allen, P.M. and Robbins, C. *Rudolph Steiner's Curative Education* (1960).
Arenson, A. *The Mission of the Ancient Hebrews* (n.d.).
————. *The Sermon on the Mount*(n.d.).
————. *The Ten Commandments* (n.d.).
Baravalle, H. von. *The International Waldorf School Movement* (1975).
Beckh, H. *From Buddha to Christ* (1978).
Bittleston, A. *Our Spiritual Companions* (1980).
Bock, E. *The Three Years. The Life of Christ between Baptism and Ascension* (1980).
Budd, C. *Prelude to Economics* (1979).
Buehler, W. *Living with your Body* (1979).
Capel, E.F. *The Making of Christianity and the Greek Spirit* (1980).
Carlgren, J. *Rudolf Steiner and Anthroposophy* (1978).
Cornish, J. *About Death and After* (1975).
Coroze, P. *A Road to the Spirit* (1950).
Davenport, Russell W. *The Dignity of Man* (New York, 1955).
Davy, J. (Ed.) *Work Arising from the life of Rudolf Steiner* (1975).
Drake, S. *The Path to Birth* (1979).
Drake, S. *Though you die . . .* (1974).
Easton, S.C. *And Another Strong Angel . . .* (1979).
Easton, S.C. *Man and World in the Light of Anthroposophy* (1975).
Easton, S.C. *Rudolf Steiner — Herald of a New Epoch* (1980).
Edmunds, L.F. *Rudolf Steiner Education* (1982).
————. 'The Scientific and the Moral in Education' (1956).*
Emmichoven, F.W. Zeylmans van *The Reality in which we live* (1964).
Faulkner Jones, D.E. *The English Spirit. A New Approach through the World Conception of Rudolf Steiner* (1935) [1982].

Frieling, R. *Christianity and Islam* (1978).
——————. *Christianity and Reincarnation* (1977).
Gardner, J.F. 'Reflections on Discipline' (1960).*
——————. 'Right Action, Right Thinking' (1969).*
——————. 'Towards a Truly Public Education' (1976).*
——————. *The Experience of Knowledge. Essays on American Education* (New York, 1976).
Glas, N. *The Fulfilment of Old Age* (1970).
——————. *The Jewish Question* (1944).
Glas, W. *The Waldorf School Approach to History* (1981).
Gordon Jones, T. *Studies in Social Science* (n.d.).
Grace, C.D. *The Task of the Curative Teacher* (n.d.).
Harwood, A.C. *The Way of a Child. An Introduction to the work of Rudolf Steiner for Children* (1982).
Harwood, A.C. (Ed.) *The Faithful Thinker. Centenary Essays on the Work and Thought of Rudolf Steiner* (1961).
Heidenreich, A. *The Book of Revelation* (1977).
——————. *Healing in the Gospels* (1980).
——————. *The Risen Christ and the Etheric Christ* (1969).
——————. *The Unknown in the Gospels* (1972).
Heisler, H. *Our Relationship to those who have died* (1976).
Hemleben, J. *Rudolf Steiner, a Documentary Biography* (1975).
Heydebrand, C. von. *The Child at Play* (1928).
Hiebel, F. *The Epistles of Paul and Rudolf Steiner's Philosophy of Freedom* (1980).
Kaufmann, G. Adams. *Christ in the Power of Memory and in the Power of Love* (1938).
——————. *Space and the Light of the Creation* (1933).
——————. *Christ and the Earth* (1927).
Koenig, K. *The Human Soul.* (1973).
Lauer, H.E. *Aggression and Repression. In the Individual and Society* (1981).
Lehrs, E. *Man or Matter. Introduction to a Spiritual Understanding of Nature on the Basis of Goethe's Method of Training Observation and Thought* (1958).
Lehrs, E. *Rosicrucian Foundations of the Age of Natural Science* (1976).
Lievegoed, B.C.J. *Forming Curative Communities* (1979).
——————. *Phases: Crisis and Development in the Individual* (1979).
Manoir, M du. *Rudolf Steiner Education* (1959).
Mayer, G. *Behind the Veils of Death and Sleep* (1st edition n.d.).
Newitt, I. *Curative Education* (1942).

—————. *Where No Light Shines* (1950).

Pfeiffer E. *Life's Resources and Esoteric Streams of Christianity* (1963).

Piening, E. and Lyons, N.(Eds.) *Educating as an Art. The Rudolf Steiner Method* (1979).

Poppelbaum, H. *Man's Eternal Biography. Three Essays on Life and Death* (1945).

—————. *Destiny and Freedom* (n.d.).

—————. *The Etheric Body in Idea and Action* (1955).

Rittlemeyer, F.W. *Rudolf Steiner Enters my Life* (1982).

Rudolf Steiner. Recollections by Some of his Pupils. Published by *The Golden Blade* (1958).

Schiller, P.E. *The Anthroposophical Path of Inner Schooling* (1981).

Spock, M. *Teaching as a Lively Art* (1978).

Stein, W.J. *West—East. A Study in National Relationships* (1933).

Unger, C. *Principles of Spiritual Science* (1976).

Wachsmuth, G. *The Life and Work of Rudolf Steiner* (1955).

Wachsmuth G. *Reincarnation as a Phenomenon of Metamorphosis* (1937).

Winkler, F.E. *Man — the Bridge between two Worlds* (1976).

—————. 'National Psychology in International Relations' (1976).*

—————. 'The Influence of Psychology on Education' (1965).*

—————. 'The Psychology of Leadership' (1976).*

* Published in the *Proceedings* of The Myrin Institute, New York.

INDEX